PRAISE FOR
THE AGE OF PERSUASION

"On fire with ideas, bursting with insights, ...taining insiders' history of persuasion takes us from the dawn of the telegraph to the future of the Internet. It's a riveting read, crammed with the very human stories of the anonymous alchemists who shape our lives and our world. Henry Ford once said, 'Nothing happens until somebody sells something.' There's never been a better exploration of that premise."

—Steve Hayden, vice chairman, chief creative officer, Ogilvy & Mather Worldwide

"I loved this book. I thought I had a pretty good idea of everything that's happened in the history of American advertising, but I didn't. I do now. The book is thorough without being heavy-handed, fun without being flippant, full of fascinating facts that fill in some voids that needed to be filled in. The only thing that might make it better would have been to include a few more quotes from me. Keep it by your bed."

—Bob Levenson, chairman and international creative director, DDB International; vice chairman, Saatchi & Saatchi, New York and Scali, McCabe, Sloves, New York

"*The Age of Persuasion* provides a wonderful romp through the history and inner workings of advertising. I am not sure what I enjoyed more, the insight and wisdom about the ad business or the wit and charm of the storytelling; either way it's a great read for all of us living in the Age of Persuasion."

—Doug Checkeris, chief executive officer, North America MediaCom

"Terry O'Reilly and Mike Tennant blend history, stories, wisdom, hundreds of facts, and just plain fun into an original, compelling, entertaining, and insightful perspective on the impact of creative communication on our culture and on our everyday lives. It is a terrific book!"
—Bob Schmetterer, author of *Leap: A Revolution in Creative Business Strategy*

"If there's one brand that advertising has failed miserably at making people understand, it's advertising itself. This book goes a long way in correcting that—now if they could only do the same for car dealers."
—Bob Kuperman, former president and chief executive, DDB New York

"As a public broadcaster, I'm contractually obligated to despise advertising, and by extension to despise those who create it. Somehow two ad men—Terry O'Reilly and Mike Tennant—slipped through my defenses. *The Age of Persuasion* will be enjoyed by those inside the ad world, but it's more than an insider's guide. It's a funny and fascinating window into a part of our culture that's too little considered by outsiders like me."
—Jesse Thorn, host and producer, PRI's *The Sound of Young America*

"Language is art. Advertising is art. Terry O'Reilly and Mike Tennant really deliver on that in this book. *The Age of Persuasion* made me stop, think, and realize that everything we do as marketers (day in and day out) can matter . . . and should be better. Because, in the end, advertising is not just about persuasion. It's about the stories we tell and how they connect with real people and what those real people do with those stories. *The Age of Persuasion* is one of those great stories."
—Mitch Joel, president of Twist Image and author of *Six Pixels of Separation*

THE AGE OF
PERSU

HOW MARKETING
ATE OUR CULTURE

TERRY O'REILLY
& MIKE TENNANT

ASION

COUNTERPOINT
BERKELEY

To CBC Radio listeners, God bless 'em.
Without whom . . .

Copyright © 2009 Terry O'Reilly and Mike Tennant.

Published by arrangement with Knopf Canada, which is a division of Random House of Canada Limited.

Library of Congress Cataloging-in-Publication Data
O'Reilly, Terry.
  The age of persuasion : how marketing ate our culture /
by Terry O'Reilly and Mike Tennant.
      p. cm.
  Includes bibliographical references and index.
  ISBN-13: 978-1-58243-724-8
  1. Advertising—Social aspects. 2. Marketing—Social aspects.
  3. Mass media and culture. 4. Persuasion (Psychology)
  I. Tennant, Mike. II. Title.

  HF5823.O68 2010
  306.3'4—dc22

                              2009052548

Cover design by Michel Vrána
Interior design by Kelly Hill
Printed in the United States of America

COUNTERPOINT
1919 Fifth Street
Berkeley, CA 94710

www.counterpointpress.com
Distributed by Publishers Group West

10 9 8 7 6 5 4 3 2

CONTENTS

I, ME, WE

We chose to write this book in first-person singular out of habit. Though we have always worked together to research, write, and produce the radio series *The Age of Persuasion,* our show has always had a single voice: that of Terry O'Reilly. And that's the voice you'll "hear" as you read this book.

Where opinions are expressed, they are shared. A few personal anecdotes might come from one or the other—but we don't expect you'll lie in bed at night agonizing over which one came from whom. All the same, the lion's share of the war stories we use—the tales from the trenches of the ad business—are taken from Terry's experiences, first as an ad agency copywriter and especially as an ad writer, director, and founding partner of the creative audio production company Pirate Toronto (and Pirate New York). It might be from all those years we've spent in radio: we just think messages are clearer when one person does the talking.

If it helps any, the authors have a lot in common: we're both Ontario boys born almost exactly a year apart, our fathers are of Irish stock, we share an encyclopaedic knowledge of NHL players of the early 1970s, we both started writing ads at private radio stations in the early 1980s, we both love to read all the credits at the ends of movies (and both of our families hate this about us), we are fathers of three kids apiece, and we both have wonderful wives. Who like some of our work.

Terry O'Reilly
Mike Tennant
Creemore / Kitchener (respectively), Ontario
March 2009

X

Advertising is the rattling of a
stick inside a swill bucket.
GEORGE ORWELL

WHAT HATH
GOD WROUGHT

Advertising is the greatest art
form of the twentieth century.
MARSHALL McLUHAN

One bracing December day in 1872, just west of the Strait of Gibraltar, a ship set out to intercept the *Mary Celeste*, a two-mast vessel bound for Genoa from New York with a cargo of industrial alcohol. The *Dei Gratia* had spotted the *Mary Celeste* a short time earlier, drifting aimlessly under partial sail. A boarding party was dispatched. A thorough search revealed no trace of its ten passengers or crew, just signs of weather damage and a metre of water in its hold. There were no notes or writings, no signs of struggle or violence, and no indications of distress. To this day, the demise of the *Mary Celeste* remains a popular puzzle for historians and mystery buffs, who pore over accounts left by the crew of the *Dei Gratia* and the intriguing, infuriating handful of clues left behind.

Now, suppose you could look at the earth with fresh eyes, like those of the *Dei Gratia*'s crew as they boarded the *Mary Celeste*. While passing from a nearby galaxy, you might notice this planet drifting erratically and drop by to investigate. You'd find everything on earth exactly as it is now—as you read this—but without a single human being to be found. What would you deduce about this world, its people, and their culture? Would you marvel at a species that produced the sonnets of Shakespeare, the prophecies of Muhammad, the solos of Miles Davis, the musings of Lao Tzu, and the engineering genius of the Robertson screwdriver?

Maybe. But not before being overwhelmed by the most conspicuous, ubiquitous force in modern culture: *advertising*.

You would see ads on billboards and posters, in bus shelters, covering the sides of six-storey buildings, infused into radio and television programming, and streamed to personal communications devices.

Monitoring the airwaves, you'd hear a loud mashing of messages transmitted for radio, TV, and satellite. You'd find ads projected onto the floors of shopping malls, broadcast on screens in elevators and over gas pumps, wrapped around buses, and planted in roadside flowerbeds. You'd see ads posted in washroom stalls, in golf holes, on taxi hubcaps, and stuffed into envelopes with utility bills.

Had you stumbled upon this planet in any other era, you might have concluded that we lived in an age of stone or bronze, an ice age, an age of reason, or an age of enlightenment. But today? You couldn't help but conclude that we live in an age of persuasion, where people's wants, wishes, whims, pleas, brands, offers, enticements, truths, petitions, and propaganda swirl in a ceaseless, growing multimedia firestorm of sales messages.

When prompted to cite the greatest influences on modern culture, most people would probably name new technologies, dominant personalities, the economy, climate change, or tribal differences. Strangely, few think to name advertising, which has insinuated itself into virtually every aspect of twenty-first-century life. The age of persuasion reveals itself in us each time we flirt, date, apply for a job, buy a car, sell a home, fight a speeding ticket, heckle a referee, write to Santa Claus, pop a breath mint, or simply dress for effect. It's a cultural force we're just beginning to understand and whose language we speak better than we realize.

Way back in 1917, novelist Norman Douglas wrote: "You can tell the ideals of a nation by its advertisements." But still, more than a century later, despite the many clues, we tend to underrate the role of advertising in daily life. It's a forgivable oversight: it's not easy to take seriously the marketing neverland where cartoon bears pitch toilet paper, where the Ty-D-Bol man patrols your toilet tank in a tiny rowboat, and where a tin of Folgers coffee can heal a marriage. Yet the influence of marketing can't be ignored: worldwide, advertisers now spend upwards of $600 billion a year trying to influence what you think, do, and buy. It took the United States four years to spend that much on its post–9/11 wars in Iraq and Afghanistan.

On a given day, at least three hundred, and as many as six thousand, marketing messages are lobbed your way. Statistics suggest that people spend more time exposed to advertising than they spend eating, reading, cooking, praying, cleaning, and making love combined. Marketing has transformed childhood games into multibillion-dollar sports empires, manufacturing heroes and sculpting our history. Does great advertising win elections? No one can say, though few doubt that bad advertising can certainly lose them.

SO . . . WHAT'S THE DIFFERENCE BETWEEN MARKETING AND ADVERTISING?

Marketing (possibly from the Latin word *mercari*, meaning "to buy") refers to all or part of the process of conceiving, promoting, distributing, and selling a product or service.

Advertising (from the Latin word *advertere*, meaning "to turn toward") is one subset of marketing. It's the act of bringing that product or service to the public's attention, often through paid announcements or commercials.

The better you understand the ad messages you receive every day, the better you'll comprehend exactly how advertising has come to drive art, culture, and communication. A striking example is the soap opera, popularized in the early 1930s because soap makers needed a way to reach a vast audience of housewives with their sales messages. In 1966 *The Monkees* TV show and its accompanying band were launched as a marketing vehicle to cash in on the rock 'n' roll craze and the eyebrow-raising merchandise machine the Beatles had become. Since the 1980s Hollywood has offered a steady diet of blast-smash-shoot-'n'-slash summer movies to attract the lucrative thirteen- to twenty-four-year-old male demographic. There may have been a time when art, music, film, broadcast, and—yes—books began with an idea and then sought an audience. But in the age of persuasion, art is market driven: a desired audience is identified, then art and entertainment are conceived—not just to reach them but to connect with them as consumers.

The age of persuasion began more than a century and a half ago, with events that, once set in motion quickly accelerated and extended beyond commerce into everyday life. This is not the story of advertising—which dates back at least as far as the ancient Babylonians—but of the living, growing, all-encompassing and relatively modern culture of persuasion. Its rise is marked by a series of what screenwriters call *beats:* key events that move a story forward. And unlike so many of humankind's pivotal moments, its beginnings can be traced to a precise time and place— to an inventor from Charlestown, Massachusetts, who tapped out a portentous, four-word message.

.— ..…—-/.….- -…./—.— -../.—-.—- ..- —.….—.—..

(WHAT HATH GOD WROUGHT)

Samuel Finley Breese (yes, *Breese*) Morse was a painter, inventor, professor, unsuccessful politician, philanthropist, and entrepreneur. In 1832, as he sailed home to America from Europe, he occupied himself with the idea of a device that could communicate over great distances by sending electrical signals through wires. A bit more than a decade later, by 1844, he had a design, and he then coaxed the U.S. Congress to bankroll his invention. On Friday, May 24, of that year, Morse gathered with assorted Washington muckety-mucks in the U.S. Supreme Court chamber to show how his contraption worked. Using his homemade code of dots and dashes, he transmitted a sentence, which was miraculously received by his colleague Alfred Vail in Baltimore, more than sixty kilometres away. A friend's young daughter, Miss Annie Ellsworth, had been given the honour of composing the historic message, and she had opted for the fashionably biblical "What hath God wrought?" From the Book of Numbers, it describes God's blessing of the Israelites. In the context of Morse's invention, however, it might be taken with a whiff of irony. It's as if the words meant "Yikes! What have we gotten ourselves into?" Morse's telegraph machine is rightly hailed for helping shrink the world, for enabling instant communication across entire continents, and a few decades later, for allowing messages to be transmitted around the world by transoceanic cable.

It also revolutionized marketing. The telegraph followed on the heels of the European industrial revolution, and in North America, manufacturing had mechanized and expanded. Rural families had gravitated to cities to work in the fast-growing factories, which in turn churned out products for burgeoning urban populations. With the rise of railways through the nineteenth century, goods could be transported overland, en masse, to distant markets, resulting in more product choices in stores. And how did the telegraph fit into the picture? It allowed manufacturers to communicate instantly with newspapers in distant cities and towns, buying advertisements to attract thousands of potential new customers.

DOT . . . DASH . . . DOT . . . AN AGENCY IS BORN

Barely a year after Morse dotted, dashed, and dotted his way into history, Philadelphia businessman Volney Palmer opined, quite rightly, that many manufacturers had neither the time nor the inclination to place ads in dozens—even hundreds—of newspapers on a regular basis. Palmer offered his services as a sort of middleman, buying large amounts of advertising space in several newspapers and then parcelling and selling it to businesses, who would have to create their own messages. And so . . . . the advertising agency was born. The explosive potential of this sexy new venture didn't prevent Palmer from hedging his bets: initially, he kept his advertising business as a sideline as he continued to sell bonds, mortgages, real estate, and coal.

Inspired by Palmer's success, like-minded advertising agencies sprouted up like daisies, buying and selling vast amounts of advertising space in distant markets to expansion-minded manufacturers. Big business and "mass" advertising had come together in a union whose rumblings would be felt throughout the nineteenth century. Outfits like Procter & Gamble and, later, Coca-Cola were pioneers in early mass advertising and rapidly grew to become international icons. Morse's gizmo did more than shrink the world; it set in motion a new era of big-league consumerism and allowed marketing to blossom into a full-blown industry.

JOHN E. KENNEDY'S THREE LITTLE WORDS

The creative side of advertising, as you see it around you right now, took root on a fine spring day in 1904 in the Chicago offices of the ad agency Lord & Thomas. Throughout the marketing industry, the legend of what transpired is still sung in ballads and told around campfires. There are many versions of what happened. Here's mine:

Ambrose Thomas was at work in his office that morning when a messenger brought him a slip of paper. It read:

> I am in the saloon downstairs. I can tell you what advertising is. I know you don't know. It will mean much to me to have you know what it is, and it will mean much to you. If you wish to know what advertising is, send the word "yes" down by the bellboy. [signed] John E. Kennedy.

Ambrose Thomas wasn't inclined to glean wisdom from some yahoo in the saloon downstairs, but the note intrigued his junior partner, twenty-four-year-old Albert Lasker. Six years earlier, Lasker had begun at Lord & Thomas as a $10-a-week office boy. Now he was commanding a princely $52,000 a year; thirteen times the average American salary at the time and more than a million dollars in today's money. One of Lasker's many remarkable and all-too-rare traits was his awareness that he didn't know everything about advertising. But he may have sensed something about Kennedy's gift for salesmanship simply by the pluck the stranger downstairs had shown, scrawling such a cocky note to the head of a major ad firm.

Lasker scribbled "yes" on the note and returned it to the messenger. A few minutes later, Canadian ex-Mountie John Ernest Kennedy, a vast, muscular giant of a man, presented himself. Lasker would later describe him as "one of the handsomest men I ever saw in my life." Kennedy introduced himself: he had recently arrived from Racine, Wisconsin, where he had written ad copy for The Shoop Family Medicine Company, who sold—of all things—a popular snake oil.

Lasker invited Kennedy to share his definition. While already impressed by the man, Lasker was utterly unprepared for the epiphany that Kennedy packed into his magical, three-word answer:

salesmanship on paper.

Today Kennedy might rework the phrase, first to neutralize gender and then to include all manner of advertising media, beginning with broadcast and Internet, but his core idea remains.

All these years later, it sounds ridiculously simple; it's now a given that advertising is about salesmanship. But in 1904 the idea was downright revolutionary. Until then the pioneers of advertising had simply invited or implored readers to visit their shops and buy their products. Hence, when Kennedy asked Lasker what he thought advertising was about, Lasker answered "news." "No," said Kennedy, "news is a technique of presentation, but advertising is a very different thing." In

Kennedy's view, it was about giving people a "reason why" they should purchase a product. Lasker would take those words to heart, and under him, Lord & Thomas would go on to transform the advertising industry, becoming the champions of "reason why" advertising, a phrase still commonly used in the marketing world.

At a time when no Lord & Thomas copywriter made more than $30 a week, Lasker bought out Kennedy's $28,000 per year contract with Shoop Family medicines and made him a sort of personal mentor-in-residence. Within two years Kennedy's salary climbed to $75,000 a year (something north of $1.7 million in today's dollars). In theory, Kennedy was hired as a copywriter. In practice, Lasker spent months tapping Kennedy's advertising insights, which ran much deeper than his deceptively simple three-word manifesto implied. By the time he retired in 1938, Albert Lasker had done very well by these lessons: a noted philanthropist (through his Lasker Foundation) and former owner of the Chicago Cubs, he's widely regarded as the richest ad executive in history.

Kennedy left Lord & Thomas suddenly—in some fit of temper—in 1906. A genius of the moody, temperamental variety, he was seen by co-workers as crude, vain, and unable to take criticism. After his abrupt departure, he drifted first to New York, where he ran his own agency and then, after the First World War, to California, to take advantage of the land boom of the 1920s. He died of pancreatic cancer in a Michigan sanitorium in 1928, by then all but forgotten in the ad world. Even today, few in my industry know of the peculiar genius of this father of modern advertising.

By introducing salesmanship into the equation, Kennedy helped make vocations of advertising strategy, copywriting, and design. No longer was it enough for an ad simply to appear in print; the *content* of an ad, the imagery it presented, the feeling it stirred, the argument it made, the unique product attributes it professed were now recognized as vital components of success. Following Kennedy's teachings, Albert Lasker would carry advertising beyond the confines of simple, bald product statements and into the limitless frontiers of emotion, effectively appealing to the right brain (considered to be the headquarters of our emotions). In the decades that followed that fateful meeting with the man in the saloon below, Lasker ruled Lord & Thomas from high atop the mountain of money it generated. Almost all the advertising you see, hear, and experience today, every enticement that causes you—consciously or otherwise—to reach for one brand over another, is rooted in the creative revolution John E. Kennedy launched with those three little words.

KENNEDY'S WASHING MACHINE

To tap insights from the mind of John E. Kennedy, Albert Lasker showed him a Lord & Thomas ad for a mechanical, hand-cranked washing machine. A line drawing showed a woman tied to an old washtub with a chain and the headline "Are You Chained to the Wash Tub?" Kennedy complained it was too negative. "The average woman is put in the position of a drudge," he explained, but subconsciously, she won't want to admit that she's been "reduced to such bestial servility." At Lasker's request Kennedy dreamed up a different ad, this time showing a woman sitting comfortably in a rocking chair, cranking the laundry machine, with the headline "Let This Machine Do Your Washing Free." It was a prime example of how effectively Kennedy's "reason why" approach reached people's imaginations. Lasker later claimed that within eight months, the company that produced those washing machines had tripled production.

THE RADIO AGE: TRUE "MASS" MEDIA IS BORN

The same year that Kennedy tromped out of the offices of Lord & Thomas in Chicago, history was made halfway across the continent. It was Christmas Eve, and over in Brant Rock, Massachusetts, Canadian-born Reginald Aubrey Fessenden was sending out the world's first radio broadcast, playing Handel's *Largo* on his Ediphone player, singing hymns and carols, and reading from the Bible for an audience of crewmembers aboard ships of the United Fruit Company. Two decades later radio manufacturers, government regulators, and fledgling broadcasters hit their stride, and broadcast, fuelled by advertising dollars, began its rapid ascent to the summit of popular culture.

Radio became the first "mass" medium to reach millions with a single voice, in their homes, at the same time. Moreover, within a decade it became the first major medium driven by advertising. And not just financially: by the end of the twenties, advertisers began buying blocks of airtime from stations and networks, creating and producing sponsored programming on behalf of their clients. Before long, "radio departments" sprouted up within major ad agencies to manage these shows. Canada Dry, then Chevrolet, vaulted vaudeville comic Jack Benny to national stardom; Maxwell House gave radio listeners George Burns and Gracie Allen. Advertisers rivalled, and in some cases, eclipsed the giants— music, publishing, and film—as kingmakers in popular entertainment.

Radio also breached a great, unseen curtain that had separated advertisers from audiences, reaching people in their homes as no other medium had before. Print ads could be skipped, set aside, or noticed at the reader's pleasure. In contrast, radio ads reverberated through people's homes on the broadcaster's own schedule, adding the evocative nuances of voice and personality, and the subconscious power of music, to the language of persuasion. Radio personalities became part of the dialogue in people's homes, in the living rooms, kitchens, and parlours where families gathered round to listen: private places where personal matters are discussed.

It wasn't the first major home invasion staged by an outside medium: the rise of the telephone had already introduced live, real-time voices from the outside world into people's private space, forever changing the idea of the home as a sanctuary.

When the uncle of a friend of mine celebrated his hundredth birthday, my friend asked him what invention, during his many years on earth, had changed his life the most. Without hesitation, he answered, "The telephone."

Still, advertisers didn't just barge into people's homes; they were invited—not necessarily as welcome guests but as parties to a Great Unwritten Contract, requiring advertisers to give the listener something in exchange for her attention. Radio wasn't free: programming was underwritten by advertisers. In exchange for a daily offering of music, drama, comedy, and information, the listener would be exposed to advertising messages. It was a great deal, and it solved a huge problem for early broadcasters, who, unlike theatres, couldn't charge admission and who, unlike magazines and newspapers, couldn't solicit subscriptions. This same unwritten, unspoken contract would form the economic template for television and, more recently, the Internet.

The contract is explored in Chapter 2.

BRAND LOYALTY— CONSCRIPTING THE KIDDIES

Radio enabled advertisers, for the first time, to form a direct dialogue with children. They quickly learned that by broadcasting kids' programs, especially on Saturday mornings and after school, they could provide a diversion for the offspring while parents cooked and did chores. And before long they discovered the power of forging brand loyalties with young listeners, who were frequently conscripted as lobbyists, urged to "remind mother to look for" Kellogg's Sugar Corn Pops, Peter Pan Peanut Butter, or Ovaltine.

BILL BERNBACH AND THE SECOND CREATIVE REVOLUTION

In 1960, less than a decade after television eclipsed radio as a home entertainment medium, a little-known New York ad agency—Doyle Dane Bernbach (DDB), headed by legendary Bill Bernbach, launched its famous campaign for the Volkswagen Beetle. Described as "the DDB shot heard around the world," it revolutionized the way marketers communicated with their audience, adding wit, intelligence, and surprise to an advertising language long mired in research, formula, and platitudes. One of the first VW print ads, headlined "Think Small," showed a Beetle, ever so tiny in the corner of an otherwise blank page, flying in the face of Detroit's "bigger is better" tradition. Another, headlined "Lemon"— an outrageous headline for a car ad—explained in magnificently written copy that the car pictured wasn't shipped because an inspector had spotted a blemished chrome strip on the glove box. Another headline played on the low cost of the Beetle—"$1.02 a Pound"—and then surprised readers by explaining that the VW, pound for pound, was actually more expensive than other cars, which was something to think about, "particularly if you haven't bought a Volkswagen because you thought they didn't cost enough." Madison Avenue had never seen anything like it.

> How outrageous was "Lemon" as a headline for a car ad in 1959?
>
> I couldn't sell it today. No car company would have the courage to take it on.

DDB followed with equally memorable campaigns for many clients including Alka-Seltzer, Avis, and the famous "Mikey likes it" ad for Quaker's Life cereal in the 1970s.

THE POLAROID "COUPLE"

One of my favourite DDB works was their wonderful Polaroid TV campaign from the late 1970s, starring James Garner and Mariette Hartley. It became so popular because of their onscreen chemistry that Hartley resorted to wearing shirts saying, "I am not married to James Garner" when she was off camera.

By raising the bar of ad language, Bill Bernbach would inspire and attract a new generation of writers, artists, musicians, and designers to careers in advertising, where they would create campaigns no less challenging, colourful, and imaginative than the content their clients sponsored. If nothing else, advertising offered the sort of remuneration artistic young minds couldn't find elsewhere. As ad giant Phil Dusenberry put it: "I have always believed that writing advertisements is the second most profitable form of writing. The first, of course, is ransom notes."

CLUTTER, NOISE, AND INTRUSION

All around you today, the age of persuasion is in full blossom. Since the early twentieth century, advertising has grown in close proportion to the economy, and since 1960, in the United States, both have grown more than twentyfold—far ahead of the rate of inflation. That represents enormous growth in the resources directed at ads that compete for your time, your attention, your loyalty, and, yes, your money.

In the 1980s deregulation begat an explosion of specialty TV channels, effectively fragmenting the "mass" TV audience. A generation is growing up with hundreds of channel choices, where their parents might have known only a dozen. At the same time, a rise in consumerism has empowered young people with spending capabilities their grandparents never dreamed of. But greater media literacy, especially among younger people, combined with an expanding onslaught of daily sales pitches, leaves each new generation increasingly immune to advertising messages.

Since the rise of the Internet in the nineties, and with the growth of texting, instant messaging, and online social networking, ad-driven mass media, especially television and print, are fast losing their power as the gatekeepers of information, music, and entertainment. People are connecting directly in groups and communities, leaving many advertisers locked outside, pawing longingly at the window. Though advertisers are spending record amounts in "traditional" ad media, major brands have begun to scale back spending in broadcast, print, and outdoor ads, instead seeking new media, new techniques, and a new language in efforts to reach an increasingly elusive audience. Broadcast and print, once the staples of any major ad campaign, are no longer an advertiser's default choice. As Yogi Berra is supposed to have said of a favourite restaurant, "Nobody goes there anymore. It's too crowded."

From the day I began as an ad copywriter in the 1980s, ad clutter has been the elephant in the room at every meeting. Back then the media universe was expanding, but we still had only a handful of magazines to choose from and not too many TV stations. Bruce Springsteen's "57 Channels (And Nothin' On)" made the point (though that represented about twenty more channels than we actually got), and advertisers could make a television campaign resonate with a large part of the population by buying airtime on only a few shows. Now there are thousands of magazines, hundreds of TV channels, and a growing galaxy of satellite radio channels. Making an "impact" is now part product, part smarts, and often a whole lot of blind luck.

In the summer of 1995, I launched a twenty-five-part radio series, *O'Reilly on Advertising*, on CBC's Radio One, eager to fill what I saw as a huge information void. Of the thousands of books, films, courses, and programs about advertising and marketing, few, if any, were created by people within the industry for people *outside* the industry. As a sweetener I loaded each show with award-winning ads, deconstructing each and telling stories of their campaigns, their techniques, and the people behind them. Braced for derisive howls from an audience horrified by a show about advertising within the ad-free oasis of public radio and hosted by (gasp) an ad guy, I was surprised to find the reception was overwhelmingly kind and curious. Feedback quickly taught me that listeners were surprisingly media savvy and hungry for anecdotes and behind-the-scenes details about the ad business.

Thus emboldened, I proposed a follow-up series, *The Age of Persuasion*, which was designed to look outward at the countless ways marketing and advertising have come to affect everyday life, why certain decisions are made in boardrooms, and why some campaigns work and some don't. This program has allowed me to fill another curious void: the thousands of works critical of the impact of advertising and marketing on modern life and culture are created, almost without exception, by people who have never worked within the advertising business. At the same time, few in the ad business ever seemed to reflect on the many ways their profession is shaping and changing the world. Response to this second radio series, also unexpectedly positive, has come from both inside and outside the ad industry. Of the many comments I receive, a favourite, frequent one is: "Love your show, still hate advertising."

Just as urgently, I wanted to undo what I saw as a common misperception about advertising and marketing: that it's a plague imposed on an innocent population by some big, bad marketing empire mothership. My observation, after some thirty years in the business, is this: we've brought the age of persuasion on ourselves. We are—all of us— its creators and its practitioners.

Behind both the radio series and this book, the authors—we'll be two authors just this once—made a vow that we would never take ourselves or our subject *too* seriously. Don't get us wrong: we're very serious about our trade and our clients, and we're convinced this is a story well worth telling. Yet we're keenly aware that a third of the world is malnourished, environmental crises loom, rogue nations are gathering nuclear secrets, and HIV/AIDS is devastating entire nations; our culture has bigger worries than fallout from a daily profusion of advertising. Never far from our minds is the wonderful line attributed to Alfred Hitchcock, dismissing the hubbub that arose with the release of the film *Psycho:* "It's only a movie."

This book gives me a welcome opportunity to expand on themes introduced on the radio show; to include war stories, anecdotes, and everyday examples that don't fit within the confines of a twenty-seven-minute broadcast. And, as with the radio series, exploring these themes, telling these stories, and raising these questions are all irresistibly fun.

1

The incessant witless repetition of
advertisers' moron-fodder has become
so much a part of life that if we are not
careful, we forget to be insulted by it.
TIMES (LONDON), 1886

CLUTTER

"You're soaking in it."
MADGE THE MANICURIST

O nly in the age of persuasion is it possible that the first thing you hear from your clock radio in the morning, and the last thing you see before your eyes flutter slowly shut at night, are advertisements.

Early each morning you might hear a half-dozen ads on the radio before your feet touch the floor. Staggering out of bed, you'll pass brand logos on your clothing as you make your way to the privy, where you're surrounded by bottles of Head & Shoulders shampoo, Colgate Total toothpaste, Speed Stick deodorant, a Gillette razor, and Ivory soap. You eye the Alka-Seltzer, remembering that glass-too-many of gin and tonic last night.

Your breakfast table resembles a logo gallery, where you sit surrounded by the images of multiple corporate brands—on a box of breakfast cereal, a milk carton, a package of frozen blueberry waffles, and a bottle of syrup. Flip on the TV and you might encounter ads for Glade air freshener, Downy fabric softener, the latest Pixar film, Ford Focus, Monistat yeast infection remedy, and a neighbourhood slip-and-fall law firm. A quick flip through your morning newspaper might reveal dozens more sales messages, from holistic healing and grocery specials to sporting goods and Jenny Craig products to men's fashions and discreet escorts, all of it before that first sip of Folgers coffee passes your lips.

That happens before you travel to work, shop, visit, or play—along roads and highways bedecked with posters, signs, murals, bus benches, billboards, and store signs—and before you turn on your car radio with its ads, traffic sponsors, station promos, and contests and before you flip open your MacBook to discover a screen dotted with banners and pop-up ads. You can see where this is headed: you may already have experienced dozens of what the marketing world calls

2

"brand exposures" and it isn't even 8 a.m. By the time you fall asleep at the end of the day to the sound of a TV ad playing, with an ad-laden magazine sagging in your hand against the duvet, you will have been targeted by hundreds, perhaps thousands, of marketing messages.

I actually counted once, noting all the ads I was exposed to one morning from 6 a.m., when I woke up, to 9 a.m., when I pulled into my parking spot at work. The total was ninety-nine.

BRANDING 101

Branding is at the core of all marketing. Different marketers have their own take on what branding really is, but to me, it means defining what a product or service promises and how it differs from the competition. For example, a Volvo is just a car, but when the idea of "safety" was added, its brand was defined. Nike is just a running shoe, but the powerful idea of "personal achievement" was attached to every single advertising message they sent out, and that gave the famous footwear its own personality. Calvin Klein's clothing line is just apparel, but when the designer linked the idea of "sex" to it, sexy clothing became his category. And then there's Coke. In a taste test once, the iconic drink was compared to an undisclosed cola. People chose Coke over the mystery item almost a hundred to one. Then the undisclosed soda was revealed: it was, in fact, Coke. The difference between the two was branding: the Coke enhances your life "idea" beat the other cola, which had no idea attached to it. When people sampled Coke, they not only tasted the sugar and water combination; they also tasted the logo and the imagery, commercials, and promotions that have accompanied the drink for decades.

YOUR DAILY AD INTAKE

3

Metaphorically speaking, the world has come to look like a NASCAR driver's racing suit, with every square inch occupied by a logo. And it's not just physical space advertisers covet: in 2007 the Chicago White Sox sold their "official start time" to the 7-Eleven convenience store chain. All weeknight games—at U.S. Cellular Field—were scheduled for 7:11 p.m.

It's impossible to measure the exact number of ads lobbed your way on a given day, but that hasn't prevented educators, researchers, and journalists from wondering, or worse, offering educated guesses masquerading as scientific fact. This game probably began in 1957 with a speech by Edwin Ebel, then a vice-president with General Foods. To make a point, he announced that he'd done a little research of his own and had found that a family of four was exposed to 1,518 ads per day. Though there's no evidence that his research was more than anecdotal, the figure was widely repeated, and in a late-fifties variation of the "telephone game," the number was soon believed to apply to an individual consumer. In his 1997 book, *Data Smog*, David Shenk set the number at six hundred. That's the same figure I often quoted while giving creative radio seminars for ad agency writers, adding, from a source since forgotten, that of all those ads, most people would retain only six and, ultimately, maybe—just maybe—remember two. Over the years, I've heard people insist, with more confidence, I think, than evidence, that you're exposed to 3,000, 6,000, even 15,000 ads per day.

The trouble is, no one can agree on criteria. Are you "exposed" to an ad if you scan it with your eyes and don't consciously notice it? Do you count a radio jingle that plays in the car while you're telling your three-year-old not to throw Cheerios at your eighteen-month old? If you glance at your underwear label as you dress, does that count? And what about the quality of each ad exposure? If you read the 250-word Verizon Wireless ad on page 31 of *Rolling Stone* magazine, should it count as much as the Nicorette ad you'd glanced at on page 21?

Then there's the sticky business of quantifying the "average" consumer, who is, at best, a figment of the statistician's oh-so-narrow imagination. In marketing, the practice of demography can be ridiculously cloudy and vague. An advertiser might brief me on wanting to reach "Canadian women, twenty to twenty-eight years old." The trouble is, that group will include an upwardly mobile Vancouver lawyer with a husband, a dog, and a mortgage; an old-order Mennonite in Wallenstein, Ontario; and an anarchistic gay barista in Fredericton. Demographers might miss the fact that a twenty-eight-year-old mother of two could have more in common with a thirty-eight-year-old mother of two than she has with another twenty-eight-year-old. Ads will affect urban dwellers differently than those in farm country. There are just too many variables to consider demographics accurate. On the other hand, "psychographics" provide more insight because they highlight attitudes and aspirations. For example, 13 percent of Wii game users are men over fifty, but my fourteen-year-old daughter is also a Wii player. No demographic is going to reveal that, but psychographics would, as both fifty-year-olds and fourteen-year-olds who like Wii share similar attitudes in the gamer category. This kind of research identifies "tribes"—groups who share the same thinking on a product or subject. And with limited budgets, smart marketers aim at larger tribes, rather than trying to find all their customers by ferreting through multiple demographic age and income categories.

TRY THIS NIFTY EXPERIMENT

For the sake of argument, let's say you're exposed to six hundred ads a day. If nothing else, my spidey sense tells me that's a reasonable, if conservative, figure. And at that rate, you'd likely be exposed to more than 15 million ads in your lifetime. But this is all academic. The daily marketing onslaught would really hit home if you played this little game: imagine yourself trying to avoid exposure to any sort of advertising message—for just one day. Ready? Go!

Suppose you begin by fleeing your workplace, though not before stopping in the privy on the way out. What do you find? Ad posters on the walls by the sink and even in the stalls. Where gender appropriate,

5

you'll find ads over the urinals or even *in* the urinals. One of my favourites was a pithy career-recruiting ad on a plastic mat in a urinal that read "Want to Be a Fireman?" And over at the sink, "admirrors" now project advertising from behind mirrors when you step up to wash your hands.

Escaping the washroom, you make for the elevator only to find . . . more ads. Not only are these high-rise sarcophagi home to poster ads; they're fast becoming home to one of the more popular new ad media: flat screen monitors that pipe ad-laced information "programs" to passengers in thousands of elevators, in hundreds of urban centres, to reach the five hundred or so people who might ride an elevator in a given office tower. Research reveals that advertising in elevators generates a remarkable 84 percent of "unaided recall"—a fancy-pants marketing term meaning that people can remember the ads without being prompted. Advertisers love elevator ads because they know they can reach specific business professionals, most of whom are seeking a place to focus their attention during the ride.

As the door opens, you run to the street and hail a cab—the one with the "HotJobs" ad on top, the special ad-covered hubcaps that remain level as the wheels spin, and the TV screen on the back of the front seat. As you escape the ad-infested city, you pass billboards, shop signs, posters in bus shelters, murals covering the sides of five-storey buildings, and people wearing sandwich boards. "Where to?" asks the cabbie in the Reebok cap. A voice deep within your psyche, recalling summers of peace and bliss, whispers a suggestion, which you promptly relay to the driver: "Take me to the beach." It's perfect. There you can relax with only the sun, the surf, the sand . . .

And the advertising. It's right there—under your bum: a message pressed repetitively into the beach by a sand-grooming machine. Years ago a New Jersey company called Beach'n Billboard found a way to impress repeated ad messages in the sand, including pleas that beach-goers refrain from littering. According to testimonials, littering has

6

decreased by more than 20 percent, while the sponsored messages—for Snapple or Skippy peanut butter, for instance—help the municipality offset the cost of beach maintenance. In beach advertising, as in life, nothing is forever: by noon beach traffic typically wears away most of the ad imprints. But they'll be back in the morning.

Suppose you seek sanctuary in, well, a *sanctuary*, as in a place of God. You've got to imagine that there's nothing like a house of worship to provide an escape from the daily volley of ads, right?

Wrong. At least it would be wrong if you chose to seek refuge at the Basilica of St. Anthony in Padua, Italy, an ancient church, which over the past few generations, had been showing its age. A few years ago, it became painfully evident that the building would require extensive, and expensive, restorations. Just imagine the elation when an Italian bank slipped ninety thousand euros into St. Anthony's collection plate. Wrapped, figuratively, around it was a caveat: in exchange for its contribution, the bank requested a favour. They wished to place a poster ad inside the basilica, effectively offering worshippers a rare opportunity to seek both eternal grace and a competitive rate on their next car loan. When viewed as a commodity, congregations put dollar signs in the eyes of cash-hungry churches, many of whom are seizing the opportunity. In thousands of places of worship across North America, the weekly bulletin—the program with the order of service in it—has become a popular vehicle for intracongregational sales pitches. A typical bulletin might include paid ads for local merchants and professionals, some from within the congregation, and for funeral homes, counselling services, mechanics, and home renovators. At least one church, in Munster, Indiana, has a Starbucks concession in the lobby, right beside the—I'm not making this up—"Heavenly Grounds" bookstore.

Many of North America's so-called "mega-churches" have little theological problem going forth and making disciples of all nations with the help of popular retail brands. Some have built compounds on

7

large acreages, offering, in effect, Christian-themed shopping malls. Ironically, some of these monoliths have become so retail minded that they've opted to cancel services on Christmas Day.

ADS IN SPAAAAAAAACE

Suppose, in your quest to escape the clutter, you cut a cheque for a tidy $20 million, sign up as a space tourist, and lift off into the cold, dark, ad-free vacuum of space? Houston, you have a problem. Not only are there ads in space, but they've been there for some time. In 1993, when an American private-sector spacecraft lifted off, its side was emblazoned with a five-word ad: "Schwarzenegger: The Last Action Hero." It was one small step for a truly B-flat film and one giant leap for advertising. Yet even that wasn't the first ad in space: since 1990 the cash-strapped Russian space program has sold ad space on their Soyuz craft for everything from Sony electronics to— no kidding—Unicharm feminine hygiene products. Tnuva, an Israeli milk company, once filmed a TV spot aboard the Mir space station. On another occasion, crew aboard the Mir deployed an oversized Pepsi can into space.

Persuasion abhors a vacuum. Such is the proliferation of ad clutter that for years I've heard it said in jest that it's a matter of time before people start selling ad space on the insides of their eyelids. People don't laugh at that one quite the way they used to.

THE RISE OF AD AVOIDANCE

In 1956 Eugene McDonald, then president of Zenith, challenged two of his engineers, Robert Adler and Eugene Polley, to create a remote control that would operate a television from across a room. When the product was launched, the ad copy (in what can be called a suicide note of sorts) crowed: "Turns set on or off . . . turns sound on or off . . .

8

changes channels . . . foolproof." It was remote TV tuning, according to McDonald, that fuelled Zenith's success the following year.

Almost unnoticed was a feature which few seem to have observed but which must have sent shock waves through the marketing world. It was the mute button. Finally, there was a way to eliminate the daily clutter of those "long, annoying commercials," and the age of "ad avoidance" was born—along with a substantial cottage industry to accommodate the new trend.

Nowadays, PVRs are programmed to skip TV commercials, "do not call" and "do not mail" lists promise—with limited success—to unsolicited marketing pitches. Peer-to-peer social networking, such as instant messaging, Facebook, and Twitter, allows us to bypass commercial radio stations and share music, information, and opinions directly. On-demand digital programming, gaming, Blu-ray and DVD technology, and music downloading are deposing commercially driven media from their traditional positions as entertainment gatekeepers. At the same time, software designers make a tidy living designing pop-up blockers and programs that detect and delete adware—and privacy legislators are scrambling, often in vain, to keep up with developments that are fundamentally altering the gathering, buying, and selling of consumer information. A kind of siege mentality has set in as those targeted by marketers try to build defences against the bullets. But as one section of wall is constructed to fend off new sales volleys, another is breached.

Ad Avoid·ance *(noun)* An industry term that gives ad people ulcers. Essentially, it's a catch-all phrase that encompasses all the ingenious ways people avoid ads. It could be the mute button on the remote, it could be triple speeding through the commercial island on a PVR, it could be simply switching radio stations when commercials come on. More radical avoiders disappear into their iPods or sell their TV sets.

CLUTTER

ACT NOW-ETH

Humorist Colin McEnroe, speaking for today's ad-fatigued civilization, once wrote that he had a disturbing dream "in which I break
through a cave wall near Nag Hammadi and discover urns full of
ancient Coptic scrolls. As I unfurl the first scroll, a subscription card
to some Gnostic exercise magazine flutters out."

THE DAWN OF CLUTTER

The first grumbling about ad clutter can be traced back to nineteenth-
century London, the granddaddy of "big" cities to emerge from the
industrial revolution. At the beginning of the 1800s, fewer than a million people lived in the British capital, but by the end of that century, the
population had grown sixfold, and during those years, sales messages
began to dominate the urban landscape.

"Of all human powers operating on the affairs of mankind,"
observed American statesman Henry Clay, "none is greater than that
of competition." Easy to say, for a guy who didn't have to spend hot
July mornings hawking mullet in London's Old Billingsgate fish
market. Competition for the attention of London's growing population required—and still requires—stifling and often backbreaking
work. In the Victorian age, merchants, tradespeople, and entrepreneurs swarmed the city, shouting to be heard over one another, and
devising ingenious, if irritating, ways to make their presence felt.
Trade cards grew in popularity. Bearing a tradesperson's name, and
perhaps a map to his place of business, these precursors of modern
junk mail were handed out and slipped under front doors. Other
ads were pressed onto coins and tokens, printed on ship's sails, and
posted inside "bathing machines"—the portable "privacy huts"
women dragged around them when they sauntered into the ocean, lest
any man should actually see their swimming attire. Posters were everywhere. Streets resounded to the noise of hawkers and the declamations

of actors performing "tableau" ads as they were carted about on portable wagons.

Deep within the swirls of this commercial maelstrom, the *Times* felt duty bound to warn its readers about "the incessant witless repetition of advertisers' moron-fodder." That itself was bold talk for a great broadsheet that tucked world events neatly in beside box ads for "Gerolstein: a perfect table water. Recommended by the most eminent physicians" and A.S. Lloyd's Euxesis, "for shaving without soap, water, or brush, and in half the usual time." Ad-driven media have wrestled with the ethics of criticizing ads ever since, prompting David Ogilvy to write: "It strikes me as bad manners for a magazine to accept one of my advertisements and then attack it editorially—like inviting a man to dinner then spitting in his eye." I agree: while the editorial department should be separated from the ad department, I do bristle when radio announcers offer up a snide remark about a product, right on the heels of an ad for that very product. It's bad form, and a call to the sales department to complain usually results in an instant make-good (ad speak for a free ad to make up for the transgression). Advertising and programming have to live in peaceful co-existence, since after all, one can't survive without the other. But when the programming people do criticize the advertising, it is usually induced by the overabundance of ads crowding the content.

DAVID OGILVY: AD GIANT

David Ogilvy will appear many times in this book. He was one of the great, wise admen, founding one of the world's mightiest advertising agencies, Ogilvy & Mather. Remarkably, however, he didn't start his agency until he was thirty-eight. Born in England, he had been a door-to-door salesman, a chef, a researcher, and a tobacco farmer, but in 1949 he started an advertising agency in New York, backed by his elder brother's British agency, Mather & Crowther. Originally called Hewitt, Ogilvy, Benson & Mather, and later Ogilvy, Benson & Mather, then finally Ogilvy & Mather, the "Mather" part didn't really exist in New York. David was the sole turbine there. Ogilvy's agency enjoyed a meteoric rise on Madison Avenue, eventually becoming one of the biggest in America, and was sold for $864 million in 1989. Ogilvy died in 1999 at the age of eighty-eight. He held firm and articulate opinions on what it took to create effective advertising, and he knew he was gifted in the ways of persuasion. A magazine once wrote an article about him with the headline "David Ogilvy: Genius?" and Ogilvy later said he almost sued them for the question mark. He wrote extensively on the subject of advertising, and his words are quoted in every corner of the advertising world to this day.

NEW TECHNOLOGIES: NEW KINDS OF CLUTTER

Newspapers themselves would soon become leading purveyors of clutter. By the late nineteenth century, new-fangled typecasting machines made it easier to print more pages—and squeeze in more ads. Newspapers that had once published editions of four, eight, or twelve pages rapidly expanded to twenty-four, thirty-six, and even forty-eight pages. Today there's even more ad space available in most major newspapers, to the point where you need a forklift to pick up their weekend editions. Advertising is a great money maker for the owners of newspapers and magazines, whose rates can remain high no matter what the sizes of their publications, on the promise that advertisers will reach a given number of readers. But running an ad in a bulky paper is a raw deal for advertisers, who pay the same but find themselves crowded by a large number of rivals, each competing for the reader's attention. For advertisers, printing more ads is like a government printing more money: the more of it there is "out there," the less value each one has.

During the early twentieth century, it wasn't just the volume of

12

advertising but also the intrusive nature of new ad media that escalated the ad-clutter crisis. When it became technologically possible for "telephones" to be installed in millions of homes, the devices were met with a growing unease about the "outside world" flooding in. Satirist Ambrose Bierce summed it up in this entry in his 1911 devil's dictionary:

> An invention of the devil which abrogates some of the advantages of making a disagreeable person keep his distance.

It's the world's loss that Mr. Bierce wasn't around long enough to define "telemarketer."

Ad clutter is a nuisance that became an annoyance, that blossomed into a full-blown media pandemic. While this is a problem for consumers, it's a catastrophe for the marketing industry, whose messages are muddled and lost within the growing din. The very onslaught of clutter is making the public immune to messages, as they have increasingly tuned them out to the point that it's now second nature for them to do so. Consumers' ad fatigue leads to an easy dismissal of most advertising and an appetite for ad-avoiding technology, such as PVRs. As their public tunes out, advertisers then heavy-up on media buys in heroic attempts to make sure their messages are heard. This, of course, has a negative effect, as their ads are buried under the very clutter they were hoping to avoid. They then resort to non-traditional methods of reaching the public, such as clever ambient marketing, but that only creates more clutter. Ad sellers, on the other hand, love ad clutter. With the increase of ad minutes per hour and the growing number of ad media, they rub their hands with glee as visions of sugarplum

Am·bi·ent ad·ver·tis·ing

(noun) Advertising that has no "traditional media" attached to it. Whereas a billboard is displayed on a paid medium (an outdoor board), a chalk-drawn ad on a sidewalk isn't. They're "ambient"—that is, they're part of the immediate surroundings.

13

profits dance in their heads. In the end, the better you understand clutter from a marketer's perspective, the more clearly you'll see why, and how, the craft of persuasion is rapidly changing.

WHY ADVERTISERS REALLY, REALLY HATE CLUTTER

They may actually hate it more than you do. I'll show you what I mean. Imagine you're sitting alone in the sixth row of a large, empty sports stadium. Empty, that is, except for one other soul sitting directly across the field from you, who is also in the sixth row—just the two of you in this cavernous space. You cup your hands to your mouth and yell your name to that person as loudly as you can. After a moment the other person cups her hands to her mouth and yells her name back. Though your voices fade a bit during their journey, each is audible— and distinct.

Now imagine that you're in the same stadium, in the same seat, but this time it's filled to capacity. You and your friend are immersed in a sea of, say, 61,371 people. The stadium is alive with distractions: couples are squabbling, babies are crying, drunks in the cheap seats are singing, hundreds of people are on the phone, and a few are snoring. The public address system is blaring out anachronistic eighties pop ballads with a subatomically tiny lyrical connection to what's happening on the playing field. The true visual focal point is the giant TV scoreboard, restlessly cycling through replays, stats, and out-of-town scores. Up and down the aisles, an army of uniformed men and women hawk the virtues of cold beer and four-dollar pretzels. There's a palpable buzz. The air is thick and alive with sensory information; Las Vegas would be proud.

Again, you cup your hands to your mouth and yell your name to the person who is still sitting across from you. But first you have to work, methodically, just to find her. Once you do spot her, you begin to wonder how to get her attention through all the noises and distractions. Your monopoly on her attention has vanished: she's been swallowed in a sea of sound and imagery. And your real troubles are just beginning. As it happens, everyone else in the stadium—61,369 others—are also cupping their hands to their mouths and screaming their names as loudly as they can, all of them intent on diverting your friend's attention to them. *Thousands* of voices meld together in one large, chaotic roar.

Does it matter who wins? Absolutely. The jobs, perhaps the careers, of every single person in that crowd, including yours, hinge on your ability to win the attention of that one person across from you. Feel that? It's a drop of sweat dripping down against your coccyx. You begin to brainstorm ways that your voice could cut through all the noise and distractions. You could shout louder than anyone else: perhaps the distinct timbre of your voice would cut through the din. Perhaps an appealing visual would attract your friend's attention: you might don a chicken suit or your birthday suit or a bright red, strapless cocktail dress. Here's an idea: you could pay the stadium to silence everyone but you for ten seconds while you holler out your name. All are viable tactics, but the trouble is this: anything you can do, your 61,369 rivals can also do.

Before long you'll notice yourself cycling through a profound series of emotions. The initial panic becomes denial, which gives way to a sense of futility. Then you become philosophical and resolved as you roll up your sleeves and begin scheming ways of conveying your message through enemy lines. When your message does get through, you feel exhilarated and untouchable—that is, until you try again, and fail. On goes the roller-coaster ride as you alternate between born-on-Krypton invincibility and snake-bit, pack-your-things-and-turn-in-your-playbook, move-to-Brazil melancholy.

Meanwhile, the person you're trying to reach feels like the lone debutante at the Cowhands Ball: overwhelmed by the number of suitors who've come a-courtin'. Some she finds attractive, some offensive, some charming, some articulate; all are struggling for a place in her heart. She can be forgiven for wanting to hide, even if it means avoiding the few she favours in order to block out the many others she doesn't.

15

Seen this way, you can begin to understand the sense of desperation that drives marketers to extreme cynicism, and on the other side, extreme artistry. The less talented know that they can drop their pants—sometimes literally—to get noticed. They're advertising's answer to cotton candy: it's irresistible for a moment but has no lasting value.

In the upper floors of marketing are great minds who base extensive campaigns on great ideas. In England, for instance, a remarkable, decades-old campaign has been built on just one line: "Heineken refreshes the parts other beers cannot reach." Twenty years of award-winning ads, all made possible by the fertile ground of that stellar concept. Another enduring campaign idea was created for Michelin, who hit the motherlode when they put a cute baby together with the line "Because so much is riding on your tires." "Unless your advertising is based on a BIG IDEA," wrote David Ogilvy, "it will pass like a ship in the night." Ogilvy proved it with resonant campaigns for Pepperidge Farms, Rolls-Royce and Hathaway shirts.

OGILVY AND THE ROLLS

I have always loved Ogilvy's classic Rolls-Royce print ad with the headline "At 60 miles an hour the loudest noise in this new Rolls-Royce comes from the electric clock." In a time when trite, glossy automotive ads ruled, it stood out as one of the few to assume intelligence on the part of the reader. The headline was completely intriguing, offering an enormous promise of upscale motoring without ever having to say it, and the copy that followed was charming, graceful, and informative—in short, a superb lesson in print advertising. Not long after that ad appeared, the Copywriters Hall of Fame made Ogilvy one of its first inductees, in 1961.

Yet even for the best in the business, great ideas are elusive. As Ogilvy confessed: "I am supposed to be one of the more fertile inventors of big ideas, but in my long career as a copywriter, I have not had more than 20, if that." So very true. In a business where one person may create thousands of ads over a career, a top creative mind may generate fewer than twenty big ideas. That is not at all a criticism of ad people but rather a stark reminder of how incredibly difficult it is to create magnificent advertising.

WHO KNEW? NOT EVERYBODY HATES AD CLUTTER

While consumers loathe ad clutter, and advertisers detest it even more, one group hopes it won't go away anytime soon: "ad-driven media." Broadcasters, publishers, out-of-home media companies, and Internet ad firms are the stadium owners in our metaphor. They are the ones who are profiting from today's ad explosion, and they are only too happy to increase the number of seats in order to accommodate growing demand—even if this means cramming their existing customers into smaller spaces. They reap financial gain from the consumers who are frustrated at having their attention parcelled and sold, and they make money from advertisers whose messages are devalued each time the clutter is allowed to grow.

Ad-driv·en me·di·a *(noun)*
Those media that are dependent on advertising for some, or all, of their revenues. Television, radio, billboards, magazines, and newspapers are all ad-driven media. They wouldn't exist without ad dollars.

Ad-driven media are the arms dealers of marketing warfare, cheerfully selling time and space to all combatants: Reebok, Nike, and Adidas; Coors and Budweiser; Apple and Microsoft. An escalation in each war can only be good for business.

FALLOUT

Of all the media, radio and television suffer most from ad clutter as programming is shrunk, subdivided, and busied by messages within messages. CP24, a news and information TV station in Toronto, is the poster child for an information-cluttered world. Where other news channels might scroll a steady stream of headlines or sports scores

17

beneath their visuals, CP24 reserves a corner of the screen for an anchor reading the news, while the rest of the screen is filled with the date, time, current temperature, a graphic showing a four-day weather forecast, a traffic camera, another graphic showing major financial indices, two station logos (one at the top with the weather, another at the bottom), two—count 'em, two—stock tickers scrawling across the bottom, and yet another graphic rotating through the major headlines of the day. The screen might contain twenty pieces of detailed information at any one time, and that's before you count the audio. The screens of mainstream broadcasters are not as cluttered as this, but they do plant their ever-present transparent logos in one corner of the screen and shove program credits to one side so they can jam in station promos, a technique known in the industry as a "squeeze-back."

MAMA'S GOT A SQUEEZE-BACK

A *squeeze-back* is the practice of literally squeezing the end credits of a program to one side of the screen in order to use the other side to promote an upcoming show. Squeeze-backs were invented by NBC in the early nineties as a way to keep people from channel hopping. By squeezing the credits over and using the remaining space to tease viewers with what was coming up next, they found they could retain them and prevent the habitual end-of-show channel hopping. In Canada squeeze-backs were used for very different reasons. Networks were limited to twelve minutes of commercial time per hour, and any promo of an upcoming American program would count against the twelve minutes. But since a promo wasn't a "commercial," it didn't generate any revenue. For every American promo, Canadian networks therefore lost money. By moving the credits over, Canadian stations could promote an upcoming American show while the credits were running. And the promo wasn't counted against their allotted commercial time because the squeezed promo was inside the program time, not outside it.

Already there are signs that this message layering is rewiring young brains. Take stacking, for instance. Kids, including mine, are becoming expert at this process: they might have a TV on while listening to music on their iPod at the same time as texting on their phones, instant-messaging on a computer, and surfing the Internet. Advertisers have caught on to this phenomenon and employ what is known as "fully integrated" marketing. This means that a product promoted on TV will also be publicized through mobile phones, Internet ads, and websites, all in the hope that every touch point will converge in one single, sit-down, "stacking" experience.

In this spirit commercial broadcasters are doing some stacking of their own: "busying" their programming and, in doing so, stuffing more commercial messages into each hour. Radio stations are phasing out sixty-second commercials, making way for shorter, more lucrative ads. Similarly, TV broadcasters have shrunk programming to accommodate more ad messages per hour: an episode of *Bonanza* in the early 1960s typically ran fifty-two minutes, allowing eight minutes for ads, promos, and station identification. Forty years later, an episode of *Desperate Housewives* might run forty-four minutes.

Broadcasters have become wary of audience backlash as their programs shrink and their commercial offerings grow—though not wary enough to actually reverse the trend. Instead, some have introduced tricks to hold audiences in spite of extended program interruptions. Some networks have taken to breaking the conventions of time, running shows past the top or bottom of the hour, starting the next one at, say, 8:05, instead of 8:00 on the nose. The theory is that viewers sticking with a program to the end will find that shows on other networks have already begun. So rather than miss the beginning of those, they might as well come back to the network they were just on and pick up the show that starts at 8:05.

Desperate Housewives experimented with some ingenious parcelling of their story "acts"—the segments that appear between commercial breaks. In some episodes, their opening segment could run as long as twelve minutes before the titles rolled: four times the length of traditional TV "teaser" segments of the sixties and seventies. The idea was to pull viewers deep enough into the story that they would stay with it—especially since it would be too late to pick up the thread of shows on rival networks. Of course, what you don't pay now, you have to pay later, which is why *Desperate Housewives* offers six shorter acts between breaks rather than follow the convention of four longer ones. In fact, some acts ran as short as four and a quarter minutes—not much longer than the three-and-a-half-minute breaks that surrounded them.

It's a far cry from 1922, when Herbert Hoover, secretary of commerce under Presidents Harding and Coolidge, oversaw the birth and early growth of the radio industry and warned "that so great a possibility as radio should not be . . . drowned in advertising chatter." And when television arrived in 1939, the government remained leery of commercials. For the first two years of TV in the United States, the Federal Communications Commission (FCC) did not allow stations to make profits from commercials and in 1945, it issued guidelines in the form of a document called *Public Service Responsibility of Broadcast Licensees* (known as the Blue Book), which limited the amount of commercial airtime each station could have.

THE GREAT "WHO LISTENS TO RADIO" EXPERIMENT

At my own company, we try to tackle ad clutter with creativity. Once, for example, we were approached by a consortium of radio stations in Toronto to create a radio campaign to advertise . . . radio. They told us their salespeople were constantly hitting a wall with retailers when they tried to sell them ad time. Why the pushback? Apparently, retailers believed that nobody "really listens to radio." Yes, radios were on but only for background noise or music. So the consortium asked us to create a radio campaign that proved people do listen to radio and that creative radio spots could break through the clutter. It was a tall order, and failure would do more damage to radio than if we had left the matter alone. However, we came up with a novel idea. We created two fictional companies and advertised them. One was called Basil's Pre-Owned Warehouse. In this campaign, a slightly stiff store owner named Basil told listeners he could save them money by selling pre-owned items, such as pre-owned business cards and pre-owned monogram shirts. The other company, Cliffhanger Publishing, advertised whodunnit books, but we gave away the surprise ending of each book in every ad.

Here's the best part: hundreds of listeners started calling the radio stations that had broadcast these ads, complaining they couldn't find Basil's store anywhere. Still others called in to say they couldn't find the Cliffhanger books in bookstores. When we finally revealed that the two companies didn't exist, a local radio talk show dedicated its evening proceedings to a discussion of the events and had to extend the two-hour show to three hours to accommodate all the calls. And the next day, the *Toronto Star* ran a front-page article on our campaign. When all was said and done, we had accomplished two things: we'd proven that people do listen to radio and we'd truly broken through the clutter. A big idea, executed with skill, has a superb chance of prevailing.

In the U.S. and Canada, regulators have begun to remove the cap on the number of minutes per hour available for advertising. "You don't regulate what you don't have to," said Konrad von Finckenstein, chairman of the Canadian Radio-television and Telecommunications Commission (CRTC). "I don't see why we should regulate advertising. It's up to the Canadian consumer to decide with his remote how much advertising he wants to see."

The program interruptions don't end at commercials either. Closed caption "sponsorships" ("Closed captioning is made possible in part by . . .") aren't counted as advertising. Many TV stations crawl brand-related messages across the screen during a program to skirt around limits on hourly commercial content, and these are considered to be outside the traditional twelve to fourteen minutes of ad time per hour currently allowed.

Contrast that with an episode of *Lux Radio Theatre* in the 1940s. Lux would be mentioned in the introduction. Then Cecil B. DeMille would introduce that evening's radio play: very often an adaptation of a popular motion picture, with the screen actors reprising their roles. Thirty minutes later, the play would break for a pitch—a minute or two long—for Lux Toilet Soap. The play would then conclude, leaving room for one more pitch for Lux. In all, perhaps five minutes of the hour-long broadcast were dedicated to the sponsor—most notably, the single sponsor—which no fan of the show was likely to forget. Today an hour of TV might include messages from a dozen sponsors, any of whom might be ignored or forgotten.

Recently I heard an hour-long program on a local radio station: a mortgage broker had purchased the entire hour and was fielding phone calls from listeners about buying and financing real estate. It was like a live infomercial, except that the broadcast was punctuated with commercials from unrelated sponsors. Similarly, some TV commercials have ads *within* ads. A commercial for a restaurant chain, for instance, might show a customer with a Molson logo on his beer glass. This kind of incremental product placement only works over time, and needs the tonnage of repeated exposures to break through.

Prod·uct place·ment *(noun)*
A product literally placed within a movie scene or TV show. In some cases, such as that of Heineken in the TV series *Mad Men*, the brand even paid to be part of the storyline.

Too many ads are, themselves, cluttered internally with information. Automotive ads are among the worst culprits, jamming the screen with graphics, prices, features, and too often, lines of tiny, completely unreadable legal jargon. In print ads, this is known as "mouse type."

22

SQUEAKY LITTLE DETAILS: MOUSE TYPE

Mouse type is an industry term for the tiny, legal disclaimer lines found in many TV and print ads. These disclaimers are required by law if an offer has strings attached, but ironically, most TV ad disclaimers end up being much too small to actually read. In print ads the type size for such disclaimers is also incredibly small, but it's generally readable. In radio the equivalent would be the super-fast "Void where prohibited; must be eighteen years of age to participate" line, read in under two seconds. In the United States most legal disclaimers have to be fully spelled out in the ad, leaving a lot of American radio ads heaving under more than fifteen seconds of "asterisk-speak." In Canada a "See store for details" usually suffices and makes Canadian ads much more bearable for the listener.

Local radio sponsors often mistakenly treat their thirty-second commercial as an elevator pitch, to be stuffed with their name (three times, please), street address, Internet address, telephone number, and if time allows, what it is they're selling. When talking to clients and writers of such ads, I used the analogy of apples. If I have five apples in my hand and I throw them at you, chances are you're going to drop them. But if I have just one apple and I lob it to you, you'll likely catch it. So it is with information in today's overly cluttered media.

> The phrase *elevator pitch* reached popular culture's top floor in the eighties and nineties, when it was used to describe an entire sales presentation packed into the duration of an elevator ride. This reduced pitch is the ultimate test for an idea: if it can be summed up in only thirty-five words and still elicit excitement, it's a winner.

According to one media consultant, TV advertising will have lost one-third of its effectiveness between 1990 and 2010 because of rising costs, falling viewership, growing ad clutter, and commercial-avoidance technologies. But in recent years, some big-money sponsors have launched bold experiments in clutter busting. In October 2003, the Season 3 debut of *24* was sponsored solely by Ford, and it was "commercial free" if you chose not to count the lengthy ads before

23

and after the show. You'd also have to ignore Ford's product-placement relationship with the series. Just as the bad guys in *Ben Hur* and *Star Wars* had British accents, in *24* the good guys drive Fords, while the bad guys drive GM vehicles. All the same, it was a rare moment in modern TV history for a single sponsor to provide an hour of programming. Even on America's "commercial-free" PBS, some programs include several fifteen-second plugs for retail brands, packaged as "funding for this program is made possible by" announcements.

For six weeks in the spring of 2006, a single sponsor—Snapple— underwrote all the programming on FNX FM in Boston. Traditional commercials were halted, in place of announcements that Snapple was sponsoring the broadcast, some Snapple-based banter from the announcers, and a few Snapple-centric station contests. One industry executive dubbed it "brandcasting"—a broadcast double whammy where clutter was tossed out to make way for messages aimed at young listeners. In spite of this new development, I wouldn't bet the farm that the "sole sponsor" trend will rescue our culture from ad clutter anytime soon: broadcasters are wary of giving so much control to a single advertiser, especially when there's more money to be made by selling the time piecemeal.

Credit the ad industry for this much: we adapt quickly. When we can't find a path to your imagination through conventional media, we start looking for another route.

24

THE MYTH OF "THEY"

In one of my favourite, long-forgotten radio ads, two men introduce themselves as "the *They* Brothers." Have you heard someone say "they" are fixing a broken water main? Or "they" are opening a supermarket? Or "they" are launching a new Mars probe? Yup, those are the guys. In this case, these "Theys" are having a sale.

In the same way, people often think of advertisers as one humungous, collective "they." Which means that "they" put up that tacky poster in a washroom stall, placed the stylish Versace ad in *Vogue,* and produced that epic Super Bowl TV spot. One could readily imagine that "they" hold regular meetings in some Dr. Evil–type lair, deep in the bowels of the high-rent district.

Here's a more accurate metaphor: think of advertisers as millions of ants in a colony, each working hard and each with its own objective. Except that in this colony, every single ant is competing *against* the others. That's the ad business. Almost every ad you see, hear, and otherwise experience is competing for a piece of your imagination. And like any cross-section of humanity, the vast, worldwide advertising community is diverse: composed of geniuses and idiots, saints and buffoons, and everything in between.

If it's any consolation, the advertising theys are a lot like you. They also watch their kung pao chicken cool as a telemarketer prattles on about replacement windows, and they cuss at the TV when a favourite movie is butchered by multiple commercial interruptions.

BREAKING THE
CONTRACT

2

I think that I shall never see
A billboard lovely as a tree.
Perhaps unless the billboards fall,
I'll never see a tree at all.
OGDEN NASH

A few decades back, Texan Claudia Alta Taylor Johnson gazed down the highway and didn't like what she saw.

Billboards blocked her view of the plains, of the distant hills, and of her beloved wildflowers. So she complained to her husband, President Lyndon Baines Johnson, who prompted Congress to pass the Highway Beautification Act, which placed limits on the spread of posters—or billboards as they're popularly known—and preserved the views that Lady Bird Johnson loved so well.

THE POOP ON POSTERS

Billboards are known as *posters* in the ad business. The term dates back centuries, to a time when printed ads were attached to public lampposts. The term *billboard* comes from the Middle English word *bill* (which refers to a written document).

In the growing cities of nineteenth-century Europe, as in North American cities, posters began littering the visual landscape. Most inflicted only a passive assault on the senses, and they rarely blocked anyone's view of anything but lampposts and buildings and construction barriers. In a few storied cases, billboards and large, busy signs have actually defined a place. In Times Square, for instance, signs and billboards embody the reputation of that locale as a bastion of money, power, and consumerism.

The new restrictions drew rave reviews, particularly from one British expat, who later wrote:

> As a private person, I have a passion for landscape, and have never seen one improved by a billboard. Where every prospect pleases, man is at his vilest when he erects a billboard. When I retire, I am going to start a secret society of masked vigilantes who will travel around the world on silent motor bicycles, chopping down posters at the dark of the moon. How many juries will convict us when we are caught in these acts of beneficent citizenship?

It's a remarkable manifesto because its author is the legendary advertising mogul David Ogilvy. Throughout his career, he railed at large outdoor posters. Also quoted in Ogilvy's rant is then governor of California, Pat Brown, who observed: "When a man throws an empty cigarette package from an automobile, he is liable to a fine of $50. When he throws a billboard across a view, he is richly rewarded."

Billboards are a symptom of a large, growing problem in the age of persuasion. While much of the work is highly creative, it, like many other media, must figure out a way to honour an implicit contract between advertisers and consumers which, simply put, promises that advertisers must give you something in exchange for their imposition on your time, attention, and space. An ad might offer useful information, an insight, or a solution to a problem. It might help pay for the TV show you're watching or the magazine you're reading. It might simply entertain you. The key is that it offers some tangible benefit.

Your job as a consumer is to discern which marketers are keeping their end of the bargain and which are not. With that knowledge, you'll have the power to reward the honest brokers and punish the transgressors. I suspect few people realize they have that power, but they—that is, you—really do. A simple letter of complaint to a brand's corporate headquarters can have a profound effect: I've seen major campaigns radically altered in response to a handful of complaints. On a larger scale, consumers can—and do—vote with their wallets.

ALBERT LASKER: HOW THE CONTRACT BUILT EARLY RADIO

Earlier I mentioned Albert Lasker, who, inspired by John E. Kennedy's famous "salesmanship on paper" note, built the Chicago-based Lord & Thomas into one of the world's largest advertising empires. Initially, Lasker paid little attention to radio as it struggled for the economic model that would sustain it. What he couldn't ignore, however, was the success of radio advertising pioneers such as Bernard Gimbel, of Gimbels department stores, and Saks Fifth Avenue. Even harder to ignore was Lasker's client David Sarnoff of RCA, who was also founder of the NBC radio network in 1926. Eventually, Lasker decided to experiment with radio advertising and asked his New York office to create a program based on some sort of Broadway entertainment as a vehicle for Palmolive. Inspired by its success, Lasker quickly embraced the new medium on behalf of other clients.

NBC president Merlin Aylesworth didn't believe in radio advertising as you hear it today, but preferred that sponsors (a word not yet invented in the late twenties) be mentioned before and after a program with a passing phrase like "The following program comes to you through the courtesy of Lucky Strike." Lasker thought differently: he reckoned that in exchange for underwriting a broadcast, brands should be offered an opportunity to present the sort of "reason why" advertising they did in print, but adapted for sound. Instead of parcels of space, they would occupy parcels of time. And that is how the broadcast "commercial," as it came to be known, was born.

In solving a problem for his clients, Lasker provided the economic model radio had been struggling to find: big-name advertisers could provide big money to underwrite high-calibre entertainment for a

30

mass audience. The bigger the audience, the greater the value to advertisers, and theoretically, the more they would pay for production.

Radio would provide top-rank entertainment, but it would not be free. Listeners would pay by allowing themselves to be exposed to an ad. It seemed just the right fit in a world of compromise. You want to go camping? You tolerate mosquitoes. You want to fly? You tolerate airports. You want Groucho Marx in your living room? No problem, provided the nation's three thousand Plymouth–De Soto dealers can tag along. And there it was: The Contract. Sponsors gave programming, and in return, they took some of the listener's time and attention.

It was Lasker, working for his client, Pepsodent, who introduced a network audience to *Amos 'n' Andy.* Today the prospect of two Caucasian actors in nineteenth-century minstrel blackface would cause marketers to squirm, but in 1928 it posed a very different problem: as strange as it sounds today, clients feared that two African-Americans (faux or otherwise) might sully the image of the toothpaste. After the sponsor's enormous initial success, Pepsodent sales eventually began to slip and Lasker theorized the problem wasn't the medium but that the brand relationship with the *Amos 'n' Andy* audience was tired. Lasker's son Edward suggested that Pepsodent shift its sponsorship to a show built around a clever young comedian, and so began *The Pepsodent Show Starring Bob Hope.* Bing Crosby also acquired his first big network exposure on a Lord & Thomas show, and L&T was a major player in the early soap operas: in fact, soaps pioneer Frank Hummert had been L&T's chief copywriter in New York in the 1920s.

L&T dominated network radio in those early days. In the first four years the networks operated, the ad agency purchased 30 percent of all network time in the United States. It was Lasker programming that pioneered the "double broadcast," where a show was performed first for the eastern time zones and later for the western time zones. In one remarkable year—during the Depression yet—L&T recorded $50 million in billings—well over half a billion of today's dollars.

31

When television took off in the 1950s, it suffered few of the birthing pains that radio had; Albert Lasker had provided a ready-made economic template. At the same time, the postwar economic boom gave consumers enough cash to buy television sets, and as TV viewership grew, the value of its audience became increasingly attractive to advertisers. Sponsors lined up to pour fresh buckets of money into the new medium. A large part of the attraction was the "mass audience" experience of the new medium; like radio, it drew millions of people to the same event during the same time span. The morning after a broadcast, it seemed that the talk was all about what "everyone" had been watching the night before: Ralph and Norton's latest get-rich-quick scheme or which dress Uncle Miltie wore on *Texaco Star Theater*. It was the shared experience, as much as the programs themselves, that caused a buzz around the broadcasts. There was a thrill in knowing that millions of others were watching the same show at the same moment. Sponsors' ads were a small price to pay.

Today the Super Bowl, the Academy Awards, and one-off events such as the Obama inauguration are among the few remnants of the big, shared experience in broadcast. One could even argue that the events of 9/11 were the first such shared experiences of the twenty-first century. Audiences have long since been scattered in a thousand directions by the explosion of multiple channels, TiVo, time shifting, and new media.

THE RISE OF BILLBOARDS

During the economic boom years that followed the Second World War, North Americans took to the road, their ears ringing to the siren call of Dinah Shore and the crooning of Pat Boone:

See the USA
In your Chevrolet.
America is askin' you to caaaaaaall
And see it in your Chevrolet.

Performance is sweeter, nothing can beat 'er,
Life is completer in a Chevy.

Times were good for postwar consumers, who could afford cars and were now demanding better roads to connect them with distant cities. Governments obliged with bigger, faster highways. Advertisers seized the opportunity to reach landscape-weary consumers.

But they broke the contract. For more than a generation, advertising had been tolerated in broadcast—in exchange for *The Shadow*, *The Great Gildersleeve*, and *The Ed Sullivan Show*—and readers accepted that box ads kept newspaper and magazine subscriptions affordable. But highway billboards? All they offered was an interruption of the experience highway driving was meant to provide. It was as if the Rocky Mountains, the wheat belt, and the rugged ocean coasts were "brought to you by" Morning Treat coffee, Coca-Cola, and Champion spark plugs.

It's worth noting that while there have been many creative billboard campaigns, some in particular have endeared themselves to highway travellers—and to many others who never laid eyes on them.

Back in the 1920s, three decades before billboards began towering over superhighways, a small company in Minneapolis was marketing an innovative new product: a shaving cream that didn't need to be mixed into a froth with a mug and brush. The formula supposedly originated with a sailor based in Burma—hence the name Burma-Shave. It was a big idea, but with no significant marketing budget. Company president Clinton Odell was approached by his son Allan with an idea for some roadside signs and a request for two hundred dollars for wooden planks and paint. The family brainstormed a series of road signs, in series of four and spaced about a hundred feet apart, to be read in sequence. That way, motorists hurtling past—at, say, thirty-five miles per hour—would read each series of signs in about nineteen seconds. Farmers were paid anywhere from $5 to $25 a year to allow the signs to be put up in their fields. At the peak of the Burma-Shave campaign,

33

seven thousand signs were placed in forty-five American states, and the pithy verse on those billboards gave Burma-Shave a special place in modern advertising lore.

> Said Juliet
> To Romeo
> If you won't shave
> Go homeo
> Burma-Shave

and

> Special seats
> Reserved in Hades
> For whiskered guys
> Who scratch their ladies
> Burma-Shave

Some moved away from the language of sale to a spirit of public service:

> When Frisky
> With Whiskey
> Don't Drive
> Cause it's risky
> Burma-Shave

Delighted motorists probably imagined an army of workers conceiving and placing those signs all over the country. Few realized that the "army" consisted of just eight vans, owned by a company that never employed more than thirty-five people. Ironically, it was the era when billboard advertising took off, in the 1950s, that the Burma-Shave campaign declined. Larger, faster highways attracted big-money advertisers, whose billboards had to be higher, bigger, and placed farther apart to be seen by the faster-moving traffic. When Philip Morris bought out the Burma-Shave company, it ended the famous campaign, and the last Burma-Shave signs came down in 1966. Without the power of the signs to sustain it, the brand soon dropped off the public's radar, but this landmark campaign, run on a shoestring budget, ranks twenty-third on *AdAge* magazine's list of Top 100 Advertising Campaigns. And in popular culture, it's regarded with fond nostalgia: ads that gave viewers fun, funny, surprising diversions during long road trips: certainly enough to honour the contract.

Decades earlier, in the 1890s, Mail Pouch Tobacco murals first appeared on the sides of barns throughout America's Midwest. Though they predated Albert Lasker's contract by three decades, they were done in the same spirit. The company offered to paint farmers' barns: but in lieu of cash, they would paint one side with an ad for their tobacco in large letters. Farmers might even receive a dollar or two per year for the privilege. Through the decades that followed, Mail Pouch murals became part of the landscape, many the work of one Harley Warwick, who reckons he painted twenty thousand barns in his time. When America's Highway Beautification Act passed in the 1960s, advertising restrictions specifically exempted the Mail Pouch barns, citing them as historic landmarks.

Time has a funny way of transforming yesterday's ad clutter into today's prized artefacts: look no further than Coke memorabilia on eBay. Or consider the story that unfolded not long ago in Jamestown, New York (known to trivia buffs as the birthplace of Lucille Ball). Workers there uncovered a billboard, ten feet by twenty-six, advertising a local appearance by Buffalo Bill Cody. The city arts council sprang into action, gathering remnants and photographing portions of the poster before wind and exposure took their toll. It's hard to imagine a team taking the same care to save a 2009 poster pitching a McChicken Sandwich.

TELEMARKETERS (*SALISBURY STEAKUS INTERRUPTUS*)

Of the many, many, supremely annoying aspects of telemarketing, perhaps the most infuriating is that it works. The Newspaper Association of America notes that telemarketing sales accounted for 60 percent of home subscriptions.

It's a low-overhead, low-yield, in-your-face ad medium, second only in its intrusiveness to door-to-door salespeople. The Internet is rife with anecdotes, rants, and audio recordings that chronicle the cat-and-mouse relationship between telemarketers and wary consumers, and consumer laws promising protection from unwanted telephone solicitations run the gamut from useless to inadequate. All in all, telemarketers neither observe nor recognize the contract: they simply interrupt your dinner, feed you a script, and content themselves with a single-digit success rate, offering nothing but a sales pitch as you stare longingly at the chicken Kiev cooling on your plate.

Popularized in the seventies, telemarketing dates back to at least the fifties and an outfit called DialAmerica Marketing. These days, it falls into three categories: inbound calling, where a marketer receives calls from its customers who have questions or gripes; outbound calling to existing customers, where your bank, for instance, might call you, trying to sell you a service or program; and the dreaded outbound cold call. These last are the scurrilous wags who ring you up, hoping your need of replacement windows outweighs your desire for a quiet meal with your family.

I dislike telemarketing because it breaks the contract, disrespecting the customer and interrupting without apology. It breaks all the rules of good marketing, which is to say it isn't pleasantly surprising or polite or humorous or meaningful. Telemarketers make no attempt to build a relationship with their clients, nor do they try to live up to that hallmark of good advertising: offering something in exchange for the customer's time. Telemarketers don't give you anything. They just call to take.

ADS IN MOVIE THEATRES: REWRITING THE CONTRACT

It seems inevitable that advertising would seep into North American movie theatres. A captive audience of like-minded people (like-minded in their choice of movie, at least) is worth a lot to theatre companies, who began selling their audiences to advertisers in the late 1980s, when the first North American ads appeared on big screens. Theatre companies have insisted that advertising helped subsidize admission prices, the way print ads keep subscription fees down. Theatregoers have argued that the price of admission should buy them an ad-free environment. Their case is a good one.

So many of the great movie theatres—many dating back to the early 1900s—were as plush and palatial as the finest concert halls, and film going was an all-evening experience, which might include a cartoon, a short film, a newsreel, a "B" picture, and the main attraction. By the 1970s, when a new wave of Hollywood icons, including Spielberg, Lucas, and Coppola redefined "blockbuster," theatres recognized that there was more money to be made attracting larger numbers of people to a wider variety of films. The moviegoing experience shifted from quality of theatre to quantity of screens. In cities and towns across the continent, the great movie palaces were divided into two, three, even six, smaller theatres. Shorter features and "B" pictures had vanished, and daytime showings were added.

Seeking new ways to increase revenues, theatres looked to Europe, where cinema ads had long been a fixture and where, historically, they haven't been regarded with the same irritation. (In North America, drive-ins featured ads designed to boost sales at the snack bar, but otherwise, most audiences were protected from ads for anything but "Coming Attractions.") I talked to a colleague in the U.K. about the theatre-ad phenomenon in Europe, and he sent me back a treasury of useful information. For instance, studies show that ritual is an important

> Many of those drive-in snack ads fit the coveted "so bad, they're good" category and have been fondly revived on YouTube.

aspect of moviegoing, which is cherished as a shared experience, and in Britain, where cinema ads have been accepted, even embraced, for many years as part of that ritual. But there's a catch: British audiences expect to be entertained by the ads. Although some North American cinema ads are lovingly constructed for theatre audiences, the majority suffer from entertainment deficit. Many, in fact, are only TV ads recycled for the big screen, and they wind up looking like . . . just that. Two key insights emerged from my chat with my colleague across the pond: one is that cinema ads featuring strong soundtracks and humour stand out; the other is that consumers believe cinema advertisers are special, and the brands publicized in movie houses are more successful. But can North American cinema ads build up that sort of reputation? Their window of opportunity is closing fast.

These days the moviegoer has been demoted from welcome guest to mere chattel, whose time and attention are commodified and sold to a growing number of advertisers. Free (but ad-laden) magazines in the lobby promote upcoming films, ads appear in pre-movie slide shows projected onto the big screen, movie times are adjusted to include cinema ads among the "Coming Attractions" trailers, and all manner of product placements might be tucked within the feature film.

It isn't the advertising itself that causes movie theatres to violate the contract here in North America. It's the erosion of the moviegoing experience, from an evening focused on giving the audience a hilarious, pleasurable, or cathartic time to a litany of non-entertaining sales devices designed to exploit a captive audience.

And for this you pay them.

MEDIA COMPANIES: THE LITTLE DEVILS ON THE SHOULDER

If advertisers are the signatories—and violators—of the contract, "media companies" are enablers, the little devils on their shoulders, tempting them with opportunities to reach new audiences—too often without giving anything back. It's media companies who erect

billboards, sell time on TV and radio, and otherwise clutter up public places and airwaves. Their
mission is to place ads in as many places as possible:
stuffed into the bottoms of golf holes, painted on
bicycle paths, projected onto the floors of shopping
malls, transmitted to televisions in classrooms.
Advertisers, rightly, take the flak; media companies
pocket the dough.

Me·di·a com·pan·ies *(noun)*
don't create ads. They buy, sell,
and sometimes own the space
and broadcast time used for
advertising. They might rent out
space on billboards they own or
buy print space or broadcast time
on behalf of advertisers. Many of
these companies are creating
new media to sell to advertisers,
such as the ads in elevators,
golf holes, and washrooms
described earlier.

The media companies' love for ad clutter, and
advertisers' contempt for it, are inversely propor-
tional. Agencies hate that you're bombarded with
ads, most of which divert your attention from ads for *their* clients.
Media companies build their business on exposing you to as many
ads as possible and on the creation of new ad media, each of which
adds another stone to the pockets of advertisers drowning in a sea
of clutter.

JUNK MAIL AND SPAM: LITTER ON THE ELECTRONIC HIGHWAY

Junk mail is the passive cousin of telemarketing
and is duly punished for it: at 1.88 percent, its
response rate is less than a third of the rate for
telephone pitches. And in these greener times,
direct mail also carries an unsavoury reputation
as a tree killer. Junk mail makes a significant contribution to ad clutter, but it's a relatively unob-
trusive medium and much easier to ignore than
a person on the phone or a film on a forty-foot
screen in a dark theatre, with surround sound. It
places a lighter strain on the audience signatories to Mr. Lasker's contract.

I was once sitting at an
advertising award show with
one of our company's music
composers. That musician
had never attended one of
those shows before, and
when the Best Direct Mail
category came up, he looked
perplexed, and then said,
"You mean this is an award
for the crap that gets stuck
in my railing?"

But then there's spam. This email version of junk mail, promising
to enhance carnal experiences, deliver real Rolex watches, and give you

irresistible savings on pharmaceuticals, dwells in a dark corner of marketing's sub-basement. Spammers lack the earnestness and honesty of advertisers who spend years, and even work up a sweat, cultivating relationships with potential customers. They're the laziest of slobs, spending the least possible amount of time, money, and effort to reach their audience by inviting themselves into your computer's inbox alongside private messages, your credit card statement, and a note from your parents in Boca Raton.

> I've been receiving spam with subject messages surprisingly similar to those of legitimate business emails I've sent. For example, after sending an email with the subject line "Send mp3s to client for approval," I might receive a spam message with the subject line "mp3s client is approval"—slightly wrong, but enough to get me to open it. This is evil.

DATA MINERS: ADDING FINE PRINT TO THE CONTRACT

Data mining is the practice of using the information gathered about you—your name, address, and spending patterns—and spinning it into gold, usually through creating and selling marketing lists. Essentially, it packages groups of consumers and presents them as prospective customers for other marketers. To ensure that lists aren't resold, abused, or "borrowed" beyond the agreed term, they are "salted." That is, the list creators sprinkle bogus names among the real ones. Then, if they receive a pitch to one of those nonexistent people, they can monitor who is using the list, when they're using it, and how. This prevents a marketer from using the list beyond an agreed term or secretly passing it to a third party.

When you fill out a contest ballot, you're turning over information to a data miner; you do the same when you oblige the cashier who asks for your phone number and postal code. Any fan of Arthur Conan Doyle's Sherlock Holmes stories might imagine what could be deduced about a person when you know their name and address and can track a number of their purchases, and retailers do use that information to tweak their business. Just as often though, they package the data and rent it to

40

unrelated marketers. The ski suit and luggage you buy at a department store might lead, months later, to a cold call telemarketer hoping to sell you a timeshare in the Laurentians—the galling part being that you're never privy to the information exchange that connected the two.

Is there an upside to data mining? Here's the argument its proponents will make: the more marketers know about you, your preferences, your habits, and particularly what you don't like, the likelier they are to offer you things you actually want and the likelier they are not to waste your time—and theirs—pitching you things you don't want. But to do that effectively, they need to gather more and more of your personal information, and that's where they smack nose first into a growing wall of privacy protection. That was my theory at least, until I had teenaged daughters.

While my wife and I are of a generation that hoards its privacy, our daughters think nothing of giving away all sorts of details about themselves online. It drives us crazy, but I've come to understand the reason. Their generation, so I'm learning, is okay with giving away private data because they want advertisers and websites to send them information that's relevant to them. And they know the quid pro quo is personal information. Having their parents grind their teeth to a fine powder, well, that's just a bonus to them.

Like movie theatres, data miners rewrite the contract, but with too-tiny-to-read print, adding new, lucrative ways to profit from their relationship with you while rarely offering you anything in return; worse, they make no effort to tell you they're doing it. What if the situation were reversed? If you were to try taking more from them than you paid for, you'd wind up doing two hundred hours of community service.

AUTHENTICITY AND TRANSPARENCY

The contract requires a brand to be authentic and transparent—that is, it must live up to its promise. Beta-carotene tanning pills promised to leave the skin bronzed, but they left some people looking like human traffic cones. A few decades back, Dr. Care toothpaste (in an aerosol can) was billed as a way to get kids to brush because spray cans are fun, but many learned that kids actually saw it as a fun bathroom redecorating tool until the product was finally pulled. And those X-ray glasses advertised in the backs of comic books in the sixties and seventies? It cost me a dollar of my hard-earned newspaper delivery money, plus twenty-five cents for shipping, to learn you couldn't use them to see people's underwear. At the heart of every brand is a promise, and those that fall short breach the contract.

Can good advertising encourage people to buy an inferior product? Sure it can—*once*. Even marketers you rarely deal with a second time, such as the company that paves your driveway or replaces your roof, must deliver on their promise. The bad ones, and the good, learn quickly that word of mouth makes and breaks brands more effectively than anything else. For any brand, overpromising is a short-term, self-destructive strategy. The smarter route is underpromise, overdeliver. Can advertising sustain a bad brand? Quite the reverse. As Bill Bernbach put it: "A great ad campaign will make a bad product fail faster. It will get more people to know it's bad."

Reputations developed by word of mouth depend on transparency, and transparency ensures that there's nothing left to be "found out," for the very act of concealing something can tarnish or destroy a brand. In the 1920s and 1930s, Grey Owl became an international *cause célèbre* as a conservationist, speaker, and author. Throughout his adult life, he insisted he was the son of a Scottish father and an Apache mother and so identified himself when he served with the 13th Montreal Battalion of the Black Watch in the First World War, where he was wounded and sent home. Following his death in 1938, however, an Ontario newspaper, the *North Bay Nugget*, revealed that he was nothing of the kind. "Grey Owl" was actually Archibald Stansfeld Belaney, who was born to a broken home in Hastings, England, and came to Canada alone at the age of seventeen. His war service, his passion for the land and its creatures,

42

and his gift for writing were all real, yet at the time that article was published, his image—his brand—was shattered.

While breaking the contract harms a brand, honouring the contract isn't always enough to help it. For an honourable, contract-abiding, low-interest product such as a brand of socks or galvanized nails, "reason why" advertising isn't enough to stand out in the daily hurricane of high-intensity, high-interest brand advertising. Everyday items like this need an edge, and that edge lies in entertainment value.

THE PERSUASIVE POWER OF ENTERTAINMENT

Entertaining an audience can do miracles, especially for a low-interest brand. In the 1980s, when I was working at Campbell-Ewald, a Toronto ad agency, I was part of a team assigned to give life to Fiberglas Pink Home Insulation, as it was then called, a low-interest brand if ever there was one. You put it behind your walls and forget it, right? The director of marketing, Grant McDiarmaid, was wonderful, smart, and candid. He actually told us, "I sell the world's most boring product. Make me famous."

First, the agency developed a consumer insight: a reason why Fiberglas Pink insulation might mean something to consumers. The obvious answer was that people could save money if they insulated properly. But when this took shape as the question "What will you do with the money you save?" a galaxy of creative possibilities opened up.

For this job, Campbell-Ewald hired the legendary TV ad director Joe Sedelmaier, whose work includes the landmark "Where's the Beef" ad for Wendy's in the 1980s. The agency came up with an idea, and set him to work on a series of TV ads featuring his trademark bizarre world with its "oom-pah ooom-pay ooom-pah" brass music and ramrod-straight, so-square-they're-hip performers. Part of his secret? He would hire non-actors, people without a whiff of on-camera experience, people who didn't know which profile was "their good side" as Joe used to say. He'd then coax spectacularly unpolished performances from them.

The first spot in the campaign (done just before I arrived) was called "Flamingos," and it hit the air on a Monday. In the spot, an odd-looking couple buys "262 bee-youtiful pink flamingos" with the money they save and stick the plastic birds in their tiny front lawn. By Wednesday, the agency got a call from Fiberglas Canada president Frank Henkelman who hadn't seen the ad prior to air. He and some of his senior executives strongly felt the commercial didn't look like Fiberglas and didn't represent the company well at all. But there was one problem: it was technically and contractually impossible to get the ads off the air right away, so they ran for the next two weeks. The brass wasn't happy. That Sunday, when the Fiberglas president was coming out of his church service, the minister said to him, "Frank, I've just seen your new Fiberglas TV commercial: it's the funniest thing I've ever seen." The next morning, the president called with just five words: "Leave it on the air." It was truly a case of divine intervention.

> Shortly after the spot became a success, the Fiberglas president thought it would be fun to plant a pink plastic flamingo on what he thought was his minister's lawn. That Sunday, the minister opened his sermon by saying he woke to a beautiful Sunday morning, looked out his window, and saw a person planting a lovely flamingo on his neighbour's lawn.

By the end of the decade, Fiberglas Pink Home Insulation had climbed to a market share of over 70 percent. We didn't create conventional ads. Instead, we isolated an insight, came up with a fresh idea, and tapped the genius of Joe Sedelmaier to create small parcels of pure entertainment.

Much of the creative revolution of the sixties was about using entertainment as a sales tool. Instead of lecturing audiences on the virtues of a product, they offered genuinely funny stories, intelligent characters, fantastic writing, and irresistible moments. Grateful audiences were left with a warm, positive impression of products and services that engaged and amused them, enhancing the brand by happy association.

And like the Alka-Seltzer ad featuring the poor schlep performing fifty-nine takes of a meatball commercial ("Mamma mia! That's a

44

spicy meatball-a"), an entertaining ad can resonate for months, even generations, after the spot's last airing and then experience reincarnation on YouTube.

Honouring the contract begins with an understanding that every ad, no matter how entertaining, is an interruption. No one worth her salt in the ad business begins conceiving an ad without that in mind; it's a thought that should be taped to the wall beside every computer in every ad agency. The content of any ad is a bonbon offered in exchange for paying attention, and when the ad is a great one, the viewer will reward the advertiser with an honoured place in his mind. The appealing content that drives great advertising borrows from the same appeal that drives TV, film, theatre, music, and, yes, publishing. In my opinion, entertainment value is by far the best way to get noticed: a kind of psychological bullhorn. For years I've advised clients that toning down ad creative—reducing the amount of entertainment in an ad—can be like giving a speech to an audience of a hundred thousand without a microphone. Great creative execution wins attention and allows advertisers to outsmart—rather than outspend—the competition. In other words, big creative ideas constitute one of the best legal means an advertiser has to gain an unfair advantage over the competition.

Why, then, are there so many ads that aren't entertaining or even interesting? Harsh as it sounds, it has been my experience that clients—the owners and keepers of a brand—sometimes tone down an ad to their own detriment. It's the client who ultimately determines the content and tone of an ad, and where and how often it runs. And in the end, it's the client who either has the courage to approve daring work or not.

Great ads are the ones you stop to watch, the ones people email to each other, the ones that yield thousands of hits on YouTube. They adorn the reels of award-winning ads that people line up and pay to see in revue cinemas. Great ad creative has revitalized Albert Lasker's contract in broadcast and print, and now it's helping redeem advertisers who had so rudely barged into hitherto ad-free sanctuaries.

A new generation of cinema ads, for instance, is slowly converting ad intrusion into entertainment. One great example of this new approach is an ad created for theatre audiences by AT&T. The scene opens with a woman tucking her young son into bed, asking if he'd like to say good night to daddy on the phone. This tender scenes is interrupted by an intruder who heads up the stairs and into the bedroom—Martin Scorsese, insisting they stop what they're doing. "This scene isn't working for me," he complains. For our purposes, the woman and son are real and stare in wonder at the great filmmaker, who has somehow infiltrated their home. Scorsese begins to direct the boy, telling him this will work better if he imagines that his father just got out of prison, and turning to the mother, he says, "You're trapped in a loveless marriage. You should be drinking from a bottle. Have you got a bottle around?" A graphic then fills the screen: "We don't interrupt your phone calls. Please don't interrupt our movies. A message from Martin Scorsese and AT&T."

Another cinema ad that gives audiences good entertainment value is a short film called *Phone Bomb*, created by GJP Advertising. I created the very detailed sound for this commercial, which looks like a trailer for a new suspense film. Then a cellphone rings in the audience and triggers the sound-sensitive detonator on the bomb. Yep, it's a public service announcement urging that cellphones and such be turned off. But it's also a beautifully crafted piece of branded entertainment for a cellphone company. Like the clever, almost-modest Burma-Shave signs, these ads perform a service by entertaining the audience. To paraphrase Confucius: a journey back to the contract begins with a single, funny ad.

It's well past time for advertisers to be held to the terms of the great unwritten contract. But that can happen only if you familiarize yourself with the terms of the contract and apply it to the ads you see, hear, and otherwise experience. Only then can you separate the sheep from the goats, rewarding the honest brokers with your time and attention and punishing transgressors by ignoring their pitch, depriving them of your business, and even complaining to those responsible. Don't believe for a moment that you can't make a difference: a handful of complaints can—and do—derail multimillion-dollar ad campaigns.

THE "SCIENCE OF ADVERTISING" MYTH

On the subject of "Advertising," the U.S. Library of Congress has tens of thousands of titles. Many of them (too many) describe the "science" of advertising, offering formulas and recipes for the perfect ad.

These are as useful as a temperance meeting in a curling rink. Advertising—or more accurately, *persuasion*—is not a science but an art. If secret tricks and formulas existed, I would be dictating this from my villa . . . in Aruba.

Which is not to say that science isn't *part* of advertising. Research helps identify strengths and opportunities that lead to great marketing campaigns. A well-handled focus group can spot flaws in a product or advertising direction before any serious money is spent. And as a copywriter, I welcome a great deal of research early in the process. I want to learn everything there is to know about the product or service I'm helping to advertise. Too often, though, research is slanted to justify predetermined conclusions. As David Ogilvy wrote, "a drunkard uses a lamp post for support, rather than for illumination."

Despite a mountain of market research, the Ford Edsel still failed in the 1950s, just as bad research contributed to the fiasco of New Coke three decades later.

Mr. Ogilvy is right: the best research is pure. It's not used as a crutch or laden with foregone conclusions. Research can reveal astounding and powerful answers, but first, you have to ask the right questions. And even then, great advertising requires a balance of insight, instinct, and calculated risk.

And therein lies the art.

When executing advertising, it's best to think of yourself as an
uninvited guest in the living room of a prospect who has the
magical power to make you disappear instantly.

JOHN O'TOOLE

THE RISE AND FALL AND RISE OF
BRANDED
ENTERTAINMENT

They say TV is free, but we pay for it
every time we hum a jingle.

JASON LOVE

n the age of persuasion, a "brand" is the emotional impression or idea that surrounds something: it could be a type of soap or it could be a celebrity. Lux, then, is a brand, and so, in a broad sense, are George Clooney, communism, the Labrador retriever, the Brussels sprout, and the Republic of Ireland. In your brain you've probably created and stored an impression of each, which becomes a sort of "recognition shorthand" whenever you encounter that particular item. Marketers know the importance of brands, and they know that ideas and emotions can be added to a product or service to make it more appealing to the public.

In July 2008, the *International Herald Tribune* reported that R&B producer Jermaine Dupri, responsible for launching such bestselling acts as Kris Kross and Da Brat, was seeking talent for a new label financed by a company just entering the music industry: Procter & Gamble (P&G). Creating what's known in my industry as a "brand extension," the label would be christened "TAG" after—yes—the name of a body spray brand P&G had acquired when it bought Gillette.

BRANDS: TO EXTEND OR NOT TO EXTEND

Brand Extension: the practice of extending the name, "feel" and emotional baggage of a brand to a new, different product. It's a risky proposition, whose success or failure hinges on consumers' ability to relate the new product to the brand's core values. Some successful brand extensions:

- Diet Coke and Diet Pepsi
- *O, The Oprah Magazine*
- Tide to Go instant stain remover

50

- National Geographic Channel

Some failed brand extensions:

- Sara Lee Frozen Dinner Entrees
- Bic underwear
- Hooters Air (an airline from the cleavage-intensive eatery brand)

It's remarkable when the planet's most formidable retail products giant plays *Pimp My Brand*, trading in its conservative P&G business suit for baggy jeans that hang four inches below its underwear band. It's even more remarkable when you consider the striking similarity to another P&G venture, launched in the darkest days of the Great Depression: the soap opera.

But first, some history. The first genuine "soap opera," if you must know, wasn't like most soap operas at all, in the sense that it wasn't broadcast nationally or sponsored by a soap brand. On Thursday, October 30, 1930, *Painted Dreams* debuted on Chicago's WGN radio. It was the creation of actress Irna Phillips, who'd been commissioned by the station to create an ongoing ten-minute radio serial "about a family." The show was relatively short lived, as it was removed from the air when a squabble erupted between Ms. Phillips and WGN over rights to the program after the broadcaster refused to sell the show to a network. What endured was the template Phillips created: ever-so-formulaic tales of "ordinary" people enduring all manner of personal woes, with key story points left hanging . . . hold it . . . wait . . .

Fear not: Irna Phillips landed on her feet, going on to create and write a number of successful radio serials. Her legacy continued on TV with such daytime staples as *The Guiding Light* and *As the World Turns*.

hang on . . . until next time. Advertising agencies had long been craving a radio vehicle that might ingratiate their clients' brands with millions of North American housewives, and the radio serial formula, as Phillips helped define it, was just what they were looking for.

51

Within months, rival serials would build on Phillips' model, revolutionizing the way major corporations communicated with housewives. Big-name advertisers in the 1930s didn't simply sponsor broadcasts as they do today. They were players—pioneers of *branded entertainment*—buying the airtime outright. Their agencies would then create, write, and produce programs on their behalf, each designed as a vehicle to expose their product or service to a vast new radio audience.

THE EARLY, EARLY, EARLY ROOTS OF BRANDED ENTERTAINMENT

Branded entertainment is a new name for an ancient practice: the act of promoting a person, product, or idea by wrapping it tightly within some form of diversion—typically, some form of art, entertainment, or amusement. If "advertising is theatre" as ex-Apple CEO John Sculley says, then it is perfectly suited to branded entertainment. In fact, the roots of this phenomenon go back thousands of years—notably, to ancient Rome, under the emperor Commodus.

If there was such a thing as a "typical" Roman emperor, Lucius Aurelius Commodus Antoninus (a.k.a. "Commodus") wasn't it. He was strong of limb if not fleet of brain, a man who preferred the lure of sport to the tedium of running an empire. Portrayed in the film *Gladiator* by Joaquin Phoenix in 2000 and by Christopher Plummer in *The Fall of the Roman Empire* in 1964, Commodus fancied himself quite the athlete and, according to scuttlebutt, imagined himself to be Hercules reborn.

> The Latin word *commodus,* referring to a person, means "agreeable, obliging, and pleasant." It's also the root of the word *commode*—a Georgian-era cross between a piece of furniture and a portable potty. Make of that what you will.

He was the only emperor to take to the arena, where his record was perfect, which is not surprising when you put yourself in the sandals of the gladiators he faced, for whom killing the emperor might be considered a career-limiting move. The emperor, never lacking in chutzpah,

52

billed the city of Rome one million sesterces for each appearance.

As you might guess, that's a tidy chunk of change. In those days a Roman soldier might earn just under one thousand sesterces per year.

So how is it that Commodus, whose CV should clearly be filed under "P" for "Piece of Work," managed to reign a dozen years? He sponsored mass public entertainments: chariot races, theatre, pantomimes, and daily contests in the great amphitheatres. There, day-long celebrations might begin with men stalking wild animals (or vice versa) before moving on to equally crowd-pleasing public executions, battle re-enactments, and gladiatorial displays. It was through these spectacles, holidays, and festivals that Commodus built his brand with the people of Rome, whose support was vital to his hold on power. After Commodus moved on to the Great Gladiator Ring in the Sky, prominent Roman politicians perfected the art of creating events to win the affection of the great unwashed. By the end of the second century, 135 "official" celebrations were packed into each year, inspiring the satirist Juvenal to coin the phrase *panem et circenses* ("bread and circuses"), a none-too-subtle dig at the people's preference for entertainment over freedom. It's a safe guess that Juvenal didn't anticipate that two millennia later, the emperors of commerce would use a modern form of *panem et circenses* to sell Ivory Flakes.

By the 19th century, political picnics had taken on the bread and circuses role. They were ingenious vehicles used to attract large crowds to political speeches and to build party membership. Crowds were wooed with promises of music, games, physical contests such as weightlifting and tug-of-war, vast amounts of food, pitchers full of lemonade, berry cordials and cider, and (shhh!) wines and spirits, should any gentleman or lady need to ward off a chill. Years ahead of his time, Canada's John A. Macdonald had so mastered the art of the political picnic that an opponent charged he was "not a man . . . but the Devil . . . who went around the country holding picnics and tempting the people."

53

THE RISE AND FALL AND RISE OF BRANDED ENTERTAINMENT

It's important to note that there's a distinct difference between entertaining people and using entertainment to build a brand. The first has no overt brand motive; it exists to entertain and attract audiences; the second is all about creating an entertainment program that features the product or revolves around the product or is connected to the brand strategically. For example, my company created a radio program called "The Job That Changed My Life," wherein celebrities and successful entrepreneurs were quizzed about the one position that changed the direction of their careers. It was sponsored by Workopolis, the online job site, because the idea of the show was perfectly in line with their strategy of transforming people's working lives. For decades, advertising has interrupted *what* people have enjoyed; branded entertainment is about *being* what people enjoy and *still delivering branding.*

RADIO AND THE RISE OF BRANDED ENTERTAINMENT

The seeds of modern branded entertainment were planted in the 1920s, a few years before Irna Phillips unleashed her first waves of anguish upon the unsuspecting housewives of Chicago and Procter & Gamble launched its first soap opera. As radio broadcasting was still finding its feet, many, including some broadcast regulators, saw it as a not-for-profit medium or a glorified hobby. Then, in 1926, the Radio Corporation of America (RCA) linked a number of its stations to form America's National Broadcasting Company (NBC) as a means of driving demand for their radio sets. A year later, entrepreneur William S. Paley linked a number of stations to form the Columbia Broadcasting System (CBS) as a means of promoting his family's cigar business. But these "networks" had an interesting side effect. For the first time in communications history, a single voice could speak to millions of people, in their homes, at the same moment. This phenomenon immediately attracted large national advertisers and led to a gigantic jump in network profits. These profits, in turn, translated into bigger budgets for programming and vastly increased the quality of production values.

54

It also hatched new programming ideas, like how-to shows, advice shows, and sponsored news.

Of course, the networks and their programs began competing with each other, and that required "big" (read: expensive) entertainment. Enter two very important, long-forgotten (even by the marketing industry) ad men: Frank Arnold and Paul Kesten. Arnold had directed the Frank Seaman ad agency and was hired by NBC to warm advertisers up to the idea of creating and financing radio programming. Kesten had worked for the ad firm Lennen & Mitchell before CBS hired him to do likewise. These rainmakers earned their keep during those early years of the Great Depression because while newspaper and magazine ad revenues declined, those of radio grew steadily. Hoping to provoke a consummation in the marriage between broadcast and commerce, CBS founder William S. Paley located his network's headquarters on New York's Madison Avenue, the very epicentre of twentieth-century advertising. Irna Phillips' shamelessly sappy style of melodrama provided advertisers with the radio device they needed to connect with housewives.

On December 4, 1933, at 3 p.m., NBC debuted Oxydol's *Ma Perkins*, the first serial created for a Procter & Gamble product. For twenty-seven years, audiences followed Ma through the ups and downs of running a lumberyard in Rushville Center (population four thousand) and the lives of her children, one of whom died during the Second World War, likely the victim of a fatal contract dispute. Rival brands, most of them soaps and cleansers, retaliated with such heart-wrenching serials as *Hilltop House* (for Palmolive Beauty Soap), *Stepmother* (for Colgate Tooth Powder), *Big Sister* (for Rinso), and *Road of Life* (for Chipsol Washday Soap).

Soaps became novels for the ear, whose stories always trumped dialogue and performance. They became a daily oasis for breathtakingly meaningless prose:

ANNCR:	On the Arizona prairie, Pascal Tyler says a silent prayer, holds out his hand, and waits for tragedy to allow itself to be dissuaded from happening, in today's episode of *Against the Storm* . . .
MUSIC:	SAPPY SOAP OPERA ORGAN SWELLS

The stations and networks of the early thirties were all too happy to relinquish control of the airwaves, for a fee, to advertisers—especially during the day, when, they reckoned, no meaningful audience could be attracted to radio. They reckoned wrong; even without sophisticated marketing research (which would become the norm years later), advertisers knew intuitively, and anecdotally, that women commanded a majority of household spending decisions. As the early trade bible *Printers Ink* said, "The proper study of mankind is man . . . but the proper study of markets is woman." Even today, the conventional wisdom among marketers has it that men may do the shopping, but women make the lists.

With marketers smelling a lucrative, captive mass audience, a parade of daily soap operas filled the air, the most successful of them the product of one of the more remarkable broadcast production factories to operate before or since: the firm created by the husband and wife team of Frank and Ann Hummert. Their production company bought enormous blocks of airtime on behalf of advertisers and filled it with formulaic, teeth-aching serials they created and produced for grateful brand sponsors. By the mid-thirties, Frank Hummert was drawing a salary and commissions totalling some $117,000—more than $1.7 million of today's dollars. His wife, Anne, scraped by on $21,000—more than $300,000 today. Together, they did for soap opera production what Henry Ford did for auto making: by creating programs and dictating storylines, they saved a bundle by hiring "dialogue writers," rather than more expensive "creator/writers." Scribes of rival soaps typically earned $200 to $400 per week, while the Hummerts paid as little as $25 for a fifteen-minute script—a considerable savings. In 1938 they began exporting scripts to Europe for broadcast to British listeners, hiring overseas writers to anglicize the stories, changing "cops" to "bobbies" and "dollars" to "pounds." By then, the Hummerts' ad agency, B.S.H., was placing orders for about one-eighth of all available national airtime on behalf of their clients—notably, P&G.

THE EARS HAVE IT

In the 1920s there was a philosophical split about the role of radio: some saw it as a not-for-profit source of information and education; others saw it as a profitable entertainment medium. Meanwhile, listeners voted with their ears. By 1934 not-for-profit stations accounted for just 2 percent of total broadcast time, while ad-driven networks were thriving. In 1929, 20 percent of commercial stations—all of them network affiliates—soaked up 80 percent of all radio ad revenue. Networks were clearly where the money was.

Radio departments within major ad agencies conceived and produced fresh radio programs, tailored to attract audiences to their clients' messages, and they flexed their creative muscles by moving well beyond soap operas to serious drama, variety entertainment, and game shows. The agency Young & Rubicam produced *Town Hall Tonight* for Ipana Toothpaste "for the smile of beauty"; J. Walter Thompson produced *Kraft Music Theatre* and *Lux Radio Theater*; Batten, Barton, Durstine & Osborne

The agency was later known simply as "BBDO." I mention the full name mostly because it's so much fun to say out loud. Go on, give it a try. I'll wait. Someone once said it sounded like someone falling down the stairs.

produced *Cavalcade of America* for DuPont; and Benton & Bowles produced *Showboat* for Maxwell House coffee. Orson Welles's avant-garde *Mercury Theatre* aired without a sponsor until their infamous *War of the Worlds* broadcast in 1938; thereafter, they became the *Campbell Playhouse*. Major ad agencies opened production offices in Hollywood and became the kingmakers of popular entertainment.

Naturally hoping for a return on their investment, advertisers watched from the wings as audiences applauded the stars they helped "create." A staple of evening radio in those early days was the hugely popular, if racially insensitive, *Amos 'n' Andy*. Stories spread that when the show aired, telephone calls dropped 30 percent across the United States and movie theatres halted performances so they could play the program for their audiences. It might easily have been forgotten that Lord & Thomas developed the show as a vehicle to sell Pepsodent Toothpaste.

An awkward tension developed between sponsors and their stars—personalities like Jack Benny, Bob Hope, and Bing Crosby— each of whom jockeyed for top billing in the listener's mind. When audiences first tuned in to hear Jack Benny, the show began: *"The Chevrolet Program,* starring Jack Benny." Later, there was the famous *"J-E-L-L . . . O"* jingle, followed by *"The Jell-O Program,* starring Jack Benny" By 1942, it was *"The Grape Nuts Flakes Program,* starring Jack Benny," and years later, with still another sponsor, Benny won the tug-of-war for top billing, with the show beginning *"The Jack Benny Program,* presented by Lucky Strike"—followed promptly by the famous Lucky Strike Auctioneer, shouting, "SOLD! to the Americaaaaan."

Sometimes the name of the show created an awkward dynamic between sponsor and star, each keen for top billing in the listener's minds, but a boat-rocking actor might find himself replaced, or worse, his character might be hit by a laundry truck or contract beriberi, or both.

Ingenious compromises were fashioned to infuse brands into the scripts or storylines of some shows. Jack Benny's greeting, "Jell-O, everyone," a line fashioned by Young & Rubicam, became a trademark. Later, an episode might include a subplot (more often a running gag), where Benny's announcer, Don Wilson, tried to devise a clever way of promoting the initialism "L-S-M-F-T" ("Lucky Strike Means Fine Tobacco").

In the 1940s, Aunt Jemima, the fictional pancake-brand icon, became host of her own sponsored radio program, offering sage, Mammy-style aphorisms ("Folks says yooo ken't buy happiness . . . but you ken *earn* it . . ."), a minstrel chorus, a double dollop of pancake-mix sales language, and a heaping plateful of nineteenth-century "yessa, yessa" African-American stereotyping. In the storied history of branded entertainment, "stars" have often become brands, but in this rare case, the reverse happened.

Throughout the thirties and forties, brand sponsors cherished their role as benefactors of popular, high-end, mass entertainment, especially when prime-time exposure translated into sales.

In the weeks following *Amos 'n' Andy*'s network debut, for instance, sales for its sponsor, Pepsodent, tripled.

TELEVISION: THE FALL OF BRANDED ENTERTAINMENT

In 1946, fewer than 1 percent of American households had a television, by 1962 the number had climbed above 64 percent, and by 1964 the number had reached 90 percent. Television had become the "it" medium, but it also spelled the demise of the "sole sponsor" tradition established on radio. In part, this was the doing of one Sylvester "Pat" Weaver, who produced radio programs for Young & Rubicam through the thirties and forties. NBC hired him to jump-start its television network in 1949, and that he did. Among his creations were *The Today Show* and *The Tonight Show*. (His daughter, Susan Alexandra, would change her name to "Sigourney" and build a tidy career for herself in Hollywood.) Another Weaver initiative was

59

an increased number of network-created programs, so NBC could have more control of the programs it aired—and a better financial return, since it could sell advertising commercial spots to a number of advertisers. Networks became the *big cheeses* of broadcast productions, and advertisers became irritants: obstacles separating audiences from their beloved programming. Even when audiences were subjected to ads, they wouldn't necessarily watch. Instead, millions of viewers would leave the room to make a sandwich, tuck the kids in, take the trash to the curb, or powder their noses, entirely ignoring the purchasing pleas of multiple advertisers. Mind you, single sponsors didn't vanish overnight. For a time, a single advertiser would bankroll the entire program, as Philip Morris cigarettes did with Lucy and Desi—and the *Beverley Hillbillies* even delivered commercials in character. Networks did experiment with subdividing "exclusive" sponsorships into fifteen- or thirty-minute segments, but the trend declined in the sixties as the number of advertisers per hour expanded in their favour.

Those of us who work in radio are proud of the fact that we can create the most vivid "pictures" using a couple of actors and a bag of sound effects, and for less than the catering budget of a typical TV shoot.

Ultimately, it was the cost of TV program production that forced advertisers from their throne as creators, producers, and creative power brokers. Television shows were many times more expensive to produce than radio broadcasts, and they represented a far heftier investment for sponsors. Advertisers, once regarded as the engines that drove television, came to be regarded as the acrid smoke that poured out its tailpipe, and networks started to ballyhoo themselves as champions of quality, prime-time entertainment.

A BICYCLE RACE AND A BOOK TO SETTLE BAR BETS

60   While marketing eggheads struggled for ways to keep their brands relevant to a mass audience, spectacular examples of branded entertainment thrived around them. In two such cases—the Tour de France and

the *Guinness Book of Records*—they came about almost by accident. The world's greatest bicycle race came onto the scene, believe it or not, as an indirect result of France's notorious Dreyfus Affair. Not the "Dreyfus Case" or the "Dreyfus Incident" or even "Dreyfusgate," mind you. Once branded, the name of an historic incident is not to be fiddled with. Alfred Dreyfus was a French army officer who, in the early 1890s, was wrongly accused of delivering sensitive documents to a foreign power. He was court-martialled, degraded, and transported for life to Devil's Island. Charges of anti-Semitism (Dreyfus was Jewish) caused an ugly debate throughout France, bordering, some say, on civil war. Later exonerated, Dreyfus served in the French army during the First World War and was awarded the Legion of Honour.

> Also known as "cashiering," degrading is the ritual by which military officers are publicly disgraced. In a formal ceremony, one's badges of office—epaulettes and insignia—are torn away, one's cap is knocked off, one's sword is broken, and one's lunch money is taken.

> So whatever happened to the Île du Diable? The tiny island off the coast of French Guiana went out of the penal colony business in 1952. Nowadays, it's a tourism hot spot (a popular photo op is Dreyfus' former hut). It also houses hardware for the French and European space agencies.

When the largest sports paper in France, *Le Vélo* (Cycling), took a stand in Dreyfus' favour, some key advertisers were cheesed enough to finance the creation of a rival paper, *L'Auto-Vélo* (Auto-Cycling), whose name was soon shortened to *L'Auto*. To draw attention away from *Le Vélo*, editor Henri Desgrange and chief cycling reporter Géo Lefèvre, concocted the idea of a trans-France bicycle race. When the entrance fee of twenty francs attracted a scant fifteen entrants, Desgrange and Lefèvre postponed the event and revised their plan, promising the first fifty riders five francs a day for expenses and offering twenty thousand francs as prize money. Not only did they attract sixty riders, but the event drew thousands of fans, who paid to watch the race. The Tour de France was an instant hit. Years later, the national road race would incorporate the coveted *maillot jaune* (yellow jersey), featuring the distinctive

THE RISE AND FALL AND RISE OF BRANDED ENTERTAINMENT

colour of *L'Auto*'s newsprint. The rest is *histoire*. Circulation soared: during the first race, in 1903, a special edition of *L'Auto* sold 130,000 copies—100,000 more than normal.

And sure enough, by 1904, rival *Le Vélo* was out of business. A century later, *L'Auto* would continue to thrive as *L'Équipe* (Team).

A less incendiary matter spawned the *Guinness Book of Records*: the question of which game bird is fastest—the golden plover or the grouse. In the spring of 1951, the question vexed Sir Hugh Beaver, head of the Guinness Brewery, during a hunting party held along the banks of Ireland's River Slaney. Finding no reference book that could settle the matter, Sir Hugh opined that similar arguments must have been raging in pubs across the country (not to say that the Irish are predisposed to argue). That's when a bright pint glass appeared over his head: he would create a book to settle bar bets.

To assemble this tome, Guinness conscripted brothers Ross and Norris McWhirter, who ran a London fact-finding agency. Three years after Guinness's hunting-party epiphany, a thousand copies of the first *Guinness Book of Records* were published and given away as a promotion for Guinness beer. The next year, a subsequent edition climbed to the top of the British bestseller list, and another edition was marketed in the U.S., where seventy thousand copies were sold. Later successes helped create an entry of its own: the *Guinness Book* became the bestselling copyright book of all time, at 100 million copies and growing. The

Qur'an and the Bible are two of the few books that outsold it. No one was more surprised by the success of the book than Beaver, who later remarked: "It was a marketing giveaway. It wasn't supposed to be a money maker." Ironically, it wasn't until the thirty-sixth edition of the

Guinness Book, published in 1989, that Sir Hugh Beaver's "fastest bird" question was finally put to rest. The answer, if you must know, is the red grouse, known to travel as speedily as 100.8 kilometres per hour over short distances.

PRODUCT PLACEMENT

Product placement is a species very different from branded entertainment, though recently, the two have begun cross-pollinating. Loosely put, product placement is the act of infusing a brand name or image into a story or film or event or broadcast. Where branded entertainment gives one item a high profile, product placement is typically an addition or afterthought: the gratuitous inclusion of Hewlett-Packard computers in *The Office* or a Kodak printer in Donald Trump's *The Apprentice*.

In contrast, by the 1960s product placement was on the wane. Shameless, if inspired, plugs for Lucky Strike like the ones in a Jack Benny dialogue and *Fibber McGee and Molly*–style promos for Johnson's Wax didn't fit into broadcasts supported by multiple sponsors. In fact, television networks catered so meticulously to the sensibilities of competing sponsors that TV-land became a bizarre, comical ad-neutral world where characters carried cigarette packs marked simply "Cigarettes," sipped from cans marked "Cola," and parked in front of stores marked "Grocer," "Book Store," and the ever-popular "Bar."

But by the eighties, familiar logos were seeping back into television and film, most conspicuously in Steven Spielberg's *ET: The Extra Terrestrial*. According to legend, the production company approached the Mars candy people about using M&Ms in the scene where Elliott uses candy to draw ET out of hiding. When Mars declined, Hershey's was approached, and Reese's Pieces were used instead. As *ET* broke box office records, Reese's Pieces sales soared, and the legend spread about how Mars missed its chance—especially given that Hershey's didn't pay to have their product used in the film. The "real-life" appear-

63

ance of an actual brand in the film and the resulting sales spike inspired a new era of product placement in Hollywood. Now deals have become routine during the pre-production stage of films and TV shows, to the point that scripts and dialogues are being altered to include plugs. And product placement companies have sprung up, to find marriages between products and scripts.

When Matthew Weiner's *Mad Men* debuted on AMC in 2007, it was impossible not to notice that everybody smokes. And drinks. A lot. In particular, they drink Jack Daniel's because they were obliged, by contract, to do so. Brown-Forman Corporation, makers of Jack Daniel's, struck a deal with the producers of *Mad Men*, through the brokerage of the Universal McCann media agency of New York. And where better to strike a product placement deal than in a show about the advertising business. In addition to running Jack Daniel's commercials during the show, the agreement called for characters to be seen drinking the product and on occasion to ask for it by name. This is where product placement and branded entertainment have begun to converge: storylines must be fashioned and dialogue steered, to make sure Jack Daniel's is as much a character in the story as Don Draper and Peggy Olson.

The Bond film *Quantum of Solace* broke all previous product placement records in 2008. A long list of advertisers, including Ford, Heineken, Smirnoff, Omega watches, Virgin Atlantic, Aston Martin, Coca-Cola, and Sony collectively spent an eye-popping $79 million to have their products placed into the storyline. The previous record was held by, wait for it, another Bond film, *Die Another Day*, which had attracted $65 million. As the website Filmonic slyly stated, "The age-old debate is whether or not product placement actually works." Is it possible for a can of Coke in a fifteen-second shot to make any impact on a viewer when it's not the focus of the scene? My feeling is, yes, it does work, but it takes a ton of media exposure for these fleeting product flashes to make a dent in people's minds. But again, context is everything. As a kid, I wanted nothing more than to be James Bond. Everything he wore, did, and said were the stuff of my daydreams, and even now, as a grown man, I leave the theatre admiring Bond. So does product placement work? It certainly can be influential for the very reason that people love to emulate heroes.

Elsewhere, branded entertainment has ventured into previously unexplored territory.

THEY WILL SELL YOU ON THE PAGE, THEY WILL SELL YOU ON THE STAGE

In 2001 author Fay Weldon released her twenty-second novel, *The Bulgari Connection*, the tale of a woman finding her way back into society after doing time for trying to run her husband's mistress down with a car. But it wasn't this attempted mistress-cide that set tongues a-wagging; it was the deal Weldon had made with an upscale Bulgari jewellery company. For a tidy £18,000, she agreed to place Bulgari's brand at least a dozen times within her novel. Bulgari originally commissioned the novel for limited, exclusive distribution to its customers. Subsequently, when HarperCollins published it for the consumer market, the howls of derision began immediately. Salon.com quoted Weldon as declaring: "Product placement or none, this is as good a novel as I've ever written." Naysayers, meanwhile, blasted Weldon's book as 192 pages of "copywriting."

The movement has since spread to the stage. In the spring of 2008, Toronto's Fringe Festival featured a new work, *Body and Soul*, by renowned playwright Judith Thompson. It contained stories and performances from a baker's dozen of nonprofessional actors about the "second act of their lives." The play was commissioned by Dove—as in the beauty bar. Harkening back to the proverb "only Nixon could go to China," only a playwright of Ms. Thompson's character could credibly attempt to create a play conceived and bankrolled by a soap brand. Ms. Thompson was quick to defend the play, which was well received and which, she insisted, never mentioned or pandered to the sponsor's product even if theatregoers did find gift bags full of Unilever products

65

under their seats.

By underwriting "conventional" art and entertainment, commercial brands such as Bulgari and Dove are taking their cue from the Roman emperors and from the clergy and nobility who sponsored the masters, from Michelangelo to Mozart. The problems connected with branded entertainment are no different from those related to any of these sponsored art forms: when subjected to ads, product placements, and promos, potential customers become suspicious of the creator's motive. How does an audience lose itself in *Body and Soul*, knowing that its funded purpose, on some level, is to brand a soap? Did readers of *The Bulgari Connection* wonder what Fay Weldon would have written had she not accepted the Bulgari deal? Or what Michelangelo might've created without those pesky clerics gawking over his shoulder?

WEBISODES

Since the Internet began its explosive growth in the nineties, marketers have seized on it as a medium for new forms of branded entertainment— notably, the "webisode," a painfully cute portmanteau describing short films made for an online audience. Among the first, and more spectacular, was a series created by the agency Fallon Worldwide for BMW titled *The Hire*, featuring actor Clive Owen as a high-end, itinerant driver-for-hire, a sort of "Have Beemer, Will Travel." Episodes were elegant, tense, and spare, each showcasing a BMW vehicle. A spectacular breadth of talent was recruited, from directors like Guy Ritchie and Ang Lee, to a head-turning list of guest actors, including Forest Whitaker, F. Murray Abraham, and even Marilyn Manson. The series was reviewed (favourably) in *Time* magazine and the *New York Times*. There was a spinoff comic and a DVD release. The

Among Fallon's litany of triumphs is the classic "Cat Herders" Super Bowl ad for EDS, the Perception/Reality print campaign for *Rolling Stone* magazine, and the post–9/11 revival for United Airlines: It's Time to Fly.

episodes live on, tailor made for eternal play on YouTube. BMW would follow up with a series for its Mini Cooper called *Hammer & Coop*, a tongue-in-cheek homage to the eighties prime-time staple *Knight Rider.* Its lighter tone was a better fit with the more playful "Mini Cooper" image.

A WHOLE NEW MEDIUM.

The Internet forced marketers and advertising agencies to learn a whole new language and acquire an entirely new skill set. In short order, they found themselves having to seek out and assemble specific Internet practitioners and establish online departments. Even after more than a century of marketing experience, the industry realized that most of the accepted methods didn't apply to the Internet, but all agreed it was the tidal wave of change that they had to understand, and understand fast.

Another conspicuous made-for-web production was *The Adventures of Seinfeld and Superman,* a series of three short, web-based films for American Express. Again, the production values were high end: Barry Levinson directed, and the brilliant Patrick Warburton loaned his voice to the animated Man of Steel. The episodes were sharp, durable, and true to the Seinfeld brand, and the troika was launched with great fanfare on *The Today Show,* complete with an appearance by Seinfeld and the animated Superman, sitting together being inter-viewed live—or so it seemed—by the show's host, Matt Lauer. Within three months, American Express reported three million visits to the Seinfeld/Superman website. With registration required to view the films, AMEX amassed a quarter-million names for its database: five times what they'd hoped for. Similar success was reported for *The Hire,* which according to *Motor Trend,* was viewed one hundred million times, and that's before you count the quality of viewership. A TV viewer might have the set on while negotiating a cup of Earl Grey and today's Sudoku puzzle. On the Internet, where an audience must search out a site, it's reasonable to assume films are viewed with a higher level of attention.

All the while, the "sole sponsor" tradition of television never completely died out. The Hallmark Hall of Fame, the crown jewel of TV drama, is one of those shows—the coelacanth of branded entertainment, a living specimen from a breed thought long extinct. Its teleplays and specials have yielded 260 Emmy nominations, 11 Peabody Awards, and 9 Golden Globes. When Hallmark aired its production of *Hamlet* in 1953, the audience for the diatribes of the melancholy Dane that night were larger than the accumulated viewers over the 350 years since Shakespeare had written the play. Nearly a quarter of all the actors who've won Academy Awards have appeared in a Hallmark drama, and because Hallmark sponsors each program, it creates its own clutter-free oasis, in which it monopolizes its audience. Boasting "more drama and fewer commercials," Hallmark ads are commonly two-minute advertising mini-dramas, designed to stir emotions in ways that few short-form ads ever could. Hallmark itself became the first TV sponsor to win an Emmy for one of its commercials: a three-minute, two-hankie story called *Required Reading*, about a sixty-something man learning to read for the first time. All the same, while branded entertainment is enjoying a revival, odds are heavily against any brand riding the same trail as the Hallmark Hall of Fame, partly because few brands are so compatible with such emotion-rich content and partly because attention spans in the marketing business are quickly shrinking. Hallmark has cultivated its brand over more than a half century of TV drama; today's marketers typically expect results in months, if not days.

BRANDED ENTERTAINMENT RISES AGAIN

We're on the cusp of an era where brands are infiltrating existing forms of entertainment and a few new ones. BBDO North America, one of the world's mightiest ad agencies, is creating and pitching TV programs on behalf of clients. Nike has produced documentaries, including a feature about cycling legend Lance Armstrong, which aired nationally on CBS television. In 2007, the Geico Cavemen, characters who star in TV ads for America's Geico Insurance, were spun into a half-hour sitcom series on ABC television until driven to premature extinction by carnivorous critics and indifferent viewers. PepsiCo produced a feature film about snowboarding, credited to "Universal Pictures in association with MD films," "MD" being (the Pepsi-owned) Mountain Dew. Burger King enjoyed a wildly successful experiment with "King Games," a set of Xbox games, featuring the rather eerie "King" character from its TV campaign. The agency responsible, Miami's Crispin, Porter + Bogusky, created the games to reach the deep-fried, meat-and-potatoes, fast-food demographic: teenaged males. Advertising trade magazines were informed that the games reached young consumers with an impact equivalent to thirteen Super Bowl ads.

WHAT AD PEOPLE READ

The most popular advertising trade magazines are *Advertising Age* and *AdWeek* in the U.S. and *Marketing* magazine and *Strategy* magazine in Canada. Their British counterpart is *Campaign*. All feature an interesting mix of news and analysis—and the best work being done in all media.

For marketers, this renaissance in branded entertainment is a necessary shift as young, marketing-savvy consumers turn away from conventional advertising. Almost by accident, major companies are reprising their role as popular culture kingmakers, creating and producing what you might call "entvertising." With clutter constantly building an almost insurmountable wall between advertisers and their audiences, the one door that remains wide open is entertainment. Just like the days of Jack Benny.

THE "ANNOY YOUBUYING" MYTH

While I aspire not to create them, I'm frequently asked about ads that annoy people. Especially broadcast ads. Some irritate potential customers by yelling or condescending or launching into hyperbole. More often, the complaint is repetition: people ask me if advertisers deliberately seek to annoy the public into purchasing a product by running the same ad over and over and over again. And I find myself answering "no, no, and no."

It's true that many commercials wear out their welcome long before they're taken off the air. Just as a convoy is only as fast as its slowest ship, advertising often appears to be only as good as its most annoying players. These are the cynics and the screamers (many of them local car dealers with outrageous hairpieces, it seems).

Think of it this way: advertising is an enormous (and growing) worldwide industry. Like any community, it's driven by geniuses, visionaries, and savants, just as its dark, damp cracks are infested with crackpots and the good ones are invited into your imagination as familiar friends and given an honoured place in that cozy chair by the fire; the bad ones are dismissed as "advertisers" and are shown the door.

Especially irritating are ads that are presented more than once during a single commercial break—sometimes back to back. A friend who buys media for advertisers told me it's never the intention of advertisers to do this but rather a mistake by the broadcaster.

Just the same, as early as the 1950s, ad giant Rosser Reeves, of the agency Ted Bates & Co., was a firm believer in the power of repetition. So much so that according to an industry joke, the switchboard used to answer the agency phone with:

"Hello, Ted Bates.
"Hello, Ted Bates.
"Hello, Ted Bates."

It's true that the very tone and manner of some ads irritate. But it's never an actual strategy to annoy anyone into buying.

PERSUADING
YOOTS

4

WHAT'S A "YOOT"?

Young people are growing so rapidly in consumer influence that the marketing world is still fumbling to classify and name them. Terms such as *youths, young people,* and *youngsters* sound too much like something my Grade 8 gym teacher would've said. More contemporary terms such as *Gen X, Gen Y, Millennials,* and the *Echo Generation* have definitions too narrow for the demographic we're putting under the microscope in this chapter. So I've decided to go with "Yoots," Joe Pesci's approximation of "youths" in the picture *My Cousin Vinny.*

P eople under twenty—"yoots"—are the new holy grail of marketing, and they know it. Children, tweens, teenagers, and young adults have enormous power to create, trash, and rebuild social trends and a collective spending clout that would have Captain Von Trapp thinking twice before wrapping his lips around that damned boson's whistle.

Marketing firms, news services, and parent groups swing the statistics—many of them conflicting—but most of them pointing to the same trend: young consumers carry an astonishing amount of consumer clout:

THE SPENDING POWER OF YOOTS

- A majority of American teenagers own cellphones.
- In 1985, 23 percent of teens aged sixteen to nineteen owned cars, and by two decades later, that percentage had almost doubled.

Those of us with kids can only nod knowingly when told that the marketing clout of young people isn't limited to the money they spend themselves; it expands to include the family spending they *influence*. So much of this begins with a major shift in the parent-child dynamic that took place with the postwar consumer boom and the tendency of kids to quickly and naturally embrace new technology. In January 2008, *Advertising Age* noted that one-third of digital music players (most of them iPods) were owned by kids six to ten years old and contained on average 125 songs, 10 TV shows, and 15 movies. Today, I wouldn't dream of buying a computer or phone or software without at least consulting my offspring, who have amassed such a vast knowledge of new products and gadgets that I suspect they're sneaking out past curfew to attend covert consumer-tech classes. The influence of young people now goes beyond whining to parents for a specific brand of breakfast cereal (though studies show parents do buy more groceries when their kids go shopping with them). Market researchers report that a majority of parents consult their kids before making major purchase decisions, even in their choice of a new vehicle. Though estimates vary, the upper-end figures suggest that each year, young people are directly and indirectly responsible for $570 billion in purchase decisions.

> The theory is that these are hand-me-down iPods: parents graduate to the newest digital players, and their teenaged kids already have their own, so Mom and Dad pass their perfectly good, old players on to their younger kids.

> The first evidence of this generation shift in expertise arrived with the VCR as parents stared blankly at their new machine flashing twelve o'clock, with no idea of how to program or set it up, and had to rely on their kids' expertise.

PERSUADING YOOTS

Whatever the number actually is, news media and advocacy groups seem firmly agreed on a few things:

- Young people are amassing enormous consumer influence.

and

- Their influence is growing. Fast.

To that let's add the phenomenon that will be keeping us in its thrall for the rest of this chapter:

- They're becoming increasingly immune to conventional marketing messages—even more than their parents are.

The rapid growth of the youth market, compared to that of other demographics, has made it the hottest property in marketing, but it's not without its own Indiana Jones–style booby trap. Young people have become adept at seeing through the sales language advertisers have honed for more than a century, and they're media savvy enough to know how the marketing machine works. What's more, they're turning away from traditional advertising-driven media, disappearing into the electronic version of gated communities as they hunker down in front of their computers, putting up fences that most marketers haven't yet learned to scale.

THE RADIO AGE: KIDS, MEET ADVERTISERS; ADVERTISERS, MEET KIDS.

This is not a biblical expression, as some believe, but is thought to have originated in the fifteenth century, when it referred specifically to young ladies.

The role of young people has undergone an amazing transformation, in a world where many can still remember a time when children were "seen and not heard." No one imagined the attitude shift that would begin as the first radio sets appeared in living rooms of the 1920s. Early advertisers, still scouting the vast *terra incognita* of broadcast marketing, were still discovering that, yes, housewives would alter their work patterns to tune into daytime programming. And they soon discovered that children's programming could occupy their offspring—but which sponsors, they wondered, might bother to underwrite programming directed at children?

An early entry, a CBS radio program called *Let's Pretend*, began its twenty-six-year run in 1929, backed by its long-time sponsor, Cream of Wheat. Children, and later their children, would perk up at the sound of this jingle:

> Cream of Wheat is so good to eat
> That we have it every day.
> We sing this song. It will make us strong
> And it makes us shout, "Hurray!"
> It's good for growing babies
> And grownups, too, to eat.
> For all the family's breakfast,
> You can't beat Cream of Wheat.

The Cream of Wheat brand was no newcomer to using verse, a mnemonic advertising form that predates radio by several decades. For example, in 1913, Cream of Wheat had run an ad in *McClure's* magazine with this verse:

> What do I care
> for snow or sleet.
> My tummy is full of
> Cream o' Wheat.

Makers of breakfast cereals were among the first serious players to use radio to communicate their brand directly to kids, and Wheaties joined Cream of Wheat on the radiowaves in the 1920s. The timing of the manufacturers of this upstart new breakfast cereal was impeccable, or lucky, or both. As an "early adopter" of radio advertising, the Washburn Crosby Company launched one of the oldest-known radio jingles, performed by an ad hoc quartet, as part of a sponsored program on Minnesota radio station WCCO. It helped that the company owned the station. (Its call letters were a short form of the firm's name at the time, though the outfit would later be rechristened "General Mills.")

Ear·ly adopt·er *(noun)* Marketing jargon, usually referring to a consumer happy to embrace new products and technologies long before the masses do, and often without so much as dipping a toe in the water first.

A CRISPY, CRUNCHY STAR IS BORN

Wheaties flakes were "discovered"—for want of a better word—by a health clinician with the Washburn Crosby Company of Minneapolis, in 1911. Goes the story: he was preparing gruel, a pasty wheat cereal, when he spilled some on a hot stove. The gruel promptly cooked and turned into small, yummy wheat flakes.

He shared his discovery with Washburn's head miller, George Cormack, who experimented with twenty-six variations of the formula until he finally created a flake that would hold together through the packaging process. In November 1924, the cereal was proudly launched as an exciting new, ready-to-eat breakfast cereal—Washburn's Gold Medal Whole Wheat Flakes, a name changed, mercifully, to "Wheaties" after the company held an internal naming contest.

So it was that in 1926, radio listeners heard the slow, sombre, hymn-like a cappella chorus

> Have you tried Wheaties?
> They're whole wheat with all of the bran.
> Won't you try Wheaties?
> For wheat is the best food of man.

They're crispy and crunchy, the whole year through.

The kiddies never tire of them and neither will you.

WASHBURN CROSBY, THE JINGLE PIONEER

Though it's hard to prove, General Mills claims that "Have You Tried Wheaties" was the first singing commercial ever to be aired. Released on Christmas Eve 1926, it featured The Wheaties Quartet, which consisted of an undertaker, a bailiff, a printer, and a businessman, who performed the song live on the air for the next six years. Each received $6 per performance.

Before long, the Washburn Crosby Company made a fascinating discovery: whenever the jingle was sung on the air, sales climbed. Granted, today this isn't the stuff of rocket science, but in a time when "reason why" advertising ruled—when advertisers believed they had to make a point-by-point case for their brand—the concept of selling a product simply by singing about it was an epiphany.

The Wheaties brand continued to blaze new trails in broadcast marketing in the early 1930s, when they struck a sponsorship deal with the Minneapolis Millers Baseball Club, whose games they agreed to broadcast on WCCO. The arrangement called for a Wheaties billboard over the left field fence where the product's new ad slogan would be displayed. That is—just as soon as they had one. Enter Minneapolis ad guy Knox Reeves. According to legend, when Reeves was asked to create a Wheaties slogan, he pulled out a pad and pencil, sketched a Wheaties box, and stared at it for a moment. Then, quicker than Malcolm Gladwell can blink, he said, "Breakfast of Champions" and plunked the pencil down. From then on, Wheaties wasn't about breakfast; it was about the emotion of victory.

It was right about here that Wheaties shifted its marketing strategy away from an adult audience and used radio to reach young people

79

with their "Breakfast of Champions" message. The man they hired to develop the right vehicle was Frank Hummert, the raja of the radio soap. (We met him and his business partner and wife, Ann, in Chapter 3.) Hummert proposed that they take "Skippy," a popular cartoon character, and adopt it as Wheaties' mascot and as the hero of a kids' radio series. All went swimmingly until a Skippy storyline—about the kidnapping of one of the hero's pals—coincided with a real-life tragedy, the kidnapping and death of the Lindbergh baby.

Hummert went back to whatever passes in radio as a drawing board and created *Jack Armstrong: The All-American Boy*. In flawless harmony with the Wheaties' brand, Jack Armstrong was a champion: he was the pride of Hudson High, who could dominate the gridiron and the diamond and the basketball court and the track—and discover lost treasure, land aircraft, and uncover international spy rings—all in time to cram for his algebra mid-term. Jim Ameche, lesser-known brother of actor Don, was the first to loan his voice to the character, who graced the airwaves from 1933 to 1951.

In 1930 Ovaltine underwrote the radio incarnation of the Harold Gray comic strip character Little Orphan Annie. During its early years, before network connections were up to snuff, the series was produced in both Chicago for the east coast and San Francisco for the west, where separate casts performed the same script. Dozens of kids' radio programs followed, many featuring popular comic strip characters. Dick Tracy went to air in 1934, sponsored first by Sterling Products, then by Quaker Oats, who used the conspicuously un-Quakerlike tactic of appealing to kids by way of firearms:

ANNCR: The makers of Quaker Puffed Wheat and Quaker Puffed Rice, those two delicious nourishing cereals that are shot from guns, now bring you another thrilling Dick Tracy detective adventure . . .

The subsequent ad explained that rice and wheat, respectively, were placed in special "guns" in the Quaker plant, where they were exploded to eight times their normal size.

Then, before kids had a chance to wrap their minds around a cereal shot from guns, they were given instructions:

ANNCR: [I]f you're a loyal Dick Tracy fan and friend, check up on the pantry at least twice a week to make sure there's always puffed wheat or puffed rice there. Look to see at the end of today's program, and if there isn't one of those famous red and blue packages in the pantry now, ask Mother to order some from the grocer's.

Hear that? That's the sound of a radio announcer forming a secret cabal with a young listener—right there in the family's living room—inciting him to lobby for a given brand of breakfast cereal. Within that speech is an implicit warning: if you don't check that pantry twice a week for Quaker cereals, well, you're not a loyal Dick Tracy fan. Radio recruited kids by the thousands as operatives, charged with ensuring that Mother didn't make the catastrophic error of showing disloyalty to Dick Tracy by picking up one of those—ugh— other cereals.

Loyalties forged among young listeners would pay dividends long after the commercials faded. And research would later affirm what those early marketers might only have suspected: children as young as two can develop brand loyalties, while children as young as three recognize brand logos. Advertisers also learned to change tack when speaking to kids, not just in their language and tone, but in their sales strategy. Rather than citing the benefits that might best appeal to mothers—economy and nutritional value, for instance—they painted on the much broader canvas of the young imagination. A cereal

81

So boasted Andy "Jingles" Devine, co-star of *The Adventures of Wild Bill Hickok,* when promoting Kellogg's Sugar Corn Pops. He was also careful to add that you can eat 'em out of a bowl for breakfast or out of the box as a snack.

Or a reasonable facsimile. Canadian law usually forbids companies to require that anyone buy their product in order to enter a contest, so advertisers had to accept a "reasonable facsimile" in place of an actual box top or coupon. While it didn't spur sales, sellers had to love the fact that kids would spend hours lovingly drawing their logos.

might be shot from guns or come ready-to-serve, with sugar already on it.

Many copywriters in those early radio days learned to embrace the phrase "Ask Mother," but Skelly Oil was even craftier. Sponsoring the *Captain Midnight* kids' serial, it once prompted young listeners to lobby Dad to buy Mom one of their new Skelgas ranges as a Christmas present. As a bonus, Skelly Oil would include a free fifty-two-piece dinnerware set (in the attractive Barcelona pattern). That, the announcer counselled young listeners, "can be your present to Mother."

Many, from Buck Rogers to Little Orphan Annie, offered club memberships with a card and often a trinket. The Orphan Annie decoder pin, which allowed club members to decipher coded messages read during the program, worked so well for Ovaltine that when they shifted their sponsorship in 1940 to the more martially inclined *Captain Midnight*, they took their decoder premium with them, adapting it to their new hero. Many "premiums" drove direct sales by requiring some proof of purchase, such as cereal box tops, Popsicle wrappers, or the inner seal from a jar of peanut butter. Not only did radio premiums ensure immediate sales and cultivate lasting brand relationships with young consumers, they also put mothers in the habit of looking for a given brand—a habit that may well have continued beyond the life of the radio promotion.

Pre·mium *(noun)* Typically a trinket or discount offered as an enticement to buy a product. Your first brush with a premium might have been the toy you dug out of a cereal box when you were a kid.

82

THE BOOMERS

Following the Second World War, months after thousands of service-men and women returned, young families beat a path to their local maternity wards. The postwar economic boom gave families confidence to expand. New highway systems, and an invigorated workforce pushed city workers into new-fangled suburbs. For a decade and a half, the "war" generation would produce the offspring—the now-ubiquitous baby boomers—who would drive marketing and culture for most of the next half century.

Raised in prosperity few of their parents knew and their grandparents never even dreamed of, the baby boomers grew up with the strong winds of consumerism gathering speed around them. They were the first born into the television age, which had overtaken popular culture by the mid-fifties, and marketers brought lessons gleaned from radio to the new medium. They realized that Saturday mornings, a traditional "dead spot" among older viewers, could be filled with programming for kids.

In December 1947 NBC launched *Puppet Playhouse*, featuring "Buffalo" Bob Smith. Within days the name was changed to *Howdy Doody*. Among his cast of characters was Tim Tremble, played by a young comedic actor, Don Knotts, and Clarabell the Clown, played by former U.S. Marine reservist Bob Keeshan. In October 1955, Keeshan created a TV institution, *Captain Kangaroo,* for CBS. Among early TV offerings for Canadian kids were *Burns Chuckwagon from the Stampede Corral,* produced not in Calgary but way out yonder in Vancouver. From Ottawa came *Let's Go to the Museum* with Robert MacNeil, later the co-anchor of *The MacNeil-Lehrer Report.* In the early 1960s, the Canadian Broadcasting Corporation would import a Pennsylvanian Baptist-minister–turned-kids'-TV-creator by the name of Fred Rogers, to develop its children's programming. He'd bring with him one Ernie Coombs, who would remain in Canada and later earn fame as *Mister Dressup.* Not all kids' shows were sponsored, though all attracted young viewers to the new ad-driven medium.

83

TELEVISION MEETS TEENAGERS

Willis was the original choice to play CIA agent Felix Leiter in *Goldfinger,* but he was relegated to the role of Leiter's sidekick, Simmons, and was thus deprived of the privilege of uttering the classic screen line "Ten'll get you one, it's either a drink or a dame." That honour went to fellow Canuck Cec Linder. (Both Linder and Willis graced my company's studios many times.) Willis, Linder, and Lois Maxwell—who played Miss Moneypenny—made for a sizable Canadian contingent in that famous Bond film.

Imagine. A device that fit in the palm of your hand, was filled with music, and came with earphones. Sound familiar? Cough. iPod. Cough.

Bandstand. It was a Philadelphia-based show, but when ABC picked it up in 1957 and renamed it *American Bandstand*, they made a household name of former disc jockey Richard Wagstaff "Dick" Clark, who at twenty-eight, would soon be crowned "America's oldest teenager." On the north side of the border, Canadian teens were swept up in the same trend with *Cross-Canada Hit Parade*, first hosted by actor-broadcaster Austin Willis. Teenaged boomers were soon surrounded by rock and roll, and by the late 1950s, radio stations formatted with "the devil's music" spread like crown vetch across the urban, and now suburban, landscape. A few years later, an invention called the "transistor radio" made this new music portable. No more were teenagers obliged to sneak into the living room to turn on the family hi-fi and fill the house with their

To be fair, a generation earlier, jazz and blues were distinguished by the "devil's music" moniker. But by the fifties, the title was tacked onto anything north of Lawrence Welk.

raucous, boogie-woogie claptrap. Now they could take their raucous, boogie-woogie claptrap with them, beyond the protective ears of Mom and Dad. The car culture of the late fifties and sixties, captured so perfectly in the movie *American Graffiti*, also propagated rock and roll as it pounded out of car radios. Needless to say, advertisers were quick to leap onto the scene, to take advantage of such fertile ground. And at the same time, a growth in part-time jobs gave young people the consumer clout to create the first serious blip on marketers' radar.

84

Youth-oriented media—especially broadcast—developed its own language and tone, or so it desperately hoped, because they were targeting an audience that was not only lucrative but also savvy. Hip cats with bread made the scene at the flicks or at some cookin' bash or just went ape (which I'm tellin' ya, man, frosted the heat). Ad copywriters, stranded with their hoods up and rads steaming on a lonely roadside outside Squaresville, struggled—often in vain—to learn the dialect and probe the inner psyche of the teenaged mind. But they gave it a good shot, resulting in copy like this:

Loosely, and rather formally, translated, this means: *In-the-know persons with disposable income revelled at the cinema or attended an invigorating party or engaged in agitated behaviour (which exasperated the law enforcement officers).*

TWO TEENS SIT IN A MALT SHOP, VIBRANT WITH OTHER TEENS, AND WITH ROCK AND ROLL GUITAR MUSIC PLAYING IN A JUKEBOX.

TEEN GIRL: *We've been going steady six weeks today.*
TEEN GUY: *They've been the best six weeks of my life.*
TEEN GIRL: *Really?*
TEEN GUY: *No foolin.' Goin' steady with you, and making the team . . . and gosh . . . I've even licked my own dandruff problem.*
TEEN GIRL: *I know.*
TEEN GUY: *[ponders a moment, then:] That crazy Head & Shoulders really works!*

As early TV broadcasters scrambled for programming that would unite advertisers with young viewers, many found themselves rooting around in the attics of their archrivals in the film industry, dusting off theatrical cartoons to be packaged as programming for young viewers. In the earliest days, these audiences were fed a steady diet of

Woody Woodpecker, Harvey Toons, Popeye the Sailor, and the ever-wonderful (pardon my bias) Warner Bros. cartoons. The market was ripe for an original, relatively low-cost, animated TV show that would unite advertisers with a fast-growing, young audience.

Enter (stage left) ex-MGM animators William Hanna and Joseph Barbera, who in 1957 formed a company to create animated programming specifically for kids. Unlike theatrical animators, such as those who created feature films for Walt Disney, Hanna-Barbera developed production methods that cut costs through more static images and repetitive backgrounds. TV cartoons would never be the same, especially after 1960, when this pair unleashed a show that was to become a pop culture institution.

It was a prime-time animated series, loosely based on Jackie Gleason's *The Honeymooners* and created for an adult audience. First developed as *The Flagstones,* the program's title evolved to *The Gladstones* before its debut on September 30, 1960, as *The Flintstones.* The kid portion of the viewership might not have mattered had the sponsor not been Winston cigarettes, who provided ads like the one where Fred and Barney sneak away from their yardwork to light a couple of darts behind the garage. The unusual marriage of Winston and the Flintstones lasted about three years: when Wilma became pregnant with Pebbles, Winston butted out gracefully, making way for the more wholesome folks at Welch's (the ones who make the grape juice). But by that time, the *Flintstones*-tobacco combo had raised questions about the imaginary curtain that separated "kids' TV" from grownup programming.

An irresistible piece of folklore has it that Fred and Wilma Flintstone were the first prime-time TV couple to be shown sharing a bed. (TV couples before them, it was said, had been relegated to twin beds.) However, the great urban legend busters at Snopes.com insist that the first-time bed-sharing honour went to one of the earliest TV sit-coms, *Mary Kay and Johnny,* in 1947. No less fun is Snopes' revelation that in *The Brady Bunch,* six kids shared a bathroom without a toilet anywhere in sight. But we digress.

THE SIXTIES

By the 1960s, as so many baby boomers reached their teens, they took a hard look at the world and didn't like what they saw. White males dominated a multigendered, multiracial world. Remnants of Vietnamese villages smouldered with the sickly scent of napalm. TV viewers watched police dogs attack civil rights protesters, and icons of change were assassinated. The heavyweight champion of the world abandoned his "slave name," Cassius Clay, to become Muhammad Ali and risked jail rather than serve in Asia, telling reporters "No VietCong ever called me a nigger."

Emboldened by their sheer numbers and by their economic clout, boomers set about using their power. Advertisers, those friendly people who once enticed them with peanut butter and pimple creams, became "the man": corporate predators, hucksters. Had they simply been jaded, that would have been hard enough for marketers, but boomers did them one better: they became media literate, and media studies classes began to spring up in high schools. Young people were gaining a sense of how marketing worked and easily saw through the old-school sales devices of slogans, rote, and the "call to action." Advertisers were like the magician whose audience knows all his tricks and now struggled to draw even polite applause.

THE THIN LINE BETWEEN KIDS' BRANDS AND KIDS' ENTERTAINMENT

On September 26, 1964, the week *The Warren Report* was published, concluding that a lone gunman had slain President Kennedy, and as the third session of Vatican II reshaped modern theology, *Linus the Lionhearted* premiered on CBS television. It was a high-end cartoon series featuring an embarrassment of top voice talent, including Sheldon Leonard, Ruth Buzzi, Jonathan Winters, Anne Meara, Jerry Stiller, and Jesse White (the original Maytag repairman). The problem? Several of its star characters, including Linus and Sugar Bear, were created to pitch specific Post Cereals—Crispy Critters and Sugar Crisp, respectively.

> I once directed Stiller in a cereal commercial. He was playing the voice of an animated honey bee. Take after take, it wasn't funny. Then I asked him to yell the entire script in the style of his *Seinfeld* character, Frank Costanza, which he did, and we all fell on the floor laughing. Stiller, hearing the laughter, asked with genuine wonder, "Why does that always work?"

Sensing that advertisers were stepping out of bounds, parents set about constructing moats around their children, and governments, reading the wind direction, developed laws and broadcast regulations limiting the relationships between marketers and children. In time several European countries and the province of Quebec banned any kind of broadcast advertising directed at children. Elsewhere, children's broadcasters faced a litany of guidelines and regulations, some of them prohibiting sponsors' products from being depicted in kids' programs. At the same time violent moments were excised from vintage cartoons.

The timing couldn't have been worse for the creators of *Linus!* After two seasons, America's Federal Communications Commission (FCC) pooped their party, passing a new regulation that prohibited advertising icons from becoming stars in children's programs, and likewise, stars of children's programs pitching products in ads. The regulation wasn't without grey areas: consider the great baritone Thurl Ravenscroft, who was a staple of both ad voiceovers (he gave voice to

Tony the Tiger) and kids programming (he sang "You're a Mean One, Mr. Grinch" in the immortal Chuck Jones cartoon *How the Grinch Stole Christmas*). The regulation restricted *characters* from appearing in both ads and children's programming, but did not extend to actors and voices.

As those children of the sixties became parents themselves, they were already wary of marketers offering sales pitches too thinly disguised as children's entertainment. And today the firewall of regulations separating children and advertisers extends beyond kids' shows. In Canada, advertisements for beer, wine, and liquor are forbidden to use celebrity endorsers who might be considered appealing to kids. That included anyone—read: anyone—who was on kids' radar. In the spring of 2003, when hockey commentator Don Cherry appeared in ads for a major beer brand, Canadian regulators ruled that his appeal to children constituted selling beer to underage viewers and ordered the ads pulled.

ADS IN SCHOOLS

Not to be constricted by broadcast regulations, some advertisers found new ways to reach young audiences, and in the spring of 1990, a new face appeared in the classrooms of four hundred American schools. It was Channel One, a daily TV news program, complete with two minutes of paid ads. Schools signing up received the hardware necessary to broadcast a daily twelve-minute current events program. The cost? Students would be subjected to four thirty-second ads tucked within each broadcast, and schools signed a contract promising to show students the broadcast virtually every school day. The shows were, as you might imagine, upbeat and fast paced. Among the energetic reporters featured onscreen was a very young Anderson Cooper, later bound for stardom on CNN.

89

Despite the objection of scores of educational organizations, and an outright ban in some jurisdictions, Channel One survived, expanding in time to more than twelve thousand schools and an audience of eight million students. By 1999, such high-powered brands as Pepsi, Nabisco, Procter & Gamble, and the U.S. Armed Forces were paying $200,000 for a thirty-second spot. But that same year, a U.S. Senate oversight committee, responding to growing public unease with ad-driven TV content in American classrooms, called Channel One brass onto the carpet and gave them the Capitol Hill equivalent of a wedgie, then sent them home to resume their programming. In Canada a similar venture, the Youth News Network, tried—and failed—to infiltrate classrooms.

There's a strong sense of farce in pretending schools are an advertising-free bubble: logos and sponsored messages have found their way into cafeterias and onto sports scoreboards for years. A fast-food pizza chain sold slices in my daughter's public school, and parents combined that with a fundraising component. In the 1990s Coke and Pepsi engaged in a fierce war for exclusive contracts within schools and universities, some worth tens of millions of dollars. This generated angst among parents and students, many of whom didn't take kindly to having themselves "sold" to major brands. Many educational institutions would, in time, ban pop machines altogether.

Ads have long been a fixture in high school yearbooks, but now they're seeping into school hallways and into, on, and on top of school buses. *Time, Newsweek,* and the *New York Times* have published special editions for classrooms, complete with advertising. A California outfit called ZapMe! provides schools with free computers and Internet, but the service comes with commercials targeting students.

In maybe the most brazen example, Tom Farber, a calculus teacher at a suburban San Diego school, was told by his school board that they were cutting supplies budgets by nearly a third. That posed a problem for Farber, because at three cents a page, his test sheets alone would cost more than $500 per year, and his annual copying budget was just $316. So he started selling ads on his test papers. As he said in an interview on CBC Radio, "Tough times call for tough actions." A local newspaper printed a story about Farber's plans, and when he came home after a three-day vacation, he discovered seventy-five email requests for ad space. His semester final is sold out. Most of the ads are for local businesses, and they play into the medium. For example, one dentist is running an ad that says, "Brace yourself for a great semester." The "ads on exams" idea is getting very mixed reactions around the country, as you can imagine, with many people taking exception to the notion of businesses paying to get access to kids. Farber first asked his students if they would be offended by the idea, and the answer was no. Parents are also supporting him. As Farber says, "We're expected to do more with less." He wants to help the kids, and advertisers are more than happy to help him.

What does all this teach young people? Quite a bit. Each generation is becoming even more media savvy than the one that came before it, and some take to rebellion.

Having taken its lumps, the marketing world is coming back with more creative and less cynical ways of connecting with students. Early in 2008 Dave Droga, of the marketing firm Droga5, launched a campaign dubbed The Million, which involved both the New York City Department of Education and Verizon. As Droga put it, the campaign reinvented the cellphone as a motivational tool. Under the Million campaign, each student received a phone free of charge, and then, by improving school attendance, participation, homework, and grades, they would be rewarded with airtime for phone calls, texting, and music downloads. And like all cellphones, the Million would not be allowed in the classroom. Campaigns like this may or may not be

Hence the wave of "culture jammers"—crusaders out to disrupt the flow of marketing messages in order to make a statement of their own. (That name was adopted by Vancouver's not-for-profit Media Foundation, which publishes *Adbusters* magazine.)

91

the most acceptable way of inviting marketers into a classroom, but it's a healthy sign that "old-school" advertising philosophies may be banished to the principal's office.

REACHING YOOTS . . . IN CODE

An eye-catching ad appeared on the sides of New York buses in 2004, for the hip hop clothing designer Akademiks. It showed an attractive woman wearing a sweater, panties, and a playful expression. She was kneeling on a book-strewn floor, looking over her shoulder, with her caboose facing the camera. On her panties was emblazoned the name "Akademiks." Beside it, the headline "Read Books. Get Brain."

To most readers older than thirty, it probably came across as a slightly saucy, street-smart ad, promoting literacy. But that was before the *New York Daily News* broke the story: "Get Brain" was street slang for oral sex. This vernacular nugget had escaped the scrutiny of the New York City Transit Authority, which promptly pulled the ads. I would be astonished if the agency behind the ad didn't fully understand the meaning of the term. They may have reasoned that, sure, it was a contentious line. But since only young people—their target audience—were likely to understand the double meaning, what was the harm? Media outfits in six other major U.S. cities were similarly taken in.

Similar campaigns are cropping up elsewhere as advertisers salt their copy with naughty slang terms detected only by a select group of young consumers. Those who get the joke feel like insiders, members of a club. They snicker as their parents did a generation earlier, when they persuaded the high school secretary to page "Bob Loblaw" or "Hugh Jorgan" to the office. Ever wonder why Abercrombie & Fitch blasts such loud music in their stores? It isn't to attract kids but to repel parents. It was a strategic decision; parents roaming around the stores killed the cool factor for younger shoppers.

The year before the Akademiks ad, Reebok ran a bitingly funny Super Bowl commercial—*Terry Tate: Office Linebacker.* The fictitious

Tate, in dress pants and a football jersey, patrolled the office, slamming, tackling, and trash talking terrified employees foolish enough to violate office protocol, such as finishing a pot of coffee without making a fresh one or not including a cover sheet on a TPS report. These moments were so much fun that few seemed to notice the company name: *Felcher & Sons.* "Felcher" is a slang term referring to one who engages in "felching": an especially unsavoury sex act. A harmless mistake? There are, after all, eleven "Felchers" in the New York City phone directory. On the other hand, ads by a brand that big, on a stage as grand as the Super Bowl, make it hard to imagine that someone didn't know the slang meaning of the name.

"F-C-U-K" apparel made quite the splash—for awhile, at least. Ostensibly it stood for "French Connection United Kingdom" when it first appeared in 1997, but the word played on the human brain's tendency to see words as patterns, rather than as groups of individual letters, filling in blanks and rearranging them as familiar terms. This phenomenon was likely in play when a potential juror was kicked out of a courtroom in Wales for wearing a F-C-U-K shirt. Meanwhile, French Connection got a lot of publicity from a lawsuit launched by a group called Conservative Future U-K.

Spinning tidily in his grave is ad pioneer David Ogilvy, who once said of print ads: "Never write an advertisement which you wouldn't want your own family to read." The rules have changed in the age of persuasion. So have consumers, and advertising writers.

WE DO AND WE DO FOR YOOTS, AND WHAT THANKS DO WE GET?

I have a friend whose twenty-year-old son settles arguments by smiling, leaning in, and declaring: "Yeah? Well *I'm* picking your retirement home." This is just evidence of the funny thing that happened as the torch was passed from boomers to their children: empowerment turned into entitlement. When they were younger, kids of this generation had bedroom walls adorned with sports awards and medals received just

93

for showing up. Their kindergarten "graduations" were marked by commencement ceremonies, complete with gowns and mortarboard caps. They were raised by adult cheerleaders chanting, "You're special," and they believed it. Their schools nurtured them, encouraged them, and then sold them to advertisers. They learned. They watched as the benevolent corporate culture of their grandparents' time—the one-job-for-life variety—devolved into a leaner, meaner, "What have you done for me lately?" headspace. They remembered. Today it isn't unusual for the latest crop of brilliant, tech-savvy, entry-level employees to dictate terms to potential employers. Major corporations are actually turning to a new breed of consultant to help them manage young employees who dress as they please, arrive when they please, and leave when it suits them, and who would think nothing of seeking work across the street if everything isn't to their liking. And despite their unprecedented spending power, the newest crop of consumers is virtually unpersuadable. This group isn't likely to bolt to the supermarket because a cute, animated doughboy asked them to.

THE "FART" INDEX

A useful measure of the edginess of advertising today is the popular use of "fart" sounds. I'm not fond of the word *fart,* and no one would have dared use flatulence in a radio ad when I started in the business thirty years go. But today, as the tone of advertising shifts to appeal to yoots, "fart" gags are common: agencies bring me "fart" scripts to produce, and "fart" spots are winning international advertising awards. In the 1980s you wouldn't have found such sounds in a radio sound effects library, but now, if you searched the word *fart* in my studio's sound effects database, you'd find more than four *hundred* entries.

This new generation is creating a crisis in ad-driven media. The attention of young people, once devoted to TV and radio, is now being spread thinner and thinner as they embrace downloaded music, texting, and instant messaging, and online communities such as Facebook and MySpace. To advertisers, they're becoming available by appointment only, and they aren't making appointments.

The blunt realities of marketing to young people are causing vast changes in the language and tone of advertising. As their attention shifts from mass media to smaller, online social networks, they're sharing information and opinions about products and brands and fashions. For the first time ever, consumers are moving much faster than brands.

TWITTER: FEEDBACK IN REAL TIME

My first experience with Twitter was while giving a speech to a tourism group. As I spoke, people were very engaged in my talk, but they were also typing furiously on their BlackBerrys. When I got back to the office, I went onto Twitter and saw that people had been sending tweets about aspects of my speech to each other *while* I was giving the speech. They were commenting on what I was saying, in real time, with others in the room and with people who were elsewhere. Later, when I mentioned this to the organizer of the event, he told me that some speakers keep Twitter open on their laptops while giving their speeches, so they can keep an eye on live feedback, allowing them to respond to comments in real time. The crowds are now way ahead of the parade.

No generation has done more than this one to cause such rapid changes to advertising. Every day the tone of ads becomes edgier, less formal, and more experimental as marketers struggle for effective ways to reach lucrative young consumers. And over the past two decades, the mean age of advertising writers, designers, and executives has plummeted as agencies hire youth to speak to youth.

95

THE "I DON'T LIKE THAT AD, SO IT DOESN'T WORK" MYTH

For all the brown-nosing and pleading and cajoling and flattering that some advertisers do, you'd be forgiven for assuming their sun, moon, and stars revolve around you. But the truth is, they don't. And many—perhaps most—of the ads you see, hear, and experience are aimed at someone else.

In these days of "niche" marketing—where many brands direct their marketing at highly specific audiences—most of us intercept ads that are targeted at someone else. Which might explain why so many messages fail to impress. An octogenarian isn't expected to "get" an edgy LeBron James ad for Nike, just as an eleven-year-old won't get too excited about commercials offering insurance discounts to drivers fifty-plus.

Ads that don't speak to you can seem tiresome or inappropriate, and this may lead some to the mistaken conclusion that those ads aren't effective. The truth is, they simply might not work on *you.*

How can you tell whether an ad is effective or not? Here's a good rule of thumb: if it irks you, ask yourself if it's advertising a product or service you might reasonably be expected to buy. And more to the point, are you part of the core audience that brand is probably trying to reach? Think beyond the simple boundaries of age or gender and ask yourself whether you're part of the social tribe that brand is trying to reach.

As you might imagine, those who complain about the tone or creative content of an ad are rarely part of the group the seller is targeting. On the other hand, if you conclude that the brand *is* trying to reach someone like you and you still hate their ad, then—yup—it could be a clunker.

The one pervading evil of democracy
is the tyranny of the majority.
JOHN EMERICH EDWARD DALBERG-ACTON,
LORD ACTON

THE YOUTUBE
REVOLUTION

The consumer isn't a moron.
She is your wife.
DAVID OGILVY

Those whose lives are turned completely upside down by revolution so rarely see it coming:

- On July 14, 1789, a mob stormed the Bastille in Paris, marking the beginning of the end of aristocratic rule in France. Just 18 kilometres away, as *la corneille* flies, at the palace of Versailles, King Louis XVI recorded in his diary: "14 juillet: rien." Nothing.

- Barely two years later, the French plantation masters of Saint-Domingue failed to anticipate the slave rebellion that would lead to the formation of the independent Republic of Haiti.

- Years earlier, England's King George III may have been too busy slipping in and out of his controversial "madness" to anticipate trouble in the American colonies. (At one point, HRH insisted that every sentence he uttered must conclude with the word "peacock.")

> Reports of George III's red urine suggest His Majesty suffered from *porphyria*, a rare blood disease. A recent theory connects his condition to his exposure to arsenic: his wigs were discovered to have contained three hundred times the minimum toxic level.

Given these precedents, the best and brightest of the marketing world might be forgiven for having slipped into their pyjamas on Saturday, April 23, 2005, sipping on their warm milk (with a dash of nutmeg), and scribbling *"rien"* in their diaries. That day, few took notice of the first video placed on a new website called YouTube. It was utterly, well, whelming: a nineteen-second video called *Me at the Zoo*, featuring YouTube co-founder Jawed Karim. (You can still find that clip on YouTube. It was uploaded at 8:27 p.m. on the fateful Saturday evening.) With elephants in the background, Karim explains that they have "really, really, really long trunks," adding "and that's cool." No saucy nuance.

98

No discernible double meaning. Watching that clip, it was clear that YouTube began its existence as a misnomer. There was no "you." Or any other audience, for that matter.

Karim had co-founded the site with partners Chad Hurley and Steve Chen. All three were financially flush from their previous jobs, helping launch PayPal, and now their idea was to fill an online void: the lack of a one-stop Internet site that accepted and shared short video clips. Their timing, of course, was impeccable, as digital cameras and cameraphones were coming of age, allowing anyone to create videos and effects not possible outside a professional studio just a few years before. With the advent of YouTube, "civilians" began scooping TV news cameras with videos of world events. Cameraphones would record the most chilling images of the tsunami of December 26, 2004. At the same time, high-speed Internet was making it possible to exchange clips promptly.

So what happened when Jawed Karim unleashed the account of his pachyderm pilgrimage on a video-hungry world? In short, *rien*. Online viewers stayed away in droves. Hurley, Chen, and Karim circulated emails to friends, pleading them to upload videos. Calls to *Wired* magazine weren't returned. A classified ad on Craigslist offered $100 through PayPal to attractive young ladies who uploaded ten videos of themselves. There were no takers.

The three partners tried a little of everything, short of tap dancing, to pump adrenalin into their site. They added a "related videos" feature—suggested videos one might want to see, relating to the one they were currently watching. They provided links to social networks, including Facebook and MySpace. They offered the ingenious "external video player"—allowing web hosts and bloggers to play any "YouTube" video from their own site. Then, finally, a miracle arrived in the form of Mentos mints and Diet Coke. Videos appeared showing the two elements combined, causing a high-powered, sticky geyser, similar to the vinegar-and-baking-soda experiment that mischievous

99

Grade 5 teachers urge their students to try at home. It drew a jaw-dropping number of viewer hits. By 2008 the top three Mentos–Diet Coke videos had drawn more than eleven million hits.

Theories abound as to why these particular videos became so popular. I have my own, and it has to do with a great characteristic of the Internet: the fact that it levels the playing field. Everyone has access, and theoretically, everyone can be heard. The Mentos–Diet Coke experiment was an extension of that: everyone could try it. You didn't need expensive equipment or materials, you just needed a couple of Mentos and a bottle of Diet Coke. Even David Letterman tried to beat the record for geyser height.

YouTube had become a destination.

THE AUDIENCE TAKES CHARGE

It was impossible not to feel the shift in power. Broadcasters and publishers felt their grip slipping from public dialogue as audiences began creating, shaping, and controlling popular conversation. It was just as inevitable that the online community would eventually commandeer copyright materials, including music clips and videos and excerpts from TV shows and films. The question was: What would the copyright holders do about it?

The first salvo lobbed was a rap-spoof created for NBC's *Saturday Night Live* called *Lazy Sunday*. Soon after the original broadcast on December 17, 2005, it was uploaded onto YouTube and drew five million hits. The promotions people at NBC were ecstatic, but the corporation's lawyers weren't. Citing copyright infringement, the network ordered the clip removed. In February 2006, YouTube obliged. But the medium—or, more precisely, the community that powered it—was not to be stopped any more than Wile E. Coyote can stop a stampede of cattle with his tiny circus umbrella. The same audience that could make and break TV shows, films, and music now ruled YouTube. That's when the producers of popular film, TV, and music also had a

100

change of heart: they stopped using YouTube audiences and started obeying them.

Users posted, edited, and parodied favourite clips at will while the copyright holders quietly applauded, or bit their lips, or both. The moguls of traditional media were no longer the gatekeepers they once were. After centuries of playing audience to mass media, people now had a megaphone all their own. Non-copyright YouTube clips began outdrawing the mightiest music videos and TV clips. The off-the-charts popularity of such videos as *The Evolution of Dance*, featuring "motivational speaker/comedian" Judson Laipply demonstrated that this new video portal would operate in ripples and waves generated by users themselves. For no earthly reason, a seemingly innocuous home video of two young children, titled *Charlie Bit Me* (the title doubles as a spoiler), quickly accrued a viewer hit-count in the tens of *millions*—and countless dozens of "response" videos: remakes, remixes, parodies, sequels, and all manner of variations-on-a-theme. The term *viral video* wove itself into the popular lexicon.

A year and a half after the day Jawed Karim posted *Me at the Zoo*, YouTube was streaming a hundred million videos daily, with seventy thousand new videos uploaded each day, and thirty million visitors each month. And each visitor spent an average of a half hour surfing YouTube. There were no programmers; no publishers; and no editors to plan, shape, or suppress messages. The audience was firmly in charge of what was, and what wasn't, popular. Advertisers circled like gulls at low tide. Google had seen enough. On October 9, 2006, it bought YouTube for

> According to Bob Garfield, writing in *Wired,* thirty-five million viewers watched *The Evolution of Dance* on YouTube in just six months, a viewership few marketers dare to dream of.

> In the mid-1990s, author Douglass Rushkoff had popularized the use of the word *viral* in the context of media and messaging in his book *Media Virus.* Think of it as "word of mouse" in the Internet age, where messages can spread worldwide almost instantly.

101

$1.65 billion. Karim, Hurley, and Chen's invention was only eighteen months old.

To marketers, the YouTube audience was irresistible, but inaccessible, unless they could find ways to draw audiences to their messages. One of the early commercials to cause a sensation on the new medium was the famous Honda Accord "Cog" spot. It was a riveting Rube Goldberg–type feat of interactions that, legend has it, took over six hundred tries to get right. The final take was attempt number 605. But in the end, the spot attracted over a million viewers almost immediately, mostly due to the technical virtuosity it displayed. Today, there are YouTube brand channels, where advertisers can create their own YouTube sites inside YouTube, with proprietary content, ads, promotions, and games, together on a page, custom-designed to fit the character of the brand. Even the Vatican has its own brand channel.

But in the early days, most marketers kept their distance, wary of the consequences of falling into disfavour with a mass audience. A few, however, ventured boldly into this new media neighbourhood, armed only with the outdated sales language of print and television. The YouTube community was waiting for them, in numbers, with shovels, rakes, and implements of destruction.

CHEVY TAHOE: FOUR-WHEELING INTO A YOUTUBE AMBUSH

In the spring of 2006, Chevrolet decided to launch its revamped 2007 Tahoe by splashily sponsoring an episode of Donald Trump's *The Apprentice*. Chevy presented the latte-fuelled herd of potential Trumps-to-be with an Internet micro-site, where anyone could cut, paste, and drag from the Tahoe maker's selection of music and pictures, to create their own tribute to the vehicle. Initially, the venture was ranked a great success, as it yielded more than half a million visitors, each lingering an average of nine minutes on the site, and fetched thirty thousand entries, most of them glowing tributes to the Tahoe.

CLICK CLICK = KA-CHING, KA-CHING

The success of an online idea is measured, in part, by the number of clicks a website gets. While that number can easily go into the millions, most advertisers are interested in "unique visitors." These are determined by counting each visitor only once, which reveals a site's true audience size. While this isn't an exact science (some computers are shared by two or more users), it's a fairly good estimate of the reach of an ad or website. Other research refines the profiles of users and the way they interact with each site by identifying the amount of time spent on each web page, the pages within a website that get the most traffic, and where the traffic is coming from. No matter what the statistics reveal, however, there is one overriding benefit related to online marketing clicks: the consumer has sought the website out. They may even have made quite an effort to find it. Because interaction with a website is not passive exposure (like TV ads, for instance), a marketer is much more likely to make an impact through advertising online than through other media.

Emphasis on *most*. Although things went smoothly at first, after awhile, the road started getting bumpy as snarky, skeptical entries began to appear. In the interests of credibility, Tahoe's ad agency, Campbell-Ewald, opted not to pull the offending ads, which promptly spilled over onto YouTube. And there, the anti-Tahoe virus gained momentum.

Over beauty shots of the Chevy Tahoe, entries included such pungent graphics as "10 miles to the gallon, who cares?" Referring to the impact of large vehicles on global warming, one read "Enjoy the long summer." Mocking the SUV as a symbol of male virility, another crowed: "How big is yours?" Parodies popped up like daisies, slamming the Tahoe for global warming, the war in Iraq, and what some saw as America's maladjusted sexual self-image.

103

As an enormous online community watched, some cheering, others recoiling (and somewhere, Madame Defarge minding her knitting), Chevy's Tahoe experiment was led to the cyber guillotine. It was official: YouTube had democratized ad messaging.

And the marketing world would learn one more important message at Chevy's expense: YouTube videos don't go away. Months after the ill-fated contest, you couldn't swing a harp seal on an ice flow without hitting a Tahoe parody ad on YouTube (remain calm—no harp seals were harmed while writing this sentence). The new medium also became a repository for TV clips of newscasters and panels commenting on the disastrous Chevy campaign. The only remnants of the great Tahoe experiment that are difficult to find are legitimate, user-generated, pro-Tahoe videos.

Ad mes·sag·ing (*noun*) The wording, imagery, or creative means by which an ad is communicated.

Democracy, as the Chevy Tahoe folks learned, can be a testy business. For decades advertisers had enjoyed a free pass, communicating one-way to consumers who were powerless to respond in such a broad-based, public way. The SUV manufacturers might have been better prepared for the debacle had they read their history and come across the story about Thomas Jefferson on the day he was inaugurated as the third president of the United States. After the ceremony, Jefferson returned to his boarding house to discover that all the places at the dinner table were occupied. Fearing that it would be undemocratic to pull rank, the new president retired to his room without eating. Similarly, Chevy had to accept the inconveniences, as well as the blessings of democracy, as cranky consumers claimed their place at the electronic table, elbowing out more positive views of the new SUV.

After this episode, consumer-produced ("you-do-it") commercials continued to be all the rage among big-brand marketers—but with one important difference. Entries were carefully vetted by advertisers before being released to the public. During the 2007 Super Bowl, for instance, after weeks of building buzz on the web and through the press, Doritos unleashed the winner of a user-generated video competition. Chevrolet was back on the scene, too, this time sponsoring a homemade TV ad competition among college students. The winner would have her work played during the Super Bowl—the queen mother of American sports broadcasts—and a job offer from Chevy's ad agency, Campbell-Ewald. In both cases, the advertisers meticulously examined entries before presenting them to the world at large. For the Chevy competition, entries and finalists were kept secret until the winner was revealed; the YouTube community wouldn't take them for a ride this time.

But the big questions remain. Can an advertiser recover its goodwill if an online idea backfires? Is there no such thing as bad publicity? I say there is. One of the sea changes that came with the emergence of the online world was that bad things never go away. They hang in cyberspace forever. In the old days, a bad brand experience might get some news coverage, but it would be quickly forgotten. Not so with the Internet. YouTube not only gave consumers a single gathering place to watch videos; it also gave them a permanent archive, and for the first time, a megaphone to comment on what they were seeing and a place to post wicked parodies and satire, many of which would be viewed more often than the original brand video.

This also raises the eternal question of what makes a good ad and what doesn't. Why are some revered by millions of viewers, while others are pilloried? As with Hollywood and publishing successes, great ads have an X factor, something special yet intangible, such as an utterly unique performance that captured a piece of the zeitgeist in a bottle. I think every ad person will tell you that their greatest successes were complete surprises and that they would have bet the house on many of their failures. Here's a case in point. In the mid-eighties, I was part of a creative team that produced a TV ad for wine brand La Piat d'Or. I hated the commercial because I thought it lacked a real idea

105

and was just a bunch of soft-focus shots of a pretty Parisian actress. But that ad ended up running for years, and stores in places where the commercial was broadcast would literally sell out after it aired. A full fifteen years later, I was in a restaurant with my wife, and the waiter suggested the wine to us. I rolled my eyes, and my wife told him that I'd helped create the launch advertising for that wine but was haunted by the commercial. The waiter's eyes lit up, and he squealed, "You did that ad? I loved that ad!" About five minutes later, I spotted the waiter in the round window of the kitchen door, pointing me out to the chef, who was smiling broadly.

Who knew?

AOL: CONSUMERS FIGHT BACK

Some of the biggest names in marketing learned hard lessons about YouTube's ability to expose their weaknesses, effectively shouting in the light what was meant to be whispered in the darkness. In June 2006, for instance, thirty-year-old Vincent Ferrari of New York called a customer service rep to cancel his AOL account. He did not (to turn around a phrase) warn AOL that he was recording the conversation for quality-control purposes. For twenty-one minutes, the calm but alarmingly obstinate phone rep looked for ways to dissuade Ferrari from leaving the fold. With the coolness and patience of a man who understood the power of the recording he was making, Ferrari persisted, like Andy Dufresne in *The Shawshank Redemption*, knowing that AOL's *judgement cometh, and that right soon.*

Armed with his evidence of the long conversation, Ferrari approached a local news station and told his story on the air. The resulting interview—including the recording—were posted on YouTube, and in six months, they were viewed over half a million times. News outfits picked up the story and reported similar experiences from other consumers, who complained it took them up to forty-five minutes to get an AOL account cancelled. The viral power of online video was too much. In full damage control mode, AOL issued a public apology and announced that "John," the phone rep who'd spoken with Ferrari, was no longer representing the company. Elapsed time from the annoying phone call: ten days.

Would the story have resonated without YouTube? Maybe. With the same speed and impact? Not a chance.

THE EVOLUTION OF VIRAL ADVERTISING

It wasn't long before savvy marketers began to understand the power of YouTube and viral videos, thus tapping into a vast, worldwide audience. An early success story was *Evolution*, a viral video made in Toronto for Dove. Created by Ogilvy & Mather, Toronto, it featured a now-famous time-lapse sequence of a young lady, who appears plain at first, without makeup or styled hair. The woman in the film was Stephanie Betts, a friend of Ogilvy & Mather art director Tim Piper, writer and co-director of the ad. The video begins—deliberately—with an almost amateurish feel, to lower viewers' expectations. Then, in a time lapse, a team transforms her, applying makeup and washing, colouring, and styling her hair as background piano music and rapid sound effects create a sense of flow. Within seconds the woman is dramatically changed. Then computer enhancements alter the way her hair falls, the curves of her face, and the size of her eyes.

> Life tends to take more time than art: the time-lapse and Photoshop effects used in *Evolution* actually took three weeks to create.

Some facial features are downplayed; others are embellished. Most startling is the slight elongation of the woman's neck—creating one of those "a-ha" moments for the viewer. Which of us civilians had noticed how a woman's neck affects her look and the way others regard her? Next, the camera pulls back to reveal the young lady's image on a billboard. By now, she's a supermodel. Two young girls walk past the billboard on the street. Then the picture slowly dissolves to a black screen, where these words appear in white type: "No

107

wonder our vision of beauty is distorted." It then invites women to participate in the Dove "Real Beauty" workshop for girls and shows a website and a logo.

> It also appeared on TV and in cinemas in the Netherlands and in the Middle East.

On a relatively low budget, and intended for the Internet, it made for irresistible viewing, accumulating more than ten million YouTube hits. It was among *Time* magazine's top ten ads of the year, made the top of the list of YouTube viral ads, scooped the coveted Grand Prix in the film category at the Cannes advertising festival, and helped blaze the trail for a new generation of viral marketers.

> Trust me, a Cannes Lion is a huge deal in itself, but Dove's low-cost viral ad won in the "Film" category, which has been dominated since 1959 by high-budget, high-falutin' TV and cinema ads. That caused aftershocks which are still felt today.

Like so many in the marketing world, Dove gleaned important lessons from the wreckage of the early explorers, such as Chevy. These new pioneers are rewriting the rules in a world where advertisers talk to consumers, and—lo!—consumers talk back. One marketing executive noted that his industry had spent most of the past fifteen years selecting the right channels to reach consumers, but they had never seen the consumer *as* a channel. David Lubars, chairman of BBDO North America, called this phenomenon "culture eats strategy." Essentially, Lubars was referring to the way the public—and pop culture—can take a well-defined advertising strategy and wreak havoc with it, twisting and reconfiguring it and sending it back to the advertiser in virtually unrecognizable form.

For about 150 years advertisers had regarded themselves as leaders and consumers as followers. To the YouTube generation, marketers are more akin to those foolhardy rakes who run with the bulls each year in Pamplona. Those who can't keep a few steps ahead find an eighteen-hundred-pound *toro* making a *piñata* of their *nalgas*.

108

THE VIRAL IDEA

A great idea drives a viral ad, just as it drives a great ad in traditional print and visual media. In 2004, before YouTube was a virtual gleam in its creators' eyes, the Miami-based agency Crispin, Porter + Bogusky launched a remarkable, user-driven viral-marketing website called The Subservient Chicken. It helped define a new language for online branding and set a tone that showed others how to survive the online veldt, where ravenous consumers wait in the tall grass for a chance to pick off the weakest of the marketing herd.

The Subservient Chicken shows a live-action guy-in-a-chicken-suit standing in a plain-looking basement rec room. A blank line beneath the frame invites visitors to "Get chicken just the way you like it. Type in your command here." When you type in "Sit," the chicken sits; when you type, "Stand on your head," he does just that. He reacts to any of hundreds of commands and offers a standard wagging of the finger in response to saucier suggestions. Word of mouth led to tens of millions of hits, with each visitor spending some six minutes on the site. Yet nowhere on the page is there any overt reference to Burger King. In fact, the link was so understated that it was regarded by many as nothing more than a rumour. The online authority Snopes.com was compelled to list the Subservient Chicken–Burger King connection among its urban legends, declaring it "true."

The Subservient Chicken lives in a postal code nowhere near that of traditional fast-food advertising, but when someone inevitably asks, "What's this chicken got to do with Burger King?" the marketing genius of the site shines through. The page and the Burger King brand are linked by a common idea: they both offer chicken "the way you like it." By leading with its content, forgoing a traditional "sales" message, and burying the sponsor, it prompts visitors to discover for themselves who is behind the idea. Besides, the clever, viral, "un-advertising" feel

109

of the site demonstrated that Burger King spoke fluent "Internet" and helped the marketing world understand that viral/interactive/online marketing doesn't convey messages through mere words and headlines, product shots and slogans, and logos and promises: it communicates through ideas that challenge, stimulate, inspire, and—especially—surprise. Not in the sense of popping a balloon behind someone's head to get their attention, but in the sense of always running a few steps ahead of the bulls.

Another brilliant, early entry into viral marketing was the series *Will It Blend?* Launched on YouTube in October 2006, it features Tom Dickson, founder of Blendtec, asking: "Will it blend? That is the question." After a brief title sequence with suspiciously cheesy, almost game-show-like music, Dickson, in a lab coat, proposes to find out if some new object can be disintegrated in a Blendtec blender. A graduate (with honours) of the "Mister Rogers" school of TV demeanour, Dickson has actually blended an iPhone, incandescent light bulbs, glow sticks, and a Coke smoothie (with the Coke still in the can). Making each episode all the more fun and engaging is some form of built-in rationale: Dickson chose to blend a Grand Theft Auto IV game disk because he learned it didn't include his personal favourite: a 1968 Mustang GT390 (Steve McQueen's car in *Bullitt*). He decimated a handful of golf balls in retribution for a bad day on the course. Remarkably, invariably, the chosen thingamabob is pulverized, usually to a fine powder, and dumped on a flat surface, with the triumphant graphic "Yes, It Blends!"

At the end of the iPhone episode, Dickson said, "Think I'm gonna put this iPhone dust on eBay." He did, and it sold for $901, which he donated to charity.

As product demonstrations, they're little different from late-night infomercials or the barkings of "ShamWow" demonstrators at home shows. What sets Will It Blend? apart is its style and its packaging. As with so many great ad campaigns, segments are tightly structured around a series of deliciously honed "moments." As the blender does

110

its work, for example, there's always a cutaway to Dickson, one hand on the blender, offering a frozen, cardboard smile, a moment that gets funnier with every viewing.

The tone is tongue-gently-in-cheek and good natured, with nary a word spoken on the virtues of the blender, no gratuitous prattle about how "no other blender can do this," and no invocation to marvel at the machine. The series' creators understand that the "star" of each film is, and should be, the destruction of some household item, harkening back to the days of David Letterman's "Throwing Things Off a Five-Story Building" and "Crushing Things with a Steamroller" routines. Dickson's deliciously dry and slightly stiff presentation is exactly what makes the videos work. Each episode also contains a surprise and is authentic—both hallmarks of a great ad campaign. The viewer is left with little doubt that the Blendtec blender can actually grind up a Wii remote, a picket sign, a baseball, or a fifteen-foot garden hose—and it can't hurt to know this, given that a high-end Blendtec might run you $800.

As with all viral campaigns, the proof is found partly in the hit-count (the series has accumulated tens of millions of hits) and in the power of the online equivalent of word of mouth. I heard about the Blendtec YouTube episodes from my daughters, who had shown no previous inclination to blow a good chunk of their freshman-year tuition on a blender and who tsk'd, "Everybody knows about them." More striking was the moment when my wife passed by as my daughters showed me the videos for the first time. Glancing over her shoulder, she said, "Wow. We need a new blender. What's it called?"

> This is viral persuasion at work. According to Blendtec, retail sales jumped 500 percent.

The lesson? Content is king, especially in the viral world. Build a better blender and the world yawns. Build a witty, well-structured, universally appealing series of viral videos and the world will beat a path

111

to your virtual door, by way of YouTube. Most traditional ads are rarely as entertaining. Great viral ads don't have to work as hard to build a brand, and there's no media money required. You can post viral ads free of charge, and among the other freedoms they offer, there are no thirty- or sixty-second time constraints.

TAGGING AIR FORCE ONE

Most people introduced to the viral video *Tagging Air Force One* could be forgiven for wondering if a couple of real-life graffiti artists (*taggers* in graffiti-speak) had somehow breached security at Andrews Air Force Base and sprayed the words *still free* on one of the engines of the president's plane. A show stealer at the Cannes advertising festival of 2006, *Tagging Air Force One* offers a link to stillfree.com, where designer Marc Ecko doesn't sell you clothes but offers a sermonette on the evils of presidential swagger. "The president can't fly around like a rock star," he said, "talking about how America is the greatest country in the world, but ignore what makes it great." He went on to congratulate himself for his "tagging" video: "The nature of this stunt would . . . create a potential pop-culture moment for us all kinda to look back on and feel nostalgic about." Behind the act of faux vandalism (yes, it was staged) was Dave Droga, the innovative mind of Droga5, who created the Million campaign. The "tagging" clip generated enough buzz to eclipse anything a television campaign was likely to have caused.

> Dave's mother used the family surname and a number to identify the clothing of each of her seven offspring. Dave was her fifth child. This irresistible story-behind-the-name is but a hint of Dave Droga's marketing smarts.

> The "Still Free" forces would boast that eighty-seven million people viewed the "tagging" video and that the story generated one hundred million news reports.

As a marketing device, the "tagging" non-stunt had two important strengths: first, no one tried especially hard to pass the film off as real (though it did prompt an investigation by the U.S. military and a denial from the Pentagon);

second, you have to scour the Still Free website for any hint that any-body's selling anything. The viral video wasn't about selling clothes: it was about branding Mark Ecko—although that ultimately sells clothes. It's a nifty gauge of how subtle "sell" has become in the YouTube era.

If you listened carefully at the Cannes advertising festival of 2006, where Still Free won the Cyber Grand Prix, you could hear the world's marketers siphoning money from their TV budgets into newer, innova-tive, viral-driven media. Advertising is changing and so are its players. Dave Droga and others of the viral-ad, YouTube era represent the non-corporate, nonconformist antithesis of the two-martinis-with-lunch, house-in-the-Hamptons, wife-at-home/mistress-downtown, send-my-wife-a-box-of-the-$25-chocolates-you-know-the-kind-with-the-gold-wrapping, *Mad Men* image of advertising's past.

Although *Will It Blend?* and *Tagging Air Force One* are both viral videos, they differ in one vital respect: one is a stunt, the other is a fantasy. One lures online voyeurs with the spectacle of a real CEO putting his iPhone into a blender. The other is a graffiti artist's wet dream, where the tagger slips past the world's most formidable secu-rity curtain to leave his mark on the president's ride. But both attracted spectacular results through millions of online hits and millions of dollars' worth of free publicity. Was the marketing world watching and learning? You bet.

PARODY PROOFING: THE NEW YOUTUBE REALITY

Television advertising now has to look over its shoulder, knowing a skeptical online community is watching and a new generation of par-ody artists are ready to pounce. In other words, today's ads need to do more than catch the imagination; they must also be parody proof, or at least repel parodies that are unflattering to the brand.

MasterCard's once-ubiquitous Priceless campaign, for example, has provided the basis for some off-colour parodies. But the campaign still has longevity because it set out a paint-by-numbers formula for

113

an ever-changing jest. It's an elaborate descendant of the knock-knock joke: its structure is fixed and immediately familiar, yet each incarnation leads to a different punchline. Online users can take that formula for a ride down any road they please: from helping the cause of breast cancer awareness . . .

> Breast exam: $100
> Discovering the lump early and sharing the breast cancer
> "scare" story with your girlfriends: Priceless.
> For everything else, there's MASTECTOMY.

. . . to crowing about a Phoenix Coyotes player scoring a penalty shot goal on a temperamental Patrick Roy . . .

> Hockey stick: $48
> Skates: $275
> Official NHL puck: $10
> Making a future Hall-of-Fame goalie cry like a little
> baby: Priceless.

"We can't manage what happens out there," conceded a MasterCard executive. The campaign "has taken on a life of its own."

The equally prevalent Get a Mac campaign that personifies the PC and the Mac has also enjoyed a long and fruitful cyber-life, for a similar reason. The campaign was developed by TBWA\Chiat\Day, Los Angeles. Ad giant Lee Clow, the agency's chairman and chief creative officer (and whom I had the pleasure of working with at Chiat\Day), created a separate unit to handle all Apple advertising and called it Media Arts Lab. Situated in a different building from the rest of TBWA, it houses about fifty staffers who work exclusively on Apple. Lee, who defines Media Arts as an "understanding of every touch point a brand has and then the artistry of using that to deliver

114

a message" has also started this initiative because of his belief that a brand can, in fact, be a medium.

The Get a Mac campaign was built around a tight, simple, easy-to-parody formula, leading with the familiar "Hello, I'm a Mac." / "And I'm a PC." The ads themselves have yielded hundreds of thousands of YouTube hits, as have their endless parodies: "Hello, I'm a Republican" / "And I'm a Democrat"; "Hello, I'm a Christian" / "And I'm a Christ follower"; "Hello, I'm Chanukah" / "Hi, I'm Christmas."

Both campaigns benefit from the viral spin of their creative formulae, using the online community to give their campaigns *oomph* unimaginable in the pre-Internet world. YouTube has emerged as the user-driven water cooler, giving voice to the tens of millions who gather daily to pass sentence on new products and campaigns and ideas. Viral campaigns, then, are not for marketing's faint of heart. Like a snowball, a viral idea is released from the top of a hill, where no one can be sure of the size and shape it will take or whether it will meet an abrupt end against an unforgiving tree.

THE SECRET OF VIRAL MARKETING: THE AUDIENCE DOES THE WORK

Samuel L. Jackson can rest easy knowing his career probably won't be measured by the empty-calorie action film *Snakes on a Plane*. His place in the public imagination might more likely be attributed to the movie's viral marketing campaign. By visiting an online site, anyone could arrange to have a customized phone call made to a friend by Mr. Jackson himself. "Terry," he began in the call I received, "this is Samuel L. Jackson." And so it was: the recording by Mr. Jackson requested that I attend the film. Better still, personal details were woven into the monologue: he knew where I worked (at an advertising company), what sort of car I drove (convertible), the name of the co-worker who organized the call (Keith), and even what I looked like (follicly challenged). Each call was customized according to a number

115

of drop-down options on the website. Industry buzz had it that the site drew a hundred thousand customized Samuel L. Jackson phone messages during its first twenty-four hours, enough to constipate the web server.

A generation ago, "big" ad campaigns typically relied on a massive (read: "expensive") media buy. Today, a viral campaign leverages a big idea by using the online community as a free medium. Ideas—not slogans or logos or catchphrases—are the hot new currency in the age of persuasion. The guiding principles in this brave new world are "Outsmart, don't outspend"; "Brain trumps brawn: film at eleven"; or "Available anytime on YouTube." The same mass online audience that can stomp giant brands like a grape can spirit others to mountaintops.

When *AdWeek* magazine asked ad executives to tell them what had the greatest impact on advertising in an end-of-year article in 2006, the respondents overwhelmingly cited YouTube. It had become the great enabler: the first hugely democratic mass medium, where any one person could speak to millions if—and it's a family-sized "if"— her idea was big enough to resonate with the masses in cyberspace.

THE MYTH OF MASS MARKETING

I f I wrote an ad for you—Maryjane—and mentioned your name throughout—Maryjane—and noted your weakness for peanut butter cookies and your habit of whistling Prokofiev when you're nervous, you might feel pretty special (if not a little creeped out). That is, you would feel special unless your name *wasn't* Maryjane, you were allergic to peanuts, and you thought Prokofiev was a backup goalie for the San Jose Sharks. And that brings us to another myth: the notion that mass marketing can reach all individuals within a vast audience with the same power and meaning that can be achieved through one-on-one contact.

The fact is, the larger the audience an advertiser strives to reach, the harder it becomes to forge a meaningful relationship with each individual customer. And the larger the army running a brand, the harder it becomes to instill a culture of treating the customer with the utmost respect and regard. I give you the patronizing, automated "hold" messages used by so many large companies.

This is what makes some brand stories—including the one about the Fuller Brush Company (see Chapter 10)—so interesting. When most in the marketing industry stampeded over to mass communications, Fuller Brush reaped the rewards of one-on-one customer service. Compare that to the modus operandi of its mass marketing antithesis: spam (the email kind), where brand relationship is sacrificed on the altar of quick transactions.

Mass marketing can reach millions; smart marketing feels like it works on one customer at a time.

GUERRILLAS
IN OUR MIDST

n the spring of 2002, a computer video game developer, Acclaim Entertainment, announced it would pay relatives of the recently deceased for the privilege of placing small billboards on their loved one's headstone, promoting their latest release *Shadowman 2: Second Coming.* They also suggested the offer would "particularly interest poorer families." Before dissecting the Acclaim Entertainment stunt, it's worth noting that popular culture has a knack for laughing at death (or *with* death if you like), not because it's appropriate but often because it's *inappropriate.* It's hard to imagine a richer subject in our culture than mortality, with the possible exceptions of God, sex, and baseball's DH rule. The institution of death has always provided fertile ground for advertising "creative."

cre·ative *(noun)* A marketing term referring to the idea, writing, and visuals that form the content of an ad.

When I give creative radio seminars to ad writers, I stress that humour is a *fatal attraction to the inappropriate.* By that I mean ad scenarios on TV and radio can yield endless possibilities when set in places with the greatest potential for inappropriate behaviour. I cite solemn occasions such as weddings, childbirths, and funerals, all of which figure prominently on reels of award-winning ads. There's also great comedic value in an over-the-top response to an incidental situation or, conversely, a tiny reaction to a life-altering event. In the 1970s, an iconic episode of *The Mary Tyler Moore Show* featured Mary's character laughing uncontrollably at the funeral of Chuckles the Clown. Even epitaphs, besides detailing one's *curriculum morte,* have long been treated as a form of art meant to inspire, advise, warn, and yes, amuse. The *People's Almanac* cites this epitaph on a headstone in a Niagara Falls cemetery:

120

Here I lie between two of the best women in the world; my wives. But I have requested my relatives to tip me a little toward Tille.

The uncontrollable gravity of a person's last words have also produced many a gem, such as those of actor Edmund Gwen when asked if he thought dying was difficult: "Yes, it's tough, but not as tough as playing comedy." And then there was Mexico's storied revolutionary general, Pancho Villa, who reportedly gave this final utterance: "Don't let it end this way. Tell them I said something." The constant unease of belonging to a species with a 100 percent death rate creates tension, and tension is the lifeblood of humour.

> Every humorous script needs a yin and a yang to work. One character smart, one not, or one fast, one slow, for instance. I always ask writers, "What is the relationship here?" If I detect no tension, I know the script is in trouble.

Ah, but there is a line, and Acclaim Entertainment strolled callously across it, whistling as they went, when they launched their ads-on-headstones stunt. It would rank among the more brazen acts in the modern trend of guerrilla marketing. Their purpose, of course, was to cause a stir, and it wasn't long before the Church of England rose to the bait. No way would it allow any of its graveyards to be used for advertising in this way, a spokesman told the *Guardian*, adding, "There was enough fuss with plastic flowers in churchyards." By no means was it the first time Acclaim Entertainment set alight a poop-filled paper bag on the front porch of popular sensibilities: prior to its *Shadowman 2* launch, it had offered £500 to the first five people willing to legally change their name to "Turok" (to mark the launch of the game *Turok: Evolution*). And they offered to pay every speeding ticket in the U.K. on the day their game *Burnout 2* was launched. When well-publicized

> It may have been a publicity-grabbing bluff, much like its claim that bus shelter posters for another release would drip realistic blood into the sidewalk. After much publicity, they announced that it wouldn't happen after all.

accusations flew that Acclaim Entertainment was encouraging speeding, the offer was withdrawn. But the advertiser rode a wave of free publicity as it so often did—that is, until it breathed its last and filed for bankruptcy in September 2004.

GUERRILLA MARKETING 101

Guerrilla marketing is a blood relative of viral marketing. It allows "little" brands to leverage a big idea—often an act, stunt, or gesture that becomes the message—using time, energy, and imagination in lieu of a large budget. The phrase was popularized by author Jay Conrad Livingston in his 1984 book, *Guerrilla Marketing: Secrets for Making Big Profits from Your Small Business*.

Roughly put, *guerrilla marketing* as it was first defined satisfies four conditions: it garners big attention; it does not rely on paid media; it's not a traditional commercial; and it's a highly unusual act or device. Rather than knocking at the consumer's front door using conventional advertising media, guerrilla marketers sneak behind the hydrangeas and force a basement window. Nowadays, many guerrilla campaigns are based on the viral power of the Internet to reach a vast audience.

To paraphrase military theorist Carl Maria von Clausewitz, guerrilla marketing might best be described as marketing by other means. The Spanish word *guerrilla* literally means "little war" (a diminutive of the word for war—*guerra*) and dates back to Napoleonic times. It was used to describe such unconventional tactics as strike-and-fade assaults, deceptions, and ambushes—saucy thinking in an age when armies killed each other by the thousands in exposed columns and lines, on open battlefields.

GOOD GUERRILLAS

122

By no means do guerrilla campaigns need to be spring-loaded with controversy. In 2005 the international humanitarian group Médecins du Monde distributed easy-to-deploy tents, bearing the organization's name, to homeless men and women in Paris. Clusters of the temporary abodes appeared in conspicuous locations, prompting a rare off-season session of the government, where it was acknowledged that homeless shelters were woefully overcrowded, and nearly $10 million was allotted to emergency housing.

True to Livingston's formula, Médecins du Monde cut through the media clutter and created the sort of buzz big corporations pine for. Like Acclaim Entertainment, they relied on a low-budget stunt to attract attention, and as in the case of the video game promo strategies, not everyone would have been pleased by their tactics. Though neither was likely to convert nonbelievers to their brand, both found effective, inexpensive ways of jumping the queue of daily ad messages and nestling in the imagination of their audiences.

A few years back, another NGO gave the guerrilla approach a try. That was the year the Brooklyn Animal Resource Coalition (BARC) created an endearing guerrilla campaign for adopting pets. They went into parks and strewed yellow Frisbees and sticks with yellow ribbons all over the ground. The type on the Frisbees and ribbons read, in effect, "Need a dog to go with this stick/frizbee? Barcshelter.org."

BAD GUERRILLAS

The makers of the animated series *Aqua Teen Hunger Force* charged into Boston with a guerrilla-marketing stunt that won them international headlines, but not before they effectively shut down the city of Boston. On January 31, 2007, suspicious LED signs were spotted, depicting the cartoon character Ignignokt, who resembled a child's drawing of a Lego block with stick-figure limbs and simple lines for eyes, mouth, and eyebrows. Oddly enough, similar signs erected in nine other U.S. cities, including New York, had caused little concern. At any rate, a Boston commuter saw one of the signs and complained

123

to the Massachusetts Bay Transportation Authority, who in turn contacted the bomb squad. The city had issued no permits for any signs of this sort. With reports of similar signs trickling in from around the Massachusetts capital, the air in downtown Boston was thick with flashing lights, squelching radios, and testosterone. One of the signs was even detonated.

The fact that the signs were part of a marketing stunt was revealed by Massachusetts Attorney General Martha Coakley in a press conference, where she revealed that the signs were part of a marketing stunt and that two men—performance artists—had been arrested for placing them. As many of Greater Boston's five million residents likely pondered suitable punishments—perhaps having them stripped to the skivvies, slathered in bacon grease, and forced to sing a couple of show tunes from the roof of the State House—they glibly announced to a scrum of reporters that they would only answer questions relating to "haircuts from the seventies."

Then Ms. Coakley offered a more interesting revelation: that the campaign had originated not with some mischievous dot-com start-up or a cocky-if-less-than-bright retailer, but with Turner Broadcasting, as in Time Warner, an outfit worth more than $75 *billion*. Turner brass promptly ended the multicity campaign, apologized, and gave the city of Boston $2 million for its troubles—half of it to cover the cost of the emergency response crews, the other half to fund Boston-area homeland security.

Turner learned an expensive lesson in violating Livingston's credo that guerrilla marketing is intended for the "little guy." A true guerrilla marketer turns to creative attention-getting because she lacks the resources to compete with bigger brands through conventional advertising. A Fortune 500 company that chooses guerrilla-marketing tactics—when it could so easily afford conventional advertising—crosses a tribal boundary. It's like watching your dad dance to Nirvana at a wedding. It's just not good.

124

Turner's final act of penance for the *Aqua Teen Hunger Force* stunt was to show its Cartoon Network VP, James Samples, the door. (Did they play Porky Pig stammering "That's all folks!"? I wonder.)

Just as the online community takes ownership of a viral idea, the marketing world has adopted and mutated the meaning of *guerrilla marketing* since it was first popularized, infusing it with a spirit of countercultural pranksterism. Livingston had never suggested that it might take the form of sophomoric stunts that would enrage clergy or paralyze major cities, but that is what it has become in some contexts today. Guerrilla marketing is open to everyone, and even FedEx has given it a try. The company planted FedEx boxes, complete with packing material, under "Stop" signs, "Don't Walk" signs, and fire hydrants, making it look as if the sign or hydrant had just been delivered.

On a much broader canvas, in 1980 Terry Fox launched his cross-Canada Marathon of Hope to raise money for cancer research, running the equivalent of a marathon each day, until his own battle with the disease forced him to stop near Thunder Bay. The original Terry Fox Run might be defined as an act of guerrilla marketing in that it met these four criteria: it garnered big attention; it didn't involve a conventional media buy; it wasn't an ad; and it was highly unconventional. Yet most people—inside marketing or out—would likely cringe at the idea of hanging a "guerrilla marketer" tag on this beloved Canadian hero.

Promoters of Hollywood films have become fond of guerrilla marketing, largely for its ability to generate the sort of high-profile, short-term buzz needed as a film debuts. And the entire industry took a lesson from the launch of *The Blair Witch Project* in 1999. Rather than investing their meagre promotion budget in conventional advertising, the producers created a website, its content devoted to

125

the fictitious Blair witch of Maryland. It was enough to whip up serious buzz prior to the film's release. The film, whose production costs were reckoned at about $60,000, grossed more than a quarter-billion dollars worldwide.

UGLY GUERRILLAS

What's worse than Boston's guerrilla stunt gone sour? Another one, in the same city, barely three weeks later. The people of Beantown had only just caught their breath after the Cartoon Network stunt when the marketing minds behind Dr Pepper launched one of their own: a treasure hunt for a $10,000 gold coin planted somewhere in the city. The idea itself wasn't inflammatory, but alas, the hiding place was. They chose Boston's 350-year-old Granary Burying Ground: the venerated resting place of Paul Revere, Thomas Hancock, Samuel Adams, Robert Paine, and Mary Goose (believed to be the original "Mother Goose"). As with the Cartoon Network stunt, no permission was sought from the city (that would be decidedly un-guerrilla-like), and before long, perceptive treasure seekers converged on the cemetery, trampling the hallowed ground and climbing over brittle, two-hundred-year-old monuments. The graveyard was promptly locked off and guarded. Dr Pepper called off the contest and announced that a winner would be chosen through a random draw.

Dr Pepper pushed the limits of taste and tolerance when it chose to stage its promotion on consecrated ground and illustrated the danger of guerrilla campaigns that cross the line. To the people of Boston, one such incident was annoying. A second, so soon after, was intolerable. As guerrilla marketing grows and thrives, it risks incurring the wrath of a stunt-wary public, and where the public gains nothing—not even a laugh or a pleasant diversion—the advertiser is in violation of the Great Unwritten Contract.

126

EARLY ANCESTORS: THE PUBLICITY STUNT

The phrase *guerrilla marketing* may be new, but the practice is ancient. The difference is that people in the olden days (those murky days prior to, say, 1980) used its direct ancestor: the publicity stunt.

On September 16, 1896, the town of "Crush" became the second-largest city in Texas. Not bad, considering it didn't exist the day before—and would be abandoned in just a few hours. It occupied a section of rail line chosen for a spectacle staged by the Missouri-Kansas-Texas Railroad, and its name was taken from railroad official William G. Crush, who for reasons lost to the ages, got it in his head that staging a train crash would somehow attract customers. Two locomotives would be brought to full speed and crashed, head-on. No admission would be charged, and a special fare of $5 would draw some thirty thousand spectators from every part of Texas.

Railway engineers had assured Mr. Crush that it was virtually impossible for the trains' boilers to explode in the collision. But explode they did. When the engines collided—each travelling at some forty-five miles per hour, a frightening blast sent chunks of searing hot metal flying. Two died; others were seriously injured.

There was one miraculous story of survival from that day: William G. Crush somehow managed to keep his job.

As urbanization in North America begat bigger cities, it also created larger audiences and sumptuous new opportunities for audacious publicity seekers to elbow their way into the daily news. Take P.T. Barnum, for instance. When he realized a field he owned in New York was within view of a busy commuter rail line, he used an elephant to plough it up, and the stunt generated national buzz. On the other side of the pond, in 1897, during a celebration of Queen Victoria's Diamond Jubilee, the Royal Navy sailed past a gathered delegation, which included the Prince of Wales.

> The incident would inspire a young Texan pianist, Scott Joplin, to create one of his earliest compositions, "The Great Crush Collision."

Over forty miles an hour. The fastest wind-driven destroyers at the time could manage only twenty-seven knots.

Crashing the party, like a mouse among the elephants, was the testicularly endowed Charles Algernon Parsons, in his new-fangled steam-turbine vessel, *Turbina*, zipping past the fleet at a gum-swallowing thirty-five knots.

A past master of the publicity stunt was Thomas Edison, who during the early twentieth century, stood to make a fortune delivering electrical power by way of his "direct current" (DC) method. His rivals at Westinghouse, including former Edison employee Nikola Tesla, championed another system: "alternating current" (AC). With a fortune at stake, Edison seized every opportunity to slam his competition, sometimes by staging public demonstrations. It's widely believed that Edison paid kids to round up stray neighbourhood cats, which he would electrocute using AC power, to demonstrate its dangers to horrified crowds. Though Edison was opposed to capital punishment, he encouraged an employee, Harold Brown, to invent the electric chair—again using Tesla's alternating current. Condemned prisoners could then be "Westinghoused"—as Edison liked to put it, a swipe at the company that backed Tesla's technology.

One atop another, Edison piled his shameless propaganda stunts. In 1903 New York was all in a flap about "Topsy," a Coney Island elephant that had killed three men in three years, including one handler who had tried feeding her a lit cigarette. When it was decided that Topsy would be put to death, hanging was proposed and then promptly dismissed by the killjoys at the SPCA. Enter Thomas Edison, who gladly volunteered to have the animal electrocuted (by alternating current, of course). As some 1,500 people watched, and Edison film cameras rolled, Topsy met her maker.

Edison lost the "battle of the currents": AC was simply the better technology and became the popular method of delivering power. But he won the PR war. He is remembered as a grandfatherly genius, while history tends to paint Nikola Tesla as a crank and a "mad scientist."

ELECTROCUTING AN ELEPHANT

The Edison film of this primitive act of guerrilla marketing has found new life, more than a century later, on YouTube. It's Edison's lasting tweak-of-the-nose to the proponents of alternating current; twenty-three seconds of classic cinematic slander, titled *Electrocuting an Elephant.*

THE MEDIUM IS THE GUERRILLA

In one strain of guerrilla marketing, it's the *medium* that's actually the guerrilla. Most of these advertising ploys come with their own buzz term, each sweet enough to make your molars ache: "egg-vertising" (ad messages stamped on the shells of supermarket eggs), "dog-vertising," and inevitably, "bra-vertising" and "ass-vertising." This last was featured in 2004, when commuters emerged from New York's Grand Central Terminal only to encounter frisky-looking young men and women flashing their buttocks. On their (clean) white underwear were the words *Booty Call.* The stunt had been staged by a local fitness club. (Picture a young lady on a pay phone calling Iowa: "Hi, Mom? I finally found a job. . . .") To some, methods like this mark a cynical new era in marketing, but within the industry they represent a survival tactic—reaching out to an audience that's averting its gaze from conventional ad media.

Marketers will take their message anywhere, and I mean *anywhere.* In February 2007, the state of New Mexico bought five hundred talking urinal cakes (a bargain at $21 each) for men's rooms in bars and restaurants throughout the state. Featuring a sultry female voice, each offered the same wiz-activated message. It began: "Hey, there, big guy" (already with the flattery) and then continued:

129

> Having a few drinks? Then listen up. Think you've had
> one too many? Then it's time to call a cab or a sober

friend for a ride home. It sure is safer, and a hell of a lot cheaper than a D-W-I. Make the smart choice tonight: don't drink and drive. Remember, the future is in your hand.

Yep: hand. *Singular.* Leave it to guerrilla marketing to boldly go where men boldly go. This New Mexico message was cleverly timed, and unavoidable: men become a captive audience in those crucial moments before they might get behind the wheel.

ALL THE WORLD'S A GUERRILLA-MARKETING OPPORTUNITY

The air was unusually still in Terre Haute, Indiana, on Monday, June 11, 2001. Outside a penitentiary, a large, strangely hushed crowd had gathered while inside, the Oklahoma bomber, Timothy McVeigh, prepared to die. His last requests had been registered: he'd asked that a nearby church perform a requiem mass. Hours before, he had asked for the customary condemned prisoner's last meal, and therein lies a guerrilla-marketing tale.

Well before McVeigh's final day, the animal-rights organization People for the Ethical Treatment of Animals (PETA) contacted him, asking that he use his final meal as an opportunity to support animal rights. More to the point, they asked to use his last meal as a guerrilla-marketing opportunity. Specifically, they wondered if he'd mind horribly making his last meal conform to vegan standards: containing no animal or dairy products. Here's what a PETA staffer had written to the condemned bomber:

> The term *vegan* sprouts from the root word (pardon the puns) *vegetable.* Variously pronounced "VEE-gan" and "VAY-gan," the word was introduced by Donald Watson, founder of the Vegan Society in 1944.

I believe that your decision to go vegan would help the movement for compassion toward animals, and I am certain that if you made the choice prayerfully, it would profit your soul. As a Christian, I believe in acts of repentance, and it seems to me that you might benefit very much from such an act.

News reports of PETA's proposition stirred outrage, which, of course, was exactly what they wanted. PETA has a history of high-test guerrilla stunts, many performed on the strength of a head-turning roster of celebrity supporters, including Sir Paul McCartney, Jackie Chan, William Shatner, Jamie Lee Curtis, Gwyneth Paltrow, Alec Baldwin, Rev. Al Sharpton, and Sarah Jessica Parker.

Alas, the high-profile roster of PETA supporters would not include Timothy McVeigh. In a terse statement released by his lawyers, he declined PETA's request to end his life with a bellyful of veggies. McVeigh's last meal was decidedly un-vegan, and included two pints of Ben & Jerry's mint chocolate chip ice cream. Shortly after eight o'clock on that June morning, McVeigh was dead. It's a safe guess that no tears were shed at the offices of PETA, who were only too happy to turn McVeigh's execution into a media opportunity. By refusing their request, McVeigh won them a tidy splash of free publicity. Had he consented, he would've won them considerably more free publicity. Either way, they won.

Since its creation in 1990, PETA has cultivated some two million members worldwide as a result of, or in spite of, a steady flow of brash guerrilla stunts. Pamela Anderson, for instance, once posed naked in the window of a Stella McCartney boutique to promote PETA's I'd Rather Go Naked than Wear Fur campaign. Prior to a presidential state of the union address, PETA sent emails with the subject line "Presidential Address + Hot Naked Chick = PETA's State of the Union Undress?" It contained a link to a video clip showing shots of a cheerful young lady on a podium, juxtaposed with stock shots of the U.S. Congress. Showcasing her gift for multitasking, the lady assesses the status of PETA's various campaigns, as well as its promise to redouble its efforts, while removing every last stitch of her clothing. No one, it seems, has mobilized to form "POOWM"—People Opposed to the Objectification of Women in Marketing.

Controversy is one of the mightiest arrows in the guerrilla marketer's quiver. Another is surprise. Just ask Karolyne Smith. If you had met her, you'd remember: in 2005 she auctioned off space on her forehead (on eBay, of course) to the highest bidder. For $10,000 cash, the Utah woman consented to have *GoldenPalace.com* (the name of an online gambling outfit) permanently tattooed on her forehead. Let's not confuse her with the likes of twenty-seven-year-old Angel Brammer of Glasgow, who, for £422, allowed GoldenPalace.com to temporarily tattoo its web address on her cleavage, by all accounts a generous canvas. One might say Ms. Smith was selling, where Ms. Brammer was merely renting. While it may or may not mitigate the stunts, it should be noted that both auctions were instigated by the tattoo-ee.

Ms. Smith's eBay initiative was tailor made for the GoldenPalace.com brand. The online gambling business has fast built its reputation on a litany of imaginative, if audacious, guerrilla-marketing stunts. Most conspicuous has been the "GoldenPalace.com streaker"—a serial streaker with a genius for breaching security and crashing major sporting events, wearing little more than the word *GoldenPalace.com* on his midriff. Such streakers have infiltrated every imaginable athletic contest from soccer finals to the Super Bowl. Never shy to offer variations-on-a-theme, GoldenPalace.com crashed a diving event at the 2004 Olympic Games in Athens, using a logo-adorned man in white polka-dot tights and a blue tutu. After he launched himself into the drink, he drip-dried in a Greek prison.

Streakers (plural), actually—though one chap has reportedly "got his kit off" for the cause more than three hundred times.

132

GURRILLAS COLLECTIBLES

GoldenPalace.com became renowned for a particularly unusual guerrilla-marketing stunt: collecting highly publicized oddities and basking in the boatload of publicity that followed. For a cool $28,000, GoldenPalace.com had the dubious distinction of winning the "miracle sandwich"—a grilled cheese sandwich purported to bear the likeness of the Virgin Mary—on eBay. Over the years they've collected a Dorito chip shaped like the pope's hat ($1,209); a potato shaped like Pete Townshend's head ($81); a VW Golf "previously owned" by Cardinal Joseph Ratzinger, later Pope Benedict XVI ($244,590.83); and a home pregnancy test allegedly used by Britney Spears (price undisclosed).

Its creator, Diane Duyser of Florida, insists the Holy Sandwich, which remained miraculously un-mouldy for a decade, brings luck. Her post-sandwich experiences include $70,000 in casino winnings. End of story? No! *Après-sale,* Ms. Duyser was inspired to have an image of the sandwich tattooed (permanently) on her chest; GoldenPalace.com picked up the tab.

The logistical advantage of guerrilla marketing is twofold: it frees advertisers from the high cost of conventional media and from the regulations that restrict them. Most countries have agencies that govern print, broadcast, and outdoor marketing, many of which seem reasonable and necessary but some of which make the cider house rules read like an anarchists' manifesto. In Canada, for instance, beer advertising regulations can be especially stringent. Here's one example: a beer ad might be turned down because it uses the phrase "to be or not to be" (a regulator ruled that since high school students study Shakespeare, this was an inducement to underage drinkers). I had a TV spot for a major beer brand refused because an actor had "toasted above shoulder level" and that was ruled "too exuberant." As I write this, it's still forbidden in Canada to show someone *drinking* beer in a beer ad. Somewhere there must be a boundless afterworld populated by countless millions of ads and campaigns—some brilliant, some ghastly, many revolutionary—but all dispatched by a regulator's red pen before they reached the public.

While many, including me, find a good number of today's guerrilla stunts viscerally wrong, they are often as hard to regulate and prevent as they are to ignore. The pallet on which some guerrilla marketers paint—tombstones, urinals, Angel Brammer's mammaries, and Karolyne Smith's forehead—are beyond the purview of advertising regulators. And well within the budget of so many smaller marketers.

So often, the choice of guerrilla marketing over conventional ad media revolves around budget. How else can a smallish brand be heard against deep-pocketed, better-established rivals? Advertising in traditional media is punishingly expensive. "Don't outspend them," I tell clients of modest means. "Outsmart them." A successful guerrilla-marketing campaign does just that.

EMILY AND STEVEN ET AL.

Marketers soon caught on to the viral power of the Internet demonstrated so well by the Blair Witch producers and from there, they began branching out into coordinated, multifaceted guerrilla campaigns. Where a conventional campaign might coordinate print, broadcast, and out-of-home advertising, these new guerrillas might spin an idea using conventional media, blogs, free publicity, and even live performance art of a sort. Here's how one of these worked:

Out-of-home advertising includes such things as billboards, bus interior and exterior ads, ads in transit shelters, posters, and murals.

In 2006 a billboard reading as follows appeared in Manhattan:

134

Hi Steven,

Do I have your attention now? I know all about her,

you dirty, sneaky, immoral, unfaithful, poorly-endowed slimeball. Everything's caught on tape.

Your (soon-to-be-ex) Wife, Emily.

P.S. I paid for this billboard from OUR joint bank account.

Word spread of a corresponding blog by "That Girl Emily," which drew a million hits within days. "Emily" promised "14 Days of Wrath," and sure enough, soon after that, a BMW was towed around New York City with the words "I HOPE SHE WAS WORTH IT" spray-painted across its side. On a busy city sidewalk, a woman with a four-alarm attitude pulled her SUV onto a curb, opened the back, and began tossing "Steven's" possessions onto the sidewalk, inviting stunned passersby to help themselves. A "homemade" clip of the tirade attracted worldwide attention through the miracle of YouTube. But central to the whole business was the blog where That Girl Emily documented her campaign against her cheating ex. The public was transfixed as it held a cyber-cup to its cyber-ear against a cyber-wall to eavesdrop on the imploding marriage. In one entry, That Girl Emily documents her discovery of the password for Steven's work email:

What did I do? I sent a simple little email to everyone in his contact list, business and personal:

Hi all,
I have gonorrhea. Just an FYI.
—Steven
President, Small Dicks Club

135

It was right about here that the marketing team behind the campaign lost control of it. Bloggers wrote that they smelled a rat, and sure enough, Internet discussion promptly revealed that there were identical billboards in Brooklyn, Los Angeles, and Chicago. When one blogger noted that an Emily blog entry was conspicuously similar to the synopsis for an episode of the Court TV series *Parco P.I.*, the secret was out. Orchestrated to promote the show, the "Emily" guerrilla campaign combined conventional ad media (billboards) with viral media (including a rash of "Have you seen this?" emails propagated by the advertiser), and a live "performance" (the irate actress, also immortalized on YouTube) and proved the key precept of guerrilla marketing: it's the idea that does the heavy lifting.

Court TV had orchestrated this buzz campaign as a precursor to a second phase—a more formal, conventional ad launch for *Parco P.I.* The trick was to hide its real motive as the buzz accumulated while sprinkling just enough crumbs along the path for a growing audience to follow until its secret could be revealed. Court TV hadn't planned on being found out quite so rapidly, and they were forced to launch their traditional ads days sooner than expected. "It's like a flash investigation took place" noted a Court TV programmer, "and within twenty-four hours we were busted."

If new forms of guerrilla marketing are to thrive, clearly they'll have to get over their adolescent infatuation with hoaxes. A ruse-wary, media-savvy audience is becoming harder to fool, even for a short time.

GUERRILLA MARKETING AS THE GREAT EQUALIZER

Guerrilla campaigns are neither fad nor fashion. They are the mushrooms sprouting atop the rising mountain of ad clutter. If popular estimates are accurate, advertisers worldwide spend more than $165 million every day, so it's not surprising that "little" advertisers are drowned out by louder, big-money brands and so have started using less expensive, guerrilla techniques. Meanwhile, the big names are finding that conventional media—broadcast, print, and out-of-home— are offering them less bang for their buck. For the same money that

136

once provided first-class treatment, they now find themselves packed into steerage with their competitors. Big advertisers, as well as the smaller ones, are leaving the urban sprawl of ad clutter and escaping to the wide-open spaces of guerrilla marketing. And just as YouTube democratizes media, viral marketing and guerrilla campaigns put the ninety-eight-pound weaklings on even terms with many of the muscle-bound marketers.

Yet major brands will likely continue to use guerrilla techniques. The payoff of a good viral campaign is too great, the potential return on investment too tempting for them to resist. Which explains why IBM was once fined $120,000 for spray-painting the words *peace, love and Linux* on a San Francisco street and why, a year later, Microsoft pasted small, hard-to-remove butterfly stickers throughout Manhattan. They were fined $50 for littering and volunteered to help with the cleanup. Giant corporations, who have so much to lose by a guerrilla stunt gone wrong will continue to flirt with guerrilla tactics. But they miss the point: at its best, guerrilla marketing appeals to people's natural affinity for the little guy and their natural aversion to giants. Imagine the outrage if Goliath tucked a smooth stone in a sling, slew David, and then cut *his* head off as a trophy.

Is guerrilla marketing the wave of the future? In some ways it will flourish: marketers will continue to reach beyond conventional media and go places ads haven't gone before, and in doing so, they'll test the limits of the Great Unwritten Contract. But in other ways, the boldness of the stunts is all about one-upmanship. As the ante goes up, so too will the strain on guerrilla marketing.

THE "ANY PUBLICITY IS GOOD PUBLICITY" MYTH

t's a simple marketing rule and it works: good publicity is good, bad publicity is bad.

I give you—

- Tylenol tampering (1982)
- Major League Baseball & steroids
- The Ford Pinto
- Halliburton
- Bre-X
- Mel Gibson
- Any airline disaster
- "Typhoid" Mary Mallon

I'll bet you could name a dozen more without trying. Great brands thrive by making a lasting, *positive*, emotional connection with their customer. And by understanding how fragile that relationship is.

Don't confuse selling with art.
JACK TAYLOR, VICE-CHAIRMAN
OF JORDAN, MCGRATH

THE LESSON OF
CLARK GABLE'S
UNDERSHIRT

Porsche. There is no substitute.
JOEL GOODSEN (PORTRAYED BY TOM CRUISE) IN
RISKY BUSINESS (1983)

At the Biltmore Hotel in Los Angeles, on Wednesday, February 27, 1935, the Seventh Annual Academy Awards were in full stride, and Columbia Pictures boss Harry Cohn wasn't happy. You'd think he would have been: his little-picture-that-could, *It Happened One Night*, was cleaning up. Its lead actress, the lovely Claudette Colbert, had just been announced winner of the best actress trophy. Heads pivoted around the banquet room, she was nowhere to be found.

True to her word, Colbert had passed on the Oscars. She'd appeared in three of the twelve nominees for best picture, but she'd made no secret of her dislike for this particular film—the one that got her the best actress nomination—by an unproven thirtysomething director, Frank Capra. Hollywood tradition has it that like her co-star, Clark Gable, Colbert was assigned to the film as a kind of penance: Colbert for daring to rebel against the brass at Paramount and Gable for running afoul of Louis B. Mayer and

In the years that followed, the number of best picture nominees has fluctuated from twelve to ten to five and more recently back to ten. That year, Academy members were permitted write-in votes that allowed them to cast a ballot for someone not on the nominee list—a concession granted when Bette Davis wasn't among the original best actress nominees.

MGM. Both had been loaned to Columbia, a poor sister among studios. (That is, "loaned" in a broad sense: it's believed Louis B. Mayer, who had Gable on a $2,000-per-week contract, hired him out to Columbia for $2,500 per week.) It's said that *It Happened One Night* had been turned down by a who's who of 1930s Hollywood actors, and Gable arrived on the set the first day, muttering, "Let's get this over with." When production wrapped, Colbert groused to a friend, "I just finished the worst picture in the world."

As her name was being announced as best actress, Colbert was already on a train, heading across country. Cohn dispatched someone to pull her off the train and whisk her to the Biltmore Hotel, where she read her speech, wearing a fashionable, two-piece travel suit, made for her by Paramount Pictures designer Travis Banton. She accepted gracefully, and as Hollywood press reported the next day, sauntered back out to catch her train. The rest is Hollywood legend: the "worst" picture won best picture. Gable, Capra, and the screenwriter Robert Riskin also won Oscars.

But it's another piece of the film's legend that transformed advertising. In one scene, the runaway heiress and the fast-talking reporter are in a motel room, where the reporter asks for privacy. When the heiress refuses, he calls her bluff and begins, nonchalantly, to peel off his clothes while reciting a neatly clipped monologue about the protocol of male disrobing. The prevailing story is that what with his topcoat, jacket, vest, tie, and shirt, an undershirt represented one layer too many for the rhythm of the scene—especially because it meant Gable would have to raise his arms aloft and possibly perpetrate the catastrophe of messing his hair. So . . . the undershirt went.

A legend then spread that Gable's bare chest caused undershirt sales to plummet. After all, who'd want to wear an undershirt if Clark Gable didn't? Some attached a number to the undershirt sales decline (75 percent is a popular choice), and many reported that the fashion industry was devastated. One manufacturer ostensibly threatened to sue Columbia Pictures.

But this is where, even by Hollywood standards, the imagination is stretched. In today's marketing-savvy world, it's impossible for one's nostrils not to fill with the distinct whiff of a studio publicity machine, especially considering that the great undershirt legend could only

141

THE LESSON OF CLARK GABLE'S UNDERSHIRT

boost the reputation of Gable, the film, and the studio. Was the undershirt industry devastated? Maybe. But in 1934, with the economy reduced to matchsticks, 20 percent unemployment, and hot prairie winds making off with untold tons of prime topsoil, "devastated" was the norm. All the same, burning in the core of this legend is an ember of reality: Gable was Hollywood royalty and could easily have set such a trend, teasing Madison Avenue with opportunities to come.

> In hard times, when the rallying cry was "make do," it's likely that many men wore old, patched undershirts, rather than buying new ones. Undershirts would make a comeback during the Second World War, where they were standard issue.

It was neither the first nor the last time that Hollywood would influence consumer fashion. Joan Crawford would champion the "shoulder pad" look; Greta Garbo would set a trend with her trench-coat-and-beret style; and Marlene Dietrich and Katharine Hepburn would lead millions of women out of their dresses—so to speak—and into slacks. Decades later Diane Keaton, if not Ralph Lauren, would help make the *Annie Hall look* part of seventies pop culture.

> It was Lauren who designed the outfits Ms. Keaton and Woody Allen wore in the film, including the former's famous collar-and-tie look.

Oddly enough, it would take decades before the inevitable marriage between marketing and art was consummated in the movie industry and the word *merchandising* would start cropping up *before* a picture was released. In the 1930s, while Undershirt-gate was or was not gripping North America, Hollywood and advertising were kept carefully separate. This was partly because movies were viewed by the public—and by investors—as being honed by great artistic minds in the lofty offices of the major studios. Radio and TV, by contrast, were seen as the poor cousins of film, who had to rely on *brand sponsors* who—gasp—actually created and produced the programming *themselves*. For those in the huckster-free sanctuary of film, this brand control over radio and television programming must have looked like shackles, confining broadcast—even reducing it—to

142

a lowly "sales" medium, a bias that is still deeply engrained to this day. The differences were infused in the imagination: *Jezebel* was seen as a star vehicle for Bette Davis, a costume epic for Warner Brothers, a splashy, oh-so-Hollywood work of art; *The Shadow* was considered to be merely a radio sales vehicle for Blue Coal. *Suspicion, Foreign Correspondent,* and *Notorious* were about escapism, *cinema noir,* and the canny storytelling of Alfred Hitchcock; the radio series *Suspense* was about selling Roma Wines. Nowhere was the difference better illustrated than in Orson Welles' "jump" to RKO. *Citizen Kane* was perceived as his arrival in the world of cinematic arts, whereas his *Mercury Theatre* was seen as a first-rate troupe of theatrical refugees, whose raison d'être was to hawk Campbell's Soup—no matter how good the writing was.

> When not engrossed in the doings of Lamont Cranston and the lovely Margot Lane, listeners were invited to phone their Blue Coal dealer to arrange for a "trial ton."

Film was an art, an end in itself. The purpose of radio was to promote the sponsor's sales. The filmmaker's job was to create with one hand, and like any self-respecting artist, stack sandbags with the other, against the inevitable seepage of meddling benefactors—a balancing act that had been going on for centuries. Just ask Michelangelo.

MICHELANGELO: EVERYBODY'S A BACKSEAT FRESCO ARTIST

You're forgiven if you haven't heard of Biagio da Cesena, even though Michelangelo immortalized him in one of the world's greatest works of art.

In 1508 Pope Julius II commissioned Michelangelo to create a fresco on the ceiling of the Sistine Chapel. Though the great artist fancied himself a sculptor, he spent four gruelling years painting that ceiling. Enter Biagio da Cesena: the pope's Master of Ceremonies and one of the art world's most infamous backseat drivers. Da Cesena was shocked— shocked!—to discover that Michelangelo had painted bare-naked figures on the chapel ceiling. With that "I'm telling!" expression most of

143

us ruefully recall from Grade 5, he complained to the pope and bully-ragged Michelangelo. In time, the Church commissioned a protégé to paint garments over the various naughty bits.

The great artist got the last laugh. After he painted the chapel ceiling, he created the magnificent *Last Judgement* behind the chapel altar. Toward the bottom right, he portrayed Minos, judge of the Underworld, leading the condemned into Hell. This character's face is that of Biagio da Cesena—but with donkey ears added—and his naked genitals are covered by a serpent.

Biagio da Cesena's birthday suit actually bore some similarities to Clark Gable's undershirt—or lack thereof. They're both about the powerful combination of art and commerce. Michelangelo's plight demonstrated the benefactor's power over an artist. Gable's undershirt taught potential sponsors a new lesson: that artists themselves also possessed enormous power over an audience, creating fashions, setting trends—even *influencing* consumer habits.

Among the millions who faithfully frequented the movie houses week after week in those days were marketers, some of them no doubt chewing their red liqorice whips from noisy cellophane packages and quite possibly pining for a world where their messages could reach such an attentive, dedicated audience. They didn't dare infiltrate movie theatres—yet—for they were just beginning to understand the marketing power embedded in motion pictures. The lesson of Clark Gable's undershirt (or lack thereof) may have taken root in the thirties, but it wouldn't be fully harvested until, well, a long time after that—in a galaxy far, far away . . .

MADISON, MEET VINE; VINE, THIS IS MADISON—THE STAR WARS MERCHANDISING EXPLOSION

144 Perhaps the only story told as many times as *Star Wars* has been viewed is the tale of George Lucas making *Star Wars*. For writing, producing, and directing the original film in the series (A *New Hope*,

released in 1977), Lucas was paid about $175,000. Oh, yes—and a percentage of the box office. And in one of those great "By the way, there's one more thing" moments, Lucas asked the studio if he could also retain the right to license *Star Wars* merchandise. They answered, in essence, "Yeah, whatever." Who cared? Until then, film merchandising was almost unknown, even though the concept had made an appearance in the late 1950s, courtesy of the Smurfs, when those characters jumped from cartoons to comic books to figurines. Seems Hollywood simply didn't notice.

But after all, the industry was just getting used to the whole idea of a $100 million blockbuster. Two years earlier Steven Spielberg's movie *Jaws*, hitherto known as Peter Benchley's novel *Jaws*, became the first genuine Hollywood blockbuster. It crossed new money-making boundaries by employing some aggressive, unprecedented marketing tactics. Never before had a motion picture been advertised on network television; never before had a picture opened on so many screens at once. Never had summer been regarded as a peak season for the film industry. Never had a film cut such a swath through the box office: it was the first picture to shatter the magic $100 million mark. Hollywood's bean-counters smelled blood.

The previous box-office champion, Francis Ford Coppola's *The Godfather*, opened in just five theatres. *Jaws* opened in 465. Until then, it had been the norm to start small, in large markets, and work slowly down to smaller cities and towns. *Jaws* begat an everywhere-at-once approach.

Since the earliest days of cinema, before air conditioning, the summer was regarded as the off-season—evidenced partly by the fact that legendary film critic Pauline Kael took summers off when she began in the early sixties. As air conditioning became widespread, films such as *Bonnie and Clyde* (1967) and *Easy Rider* (1969) helped build the summer-movie trend.

Steven Spielberg tells the wonderful story of the panic attack he had when completing *Jaws*: he'd run hopelessly over schedule, and at some $12 million, had spent three times his reported budget. But he needn't have worried. By 2001 *Jaws* had grossed $260 million in the U.S. alone.

But *Star Wars*, with its sophomore director Lucas, hardly looked like a blockbuster. The movie would open on fewer than forty screens—and only after the studio, Twentieth Century Fox, had strong-armed theatres into taking the flick by saying: if you want to show the much-anticipated *Other Side of Midnight*, well, then, you'll have to show this two-bit space opera as well.

> "Sophomore" only in a loose sense. Lucas had made several films previously, but his first major feature was *American Graffiti*.

To be fair, nobody saw the *Star Wars* phenomenon coming. But suddenly all things *Star Wars* were in huge demand among young filmgoers and consumers' wallets were holstered like blasters, with a gloved hand at the ready. Yet Lucas had no merchandising plan. With Christmas coming, the *Star Wars* empire was caught with its pants around its ankles. A marketing team feverishly went about the business of cashing in.

> While working with Mr. Skywalker himself (Mark Hamill), I discovered that we were both big Beatles memorabilia collectors. I always found that amusing, since Mark himself is a collectible.

Most major toy manufacturers turned down licensing deals. Only one—Kenner—was interested. But their toys wouldn't be ready for Christmas. So began the storied "voucher" campaign. Commercials promised Star Wars toys *some time next year*, provided customers bought a voucher before Christmas. Nothing says "Christmas" like a promise on a piece of cardboard. The Kenner deal involved an annual fee of $100,000 a year for Lucas—plus a royalty—for rights to market Star Wars toys.

> In 1991, when Hasbro bought Kenner, Star Wars toys were a nonentity, so Hasbro discontinued payments, a move they would soon regret. When Lucas announced plans to produce his prequel trilogy, Hasbro asked to reactivate the partnership, but by then, Lucas had struck a deal with another toy maker, Galoob, of San Francisco. In the end, the two companies split the business, with Lucas reportedly collecting royalties of 15 percent.

From that $175,000 writing, producing, and directing job and that "oh-by-the-way" merchandising clause, Forbes reckons Lucas has built an empire worth some $3.5 billion, give or take a hundred million. *Jaws* and *Star Wars*, their makers, their timing, and their wildly unorthodox approach to marketing would change the attitude of the film industry. Spielberg, and especially Lucas, had broken down a barrier, and that barrier would soon be a distant memory. Take a film like *Wall-E*. It's a story about the excesses of consumerism, yet in its first run, more than thirty tie-in toys were available. As a matter of fact, kids were handed a Wall-E promotion as their ticket was taken in the theatre. It's hard not to trip over the irony there.

THE BILLION-DOLLAR WIZARD

What does the marriage of film and merchandising look like today? Picture an adolescent boy with a wand, round glasses, and a billion-dollar touch.

Billion dollar? In 2007 *Advertising Age* estimated the economy generated by the Harry Potter franchise to be worth upwards of $15 billion. They factored in both expenditures (hundreds of millions spent advertising Potter books, films, and peripherals) and income, including book, film, music, and merchandising sales; home video rentals; ad revenue generated through TV screenings; licensing of packaged goods; and projected revenue from a Universal Studios "Harry Potter" theme park in Orlando.

WILL YOU HAVE FRANCHISE WITH THAT?

The term *franchise* has a French root meaning "free," and it first referred to one's right to vote, then to one's right to carry out commercial activities, and finally to territorial membership in a sporting or corporate group. What better symptom of the Hollywood shift from art to commerce than the application of the word *franchise* to the likes of *Star Wars, Star Trek, Harry Potter,* and no end of comic book superheroes.

147

By then, the avaricious fantasies swirling through the industry following the runaway success of *Star Wars* manifested themselves in the world created by rags-to-riches single mom Joanne Kathleen Rowling. Unlike Lucas, who scrambled to keep up with unexpected success, the marketing minds behind Harry Potter plotted every facet of its multimedia, multitiered, perfectly timed campaign. The industry's early mistakes would not be repeated.

Born "Joanne Rowling," the middle initial was added at the behest of Ms. Rowling's publisher. Scuttlebutt has it that initials were favoured, lest a woman's name deter boys from reading the book. She chose "K" for "Kathleen," an homage to her favourite grandmother.

The Harry Potter series has been the high-water mark of the era of *convergence*. That's a fancy-pants corporate term meaning that Time Warner—whose company produced the film—could work all its tendrils at once to maximize exposure, and profit. Its media—from CNN to *Time* magazine to Turner Broadcasting—could work together to advertise and promote the film, all within the corporate family. The soundtrack, video games and DVDs are sold through Warner Bros. Home Entertainment Group.

And merchandising? That's where the real magic happens. Surf by the online Harry Potter Shop, and with a wave of the credit card, hundreds of possible purchases will unfold—from clothing, clocks, and backpacks to board games, scarves, ties, chess sets, wands, bedding, key chains, plush toys, puzzles, bookmarks, stationery, journals, snow globes, sheet music, costumes, wall hangings, lunch boxes, and the coveted Death Eater Mini Bust. Elsewhere, you can find licensed Bertie Bott's Every Flavor Beans in such memorable varieties as black pepper, booger, earthworm, dirt, earwax, sardine, soap, and—no kidding—*vomit*.

Meanwhile, another important media shift had taken place. Among nostalgia-starved boomers, a market developed for big-screen versions of their favourite small-screen shows. The floodwall broke with the first of the *Star Trek* features in 1979. In time a steady parade of TV properties migrated to the local multiplex: from *Scooby-Doo* to *SWAT*, from

148

The Flintstones to *The Fugitive*. And a new generation could buzz to the cinema for *Beavis and Butt-head* or *South Park*, then rush home to watch . . . *Beavis and Butt-head* or *South Park*. In 2007 *The Simpsons* could saunter across the street from TV to the big screen, pull in more than a half-billion dollars from *The Simpsons Movie*, and saunter back without missing a beat. Production companies now travelled freely between media, and nobody was forgetting to pack their wallet.

At the same time, the wall that used to segregate the creation of books from film from music from merchandise has now vanished. Today, popular "properties" are created with all these facets in mind from the very beginning. Marketing people are hard at work while scripts are still in development. Release dates and marketing campaigns are carefully orchestrated for maximum *oomph*. It took decades, but the trumpet kept sounding and the Wall of Jericho separating massive merchandising and film finally dropped unceremoniously floorward.

The powerful marriage of art and commerce has also been forged in other galaxies of the entertainment industry. If films—and film stars—influence fashions, drive sales, and create demand for new products, then certainly music and musicians do the same. As in any art form, artists first develop a new medium and use it to persuade their audiences to accept their personal messages and viewpoints. Then, inevitably, advertisers figure out how to harness this new medium in the market-place. Persuasion precedes marketing. Consider the cultural influence of the Beatles in the sixties: they induced a generation of young men to grow their locks, and led their followers into (and then, for many, out of) transcendental meditation, they made a worldwide fashion of sitar music, and they personified the movement of peace and love. At the same time, they virtually pioneered pop-group merchandising through their subsidiary company Seltaeb Inc., which sold over 150 different products in 1964. Their manager, Brian Epstein, negotiated only a 10 percent royalty, never dreaming that revenue from Beatles

Seltaeb is *Beatles* spelled backwards.

products would amount to much. While Colonel Tom Parker had developed some Elvis merchandising by the late fifties, it was the Beatles who were the true mass-merchandising pioneers but didn't emphasize it, keeping their sights more firmly fixed on record sales and tour revenue. Today, there are a gazillion recording artists and a gazillion products and brands, all trying to win a place in the consumer's heart. And they're learning to help each other out.

STING AND JAGUAR: PIMP MY ALBUM

Sting's 1999 song "Desert Rose" is a landmark example of how music and commerce have become entwined. In the video version, Sting is being whisked through a desert in the back seat of a Jaguar S-Type sedan (which vehicle the director thought was a perfect fit for Sting's image). Getting to the desert had been easy, but for Sting, his album *Brand New Day*, and his new single, getting *out* of those arid acres would be another matter altogether. Radio stations were giving the song little airplay, and competition for a place on station playlists grew increasingly brutal. Audiences, meanwhile, were scattering—to other radio stations, to the Internet, to file-sharing communities. It appeared that the song born in the desert would die there as well.

That's when Sting's manager, Miles Copeland, screened the *Desert Rose* video and, by his own account, said, "My God, it's a car commercial." (He meant it as a *good* thing.) In 1999 that connection had a sweet whiff of opportunity. Soon, a branch of Ogilvy & Mather, who handle the Jaguar account, received a call from Copeland with an irresistible proposition: how would they like to re-cut the *Desert Rose* video as a TV ad for the Jaguar S-Type? Sting, for his part, would loan his image and his song at no cost, on one condition: that the final commercial look like an ad for the recording. The deal was done.

150

The ad begins with Sting's video, where he's performing the song at a club. It slips away to an animated graphic, noting the song and the album. After some more concert footage, there are further graphics:

"Everyone dreams of becoming a rock star. / What then do rock stars dream of?" Cut to Sting from the original video footage, entranced, hurtling through the desert in the back seat of the Jag. A couple of beauty shots of the Jag are inserted. It's dusk. Sting, lost in his dream, disappears down the road, toward the distant desert city, where, presumably, he'll play his gig. It ends with the graphic "Jaguar S-Type. The Art of Performance."

What happened next? Everything. The record label had budgeted $1.8 million to promote "Desert Rose"—$800,000 of that going to video production—and Jaguar, meanwhile, bought $8 million worth of ad media to feature the Sting commercial. And rather than grovelling for radio airplay, the Sting song jumped the queue, beaming directly onto the TV screens of a mass audience. "Desert Rose" caught on: 180 contemporary hit stations picked up the song, and sales soared. The label had anticipated sales of a million albums—modest by Sting standards, but sales for *Brand New Day* reached four million albums in the U.S. alone. It was Sting's biggest solo album. Jaguar, meanwhile, believes the association with Sting added all kinds of horsepower to its S-Type brand.

Copeland held up the "Desert Rose" deal as a model for others to follow—and other artists did team up with advertising partners to promote their recordings. One of them was Paul McCartney, though his experience in this new domain was not without its share of Maalox moments.

FIDELITY AND MCCARTNEY

In the fall of 2005, Sir James Paul McCartney, legend and icon, launched a tour, timed with his new release, *Chaos and Creation in the Backyard*. What turned heads was his announcement of a partnership with Fidelity Investments. McCartney, having honed his marketing skills for more than four decades, had struck a deal with Fidelity to help underwrite the cost of staging his concerts. They'd also kick in $1 million for The Music Lives Foundation, a group that provides and promotes music education for underprivileged American kids. For his part McCartney would loan his name and image to a pair of TV ads for Fidelity. What TV viewers saw was a brief bio of "Paul": Quarryman, Beatle, Wing, poet, father, front man, producer, business mogul, painter, and if that wasn't enough, knight. The key was the tie to Fidelity: "Never stop doing what you love." That is, the viewer was urged to start the next chapter of life with help from a Fidelity agent.

Where Sting had enjoyed a refreshing and lucrative drive through the desert, Sir Paul found himself on far bumpier terrain. Critics were quick to pounce. One headline read, "Rubber Sold" and another mocked, "I am the *Ad* Man, Goo Goo G'joob." For Sting, an advertising partnership raised a struggling album, quadrupled projected sales, and put Sting back on the sales map. But for Paul McCartney, a partnership with Fidelity drew negative PR.

Why the difference? Two reasons. First and foremost, Sting, though stellar, is mortal in comparison to McCartney, who is the living remnant of one of the greatest music phenomena of modern history. On the highway of popular culture, he's several exits past a mere superstar like Sting. I've heard of many celebrities who've remarked that there are rock stars and then there are Beatles. In a very real sense, McCartney's career has been heavily shackled by hundreds of millions of fans who cut their teeth on Beatles music. They have an acute sense of proprietorship over him. They hold him up to a higher

> Beatles purists, of whom I am a card-carrying example, would quickly tsk this. Though credited to "Lennon/McCartney" (as were all their Beatles songs as per an agreement they made as teenagers), "I Am the Walrus" was a John Lennon composition. I once saw a forty-five of that song, signed by Lennon, where he had scratched out McCartney's songwriting credit and written, "Me mostly" instead.

> In 1974 Lennon went to a party with date May Pang. The place was full of rock stars, but almost nobody came up to speak to him. Lennon soon left, and on the way home, turned dejectedly to Pang and said, "I guess none of them like me." Pang just stared at Lennon and screamed, "Are you kidding? They were all too intimidated to talk to you!"

standard, and they're not so sure about his taking money from an investment company. No matter how Fidelity handled the ad, McCartney was going to take some collateral damage.

Second, it's a long walk from people's image of Paul McCartney to their image of Fidelity Investments (even though McCartney is a hugely successful businessman). It's a hop and a skip, meanwhile, from the free-spirited, casual sophistication of Sting to the Jaguar S-Type. Compatibility between a celebrity and a brand sponsor is a touchy business and it's difficult for fans to wrap their heads around a Beatle pitching an investment firm.

Or is it? Ironically, many critics had forgotten a Super Bowl ad released at about the same time that Sting was taking his Jag for a spin. The commercial, for Schwab Investments, showed members of a rock band in a rehearsal room, struggling to create a lyric to rhyme with "elation." Suggestions are offered and dismissed. Then, over the familiar piano line of Barrett Strong's "Money (That's What I Want)" (covered by the Beatles in 1963), we hear a familiar voice offering possibilities: "dividend investment participation," "market capitalization," "European market fluctuation," and "industry globalization." Why it's . . . yes . . . Ringo Starr, Schwab investor (so a graphic informs us). It was a funny ad, and no one remembers a flap about *it*. Even the distance McCartney created by not actually "acting" in the Fidelity ad didn't seem to help. Clearly, the standard critics seem to apply to Paul McCartney was unique. All Beatles, it seems, are not created equal.

When California's elections of 1970 neared, activist Timothy Leary announced plans to run for governor. The slogan he chose was "Come together, join the party." When Leary was busted for possession, the campaign promptly collapsed but not before he commissioned his friend John Lennon to write a campaign song—"Come Together." Odd as it may seem for the most revolutionary of Beatles, John Lennon embraced advertising. Late in his short life, he and Yoko Ono launched their War Is Over! If You Want It billboard campaign in eleven cities. "Come Together" was later rejigged and slowed down by McCartney, and the song that began as an election ad became the first cut on *Abbey Road*. Granted, a Timothy Leary campaign song (designed to unseat Ronald Reagan) is not the stuff of a classic Madison Avenue sellout.

It's a safe guess that those upset about the Fidelity deal were old enough to laugh if their kids asked, "Did Paul McCartney have a band before Wings?" and old enough to rant, "When I was your age, I had to *get up* to change the channels!" Those who complain are just as likely to have gasped when Bob Dylan appeared in a TV ad for Victoria's Secret and when the Rolling Stones made a sponsorship deal with Ameriquest Mortgage Company or when they licensed their song "Start Me Up" to Microsoft for the Windows 95 advertising campaign.

> It was rumoured that they pocketed over $10 million. It was the first time the Stones allowed their music to be used in advertising. (We won't count the Rice Krispies jingle they performed in the sixties before they hit it big.)

These campaigns and the McCartney deal have shocked even those who are alarmingly conscious of the business side of their culture and can rattle off the salaries, contracts, and incentive clauses of star athletes the way their parents grew up reciting ERAs and goals against averages. What's most striking about the McCartney story, however, is that it *isn't* about a breach in the wall separating popular musicians from advertisers; it's that such a wall never really existed.

THE PERSUASIVE POWER OF SONG

The music industry learned the lesson of Clark Gable's undershirt (or lack thereof) much faster than the film industry, and for good reason.

> **Mne·mon·ic** *(noun)* A sound effect or a catchy musical punctuation designed to tie emotionally to a brand in the consumer's mind.

Music and rhymes have been used as marketing tools since at least the nineteenth century. Before there was broadcast, nineteenth-century advertisers used verse and rhyme as "mnemonic" devices to sell brands. And in the 1920s, marketers used their own art form—the jingle.

154   Wheaties helped pioneer the radio jingle—see Chapter Four—and when they broadcast their first such ad, sales climbed each time the song was played. Very soon, the pioneers of broadcast advertising

grasped the power of the infectious combination of music and verse and others got into the game:

> Pepsi-Cola hits the spot,
> Twelve full ounces, that's a lot!
> Twice as much for a nickel, too, [cowbell]
> Pepsi-Cola is the drink for you!
> Nickel nickel nickel nickel . . .
> Nickel nickel trickle trickle . . .

They had a stickiness to them—enough for some to rattle around in people's heads a half century after they hit the airwaves:

> You'll wonder where the yellow went
> When you brush your teeth with Pepsodent.

At first, jingles and popular music were set apart in people's minds the way Hollywood films were separate from ad-driven broadcast. But the music line didn't take as long to blur. There was Frank Sinatra, for instance, who crooned, "Halo everybody, Halo" for the famous shampoo in a 1950's TV ad. And Canada's Four Lads converted their 1956 hit "Standing on the Corner" into:

So did Peggy Lee and Eddie Cantor, for those keeping score at home.

> Standing on the corner
> Watching all the Fords go by.

A Frank Loesser number from the Broadway show *The Most Happy Fella.*

Beginning in the sixties, during an especially prolific outbreak of hostilities in the storied Cola Wars, Pepsi and Coke recruited, commandeered, and otherwise enlisted the who's who of popular music in their cause. Coca-Cola chose a bevy of current stars, from Tom Jones to Petula Clark to the Moody Blues. Retaliating for Pepsi were the

155

B.J. Thomas, of "Raindrops Keep Fallin' on my Head" fame, has the distinction of crooning for both Coke (ca. 1969) and later, for Pepsi (ca. 1972). All's fair, it would appear, in love and cola marketing.

Prime among the many amazing stories in ad veteran Phil Dusenberry's memoir *Then We Set His Hair on Fire: Insights and Accidents from a Hall of Fame Career in Advertising* is a behind-the-scenes story of Jackson's infamous accident during the Pepsi shoot Dusenberry was overseeing, when Jackson's hair ignited.

likes of Martha Reeves and the Vandellas, Johnny Cash, and B.B. King. And after these came performances by a steady parade of the usual suspects of pop music, from Michael Jackson and Madonna to Britney Spears.

PINCHING POPULAR SONGS (SO TO SPEAK)

Over the years the music industry has produced some notable holdouts—artists who refused to work and play nicely with advertisers. Some advertisers, meanwhile, have played a little too fast and loose with copyrighted music.

REAGAN, SPRINGSTEEN, McCAIN, AND MELLENCAMP

When Ronald Reagan tried to co-opt Bruce Springsteen's song "Born in the U.S.A." while making a campaign stop in 1984, Springsteen's office was quick to rebuff the connection. Ironically, the song is a barbed comment on the effects of the Vietnam War on America, suggesting Reagan's people must have listened only to the chorus. Decades later Republican John McCain used John Mellencamp's songs "Our Country" and "Small Town" at his rallies, hoping these upbeat heartland numbers would persuade voters to swing to his cause. But Mellencamp's office quietly asked McCain to stop using them—seems Mr. Mellencamp is a diehard Democrat.

The precedent-setting case was Bette Midler versus the ad agency Young & Rubicam. The agency had used Midler's cover of the Bobby Freeman song "Do You Want to Dance?" in a 1985 Ford commercial, and hired one of her backup singers to "imitate Midler as closely as possible." Young & Rubicam argued that it was trying to create "credible renditions of the original recording" but not of Ms. Midler's voice. Her lawyers argued the distinction was meaningless. Midler asked for $10 million in damages; the court awarded her $400,000.

In November 1988, Tom Waits was being interviewed on a Los Angeles radio station when he heard a familiar voice during a commercial break: his own. Okay, not *exactly* his own: but that of Stephen Carter, a musician whose band covered a number of Waits' tunes. The ad had been produced for Frito-Lay, and it had been distributed to 250 radio stations in 61 markets. Waits didn't like the implication that he was endorsing Frito-Lay, so he took the chip makers and their agency to court and was awarded nearly $2.5 million. There was also an ironic twist: the Waits song that had inspired the Frito-Lay ad was "Step Right Up"—a Tom Waits rant against hucksterism—slipping the iron fist of satire within the velvet glove of dexterous jazz and nimble scat phrasing.

> Initially, Frito-Lay approached Waits about hiring out his song for the campaign, but he firmly refused.

> When Waits later sued Levi's for using one of his songs, the jeans maker agreed to cease using the song and took out a full-page ad in the music news magazine *Billboard* to apologize. Waits won similar suits in Europe against auto makers Audi and Opel.

Recently, advertisers have fallen more frequently into the practice of acquiring rights to songs they think fit their brand, a phenomenon known in my trade as *borrowed interest*.

Yet a closer look reveals that many of these song-brand relationships are woefully incompatible.

BORROWED INTEREST

Here's what *borrowed interest* means. Rather than investing time in a long-term campaign, many brands embrace a strategy of hitch-hiking on an element of popular culture to get immediate attention. This means looking for emotional shortcuts. Solution? Advertisers borrow emotions—by licensing, and often rearranging, hit songs that have built-in emotional baggage. Lyrics are often changed to suit a strategy. Iconic images, from the Mona Lisa to the Great Pyramid of Giza, are similarly commandeered.

Consider the cruise line that chose to use Iggy Pop's "Lust for Life." Great music, great title—but did anyone notice the lyrics were about liquor, drugs, and doing a striptease?

Fashion lines and birth control brands have used "There She Goes," originally by The La's, and covered by Sixpence None the Richer. A lovely ballad . . . about a heroin addict. The Best Buy chain once used Sheryl Crow's "Soak Up the Sun," which packs a double-dollop punch of anticonsumerism.

The "instant recognition" advertisers win through this borrowed interest comes at a cost that's not just financial: people might remember Katrina and the Waves' "Walking on Sunshine" but quickly forget the product the song is meant to sell—especially when the same hit crops up in campaigns for several unrelated brands. Or worse, people might just resent the commandeering of a favourite memory.

COKE: I'D LIKE TO TEACH THE WORLD TO SING

In rare moments when the cosmic tumblers of marketing align, a powerful piece of original music emerges—created for a brand but worthy of a place on the music charts. The classic example is Coca-Cola's "I'd Like to Teach the World to Sing," a ditty that owes much to serendipity.

On a foggy Thursday afternoon in February 1971, a man sat among a crowd of fog-bound passengers in Ireland's Shannon Airport. He was Bill Backer, creative director of the Coca-Cola account for the agency McCann-Erickson. He was on his way to England to meet an arranger with the band the New Seekers to discuss some original music for a new TV campaign for Coke.

Hours had passed before Backer noticed something: stranded passengers who'd been livid just a few hours before were now sitting in the lounge sipping Coca-Cola with strangers from all around the world, laughing and swapping stories. Backer imagined the same scene must be happening around the world, with people from every country imaginable, all finding common ground through a Coke. Around this very warm, very real human insight, Backer and his team went to work writing a song that might capture that sentiment.

The TV ad was supposed to have been set on the cliffs of Dover. But three days of heavy rain moved the production to a hillside in Italy. Helicopter shots of the group on the hill were punctuated with close-ups (which were actually shot separately at a racetrack near Rome).

When "I'd Like to Teach the World to Sing" first aired in North America in July 1971, radio stations took calls requesting that they play the song. A single was quickly recorded, omitting mention of Coke and it's signature line: "It's the real thing." The folks marketing Coca-Cola didn't mind a bit. They knew the association with their brand was already established—and "I'd Like to Teach the World to Sing" would climb to number 7 on *Billboard*'s U.S. singles chart.

South African Coke bottlers requested a version of the ad without any black people. Their request was denied.

T-BONES FOR ALKA-SELTZER

A case of a song migrating from advertising to the pop charts (rather than the by far more common reverse) was not without precedent: Six years before the famous Coke ad, a group of studio

159

Until the 1990s advertising and music came together for only short, surreptitious trysts, as awkward as two porcupines pitching woo. It took a slight, humble, understated revolutionary to deliver the lesson of Clark Gable's undershirt to the music industry.

MOBY: PERSUASION, IT'S A-CHANGIN'

He was born Richard Melville Hall on September 11, 1965, in New York City. His parents gave him the nickname "Moby" when he was a child because Herman Melville, the author of *Moby Dick*, was a distant relative. In 1999 he released an album called *Play*, which did little to interest radio stations. Not to worry: just as Moby wasn't your run-of-the-mill DJ-turned-techno-king (he's a vegan and a born-again Christian), *Play* wasn't a typical release. Each of its eighteen songs was licensed for use in advertising, on TV, and in movies. Moby songs wound up behind *Dharma and Greg* TV promos and, notably, in a Nike ad, featuring Tiger Woods playing a round of golf on the streets of New York. *Wired* magazine reported that the songs were licensed to hundreds of buyers and made *Play* a financial success before it sold a single copy.

Melville was his great-great-great uncle.

Moby had bypassed the traditional radio-airplay route and got *Play* "out there" through commercials and TV shows and in film. In doing so he helped reinvent the relationship between marketing and music. As Moby defined the terms, his music became, in effect, a free agent: listeners could enjoy it on their iPods and it could sell golf shirts like nobody's business, yet it never truly belonged to anyone except its creator. Moby, like the millennials who consume his songs, is in business for *himself*.

How does all of this affect you? As marketing seeps into feature films, arts, popular music, and even literature, it changes the relationship between the arts and audiences. Boomers grew up accustomed to escaping to movie theatres. Today, they find themselves "sold" to advertisers as a captive audience, for ads before the film and for product placement within. While boomers pout about this new state of affairs, their kids aren't taking it so hard. They've grown up expecting product placement in films and ads in theatres, on school buses, and even in their classrooms. All their lives they've seen major sports leagues paralyzed by multimillionaires squabbling over money. While their parents shake their heads ruefully, they shrug their shoulders and wonder what the flap is all about.

Yeah, *them* again: those pesky young consumers. Marketers are beginning to understand that to reach this new breed of consumer, they need more than ubiquitous messages, attention-grabbing guerrilla tactics, and infusions of sales messages in popular culture. They need to create a whole new language.

THE MYTH OF WHO LEADS AND WHO FOLLOWS

Advertisers are constantly accused of creating trends, shaping attitudes, and planting new behaviour in consumers. But in fact, the opposite is true: advertising doesn't set trends, it follows them. Bold new ideas are embraced in advertising only after society has long since accepted them. Advertising is the great mirror of society.

Case in point: I once attended an all-male focus group for a beer brand (men being the main consumers of suds). At that august gathering, we tested some innovative creative that didn't include the usual parade of scantily clad women. The focus group balked: they *wanted* scantily clad women. Guess what? Out went the innovative new creative and in came the beer bunnies, though none of us on the agency's creative team wanted the beer bunnies to win. In fact, we didn't even want the beer bunnies presented as an option. Would the pioneering approach have worked? Maybe. But it was a path less travelled, and for the beer brand, it represented too great a risk.

Advertisers have been among the last to liberate women, provide equality among races, and free the gay/bi/transgender community from its closet. In a way, it's this very conservatism that makes advertising so powerful. It's so safe, so unwilling to challenge public sensibilities that when it does shift to reflect new thinking, it actually normalizes—or even consecrates—the trend. When an ad shows a female boss or a same-sex or mixed-race couple, or when it stops showing smokers, it implies a prevailing view.

Advertising loves a parade, but it never, ever, seeks to be grand marshal.

Advertising practitioners are interpreters. But unlike foreign language interpreters, ad people must constantly learn new languages. They must understand the language of each new product, and speak the language of each new target audience.

JEF I. RICHARDS

THE LANGUAGE OF PERSUASION

8

**S**mall is dead. To honour its memory, please join me in four lines of silence.

Thank you.

After a long decline, *small* was quietly euthanized by the Starbucks coffee chain. It is survived, throughout the upscale coffee industry, by a large—no, a *grande*—family of euphemisms. And if you seek proof that the pervasive advertising culture influences everyday speech in the age of persuasion, Starbucks is a cozy place to begin.

Pity the uninitiated soul who strolls unknowingly into one of these coffee shops only to find her mind swimming in a sea of menu-board variables and, utterly rattled, blurts out an order for a *small* coffee. There's a palpable intake of air through the collective nostrils of the regulars, exhaling in a silent "oh dear, oh dear, oh dear." With great patience and care, this newcomer to the Valhalla of caffeine is brought up to speed: there is no such thing as *small*. *Small* is gone. Banished. Vamoosed. Adios. Like Elvis, it has left the building. In Starbucks-speak, *small* isn't small, it's *Tall*. Already you can see its back a little straighter and its tummy sucked in. Medium is *Grande*. Large is *Venti*, presumably from the Italian word for "twenty"— as in twenty ounces. Before long, the newcomer will stand cockily among the knowing, ready to titter inwardly at the next poor schlep to stammer out a request for *small*. Pfffft. Rookies.

> Strictly *entre nous,* it may not be on the board, but you can order a "short" coffee (which, yes, is smaller than *Tall*), provided you can weather the public ridicule.

The word *small* posed a marketing problem for Starbucks, the Seattle retailer that rose rapidly in the nineties to worldwide dominance of the designer coffee market, with thousands of stores spread through more than thirty countries. Upscale coffee also means upscale prices. In a fast-food world, people might be outraged at the prospect of paying well north of a dollar for a *small* coffee. Ah, but slapping down that same money for a *Tall*, well, that's different. To break this psychological barrier, Starbucks didn't change the size or the price of its coffee: it changed the language.

In fact, the coffee culture championed by Starbucks has millions of customers speaking in tongues. With its baristas serving *iced quad Venti with whip skinny caramel macchiatos*, they draw customers into the Starbucks culture, complete with its unique language, creating an exclusive club and community. In centuries past, the who's who among the cultural elite spoke French. Today, they speak "coffee." Learning the language and immersing themselves in that culture might leave people with a sense of belonging and inclusion. Brand loyalty won't be far behind.

THE ADVERSARIAL SYSTEM

The essence of marketing language goes way back—to long before the rise of "reason why" advertising—at least to the days of King Solomon.

Judeo-Christian tradition has it that Solomon made his reputation in the wisdom game when asked to judge a dispute over a baby by two women, each of whom claimed to be the mother. As was the custom, Solomon heard each woman's argument. Then he offered to cut the baby in two and give half to each. Spoiler alert: Solomon knew that the woman who'd sooner give up the baby than allow it to be harmed was the true mother. Case closed. Call in the next plaintiff.

This was the adversarial system, where opponents make the strongest case for their side and a decision is made based on the arguments. It forms the foundation of most court systems, elections, reality TV shows, pie-eating contests, courtship rituals, beauty pageants, job interviews, and figure skating championships, and it's at the root of the business of persuasion. Since the heyday of "reason why" ads, there has been an unwritten understanding between marketers and consumers that advertising is a one-sided argument for a brand, product, or idea. Competitors argue their case. You vote with your wallet.

It's implicitly understood: no one expects advertisers to cast themselves in an unfavourable light, just as no one expects young siblings to play nicely in the back seat during long car trips and just as no one thought John Scopes' defence lawyer, Clarence Darrow, would leap to his feet and bellow, "Sinner repent, the Lord's judgement is nigh!" when the high school teacher was on trial for teaching Darwin's theory of evolution. The language of advertisers is traditionally confined to a world where their brand is the only one for you and you are the only star in their firmament. They tell you, in effect, "We're good. You're good. Together we're great." Your job, as consumer, is to be the judge, ever aware that the evidence presented favours the advertisers. Children understand this before many are old enough for school, while some ad-fatigued adults complain that advertising should be more "balanced" and "honest," as if they never got the memo.

> With the exception of U.S. pharmaceutical TV ads, who are required by law to warn that some of their products may cause nausea, dizziness, or a sudden and potentially dangerous drop in blood pressure. Pharmaceutical ads are not right for everyone. See your doctor immediately if they cause you to experience open sores, hiccups, vertigo, hives, shingles, cankles, boils, bunions or lumbago. If you are pregnant, red-headed, warm-hearted or ham-handed, see your doctor before viewing pharmaceutical ads.

Within the confines of seller-consumer fantasy, advertisers forged their own lexicon of crisply starched platitudes: the official language of the land where whites are whiter, your husband got the promotion because his boss loved your pie, and a little acne isn't gonna stop Tom from asking Jessica to the prom.

In each brand's quest to elbow ahead of the competition, superlatives became the cheapest of commodities. Even our great-grandparents

166

rolled their eyes in response to promises of "best, brightest, fastest, slowest, hardest, easiest, cleanest, heaviest, lightest, kindest, gentlest, and dentist-preferred." Where a superlative wasn't possible, a parity statement would do: "No cleaner removes tough stains more quickly," "No airline flies to more destinations worldwide," "Nobody beats our prices," or while we're on the subject, "Nobody Does It Better" as Carly Simon put it. They're not saying the competition isn't just as good; they're only promising nobody's *better.* Tricky stuff, this copywriting.

Through its relatively short history, ad copy has explored its share of zeniths and nadirs, like the subject of Longfellow's poem:

> There was a little girl
> Who had a little curl
> Right in the middle of her forehead;
> And when she was good
> She was very, very good,
> But when she was bad she was horrid.

In radio, where I live, a lazy copywriter will introduce any subject by opening with the phrase "When it comes to," as in "When it comes to choosing a steel roof," "When it comes to dishwasher spots," or "When it comes to freshwater plugs and lures." Another chestnut is *For all your* [your brand category here] *needs*—as in "For all your roofing needs" or "For all your pet-care needs." One Canadian outfit uses the tagline "For all your steel needs." What exactly are "steel needs"? On second thought, don't answer that.

Wherever the old salts of my business gather, conversation oft turns to copywriting bloopers: cow-pies of my trade, into which junior copywriters step, failing to sense danger until it's too late. Take for example lines like these, which I've actually encountered in my career: "At prices like these, our appliances won't last long!," "Break the wind—with windbreakers—just $11.99," and "Panties and bras, half off!"

167

REAL ESTATE–SPEAK

Ever bought a house?

No. You haven't. Even if you have, you haven't, because in the real estate business, they aren't houses anymore, they're "homes."

This is real estate–speak, or *propertese*, as the great speechwriter and columnist William Safire described it. It's the official language of the world where a six-figure mortgage buys enough euphemisms to add a third shift in the Webster's factory. One casualty within the real estate lexicon was the term *row house*, which over the past generation, somehow became *town house* before changing again into *town home*. Even the word *home* has become homely: cast aside for the more romantic *villa*, *chateau*, *manor*, or *estate*. Meanwhile, *small* has become *intimate*, and *ramshackle* has become *rustic*, while there are no *developments* or *subdivisions*—just *new communities*. And if you must know, one doesn't *buy* a home: one *invests* in it.

In the realm of propertese, a *country kitchen* is large, an *efficient kitchen* is tiny, and a *gourmet kitchen* has an island with a faucet. If built beside a freeway, a home is "convenient to major transportation." The sort of shack that a stiff breeze might reduce to matchwood is a "handyman's dream," "perfect for the DIYer." In real estate, as in all upscale marketing, *executive* means *expensive*. But if your dream home is a little too "executive" for your budget, at least you won't be reduced to buying a "used" car because they don't exist anymore. Nowadays, cars are *pre-owned*, *previously enjoyed*, or even *previously loved*. It's the same imaginative language that probably inspired one retailer to offer products "with no previous experience."

CHANGING FASHIONS, CHANGING LANGUAGE

168   There are fashions in language, just as there are in clothing, music, and architecture, and when those fashions change, marketers often find themselves trapped. During the gas crisis of the early 1970s, for

instance, when fuel prices shot skyward and as the world broadened its vocabulary to include the acronym *OPEC* and the adapted Spanish word *embargo*, automakers received a language lesson of their own. Almost overnight, "full-size" automobiles—or "luxury cars"—once a definitive status symbol, became "gas guzzlers," "road hogs," and "oil barons." North American automakers turned their attention to small cars, but the word *small* posed a problem: consumers had been conditioned to believe that bigger is better (or Grande, or Venti, as one might say today). The auto industry responded, retooling some of its automobile designs and its language. In autospeak *small* became *compact*. When cars got smaller still, they became *subcompact*.

> The VW Beetle, marketed so beautifully in the sixties *against* the bigger-is-better mentality of Detroit, suddenly found itself on the inside looking out in the seventies.

Meanwhile, back in the food and beverage category, "small" may not be dead either: though it may have migrated. In the spring of 2006, the Wendy's restaurant chain changed course: it abandoned its signature *Biggie* sizes and got smaller. Sort of.

Baby boomers were getting older—and mortal. The dangers of obesity, cholesterol, and high blood pressure had become a fashionable topic. "Bigger," in fast food and the midriffs of those who consumed it, was not better. That, at least, was the theory. In practice, countless millions still lined up for burgers and fries.

Pop quiz: you're a multibillion-dollar fast-food chain: what do you do? You'd probably do exactly what Wendy's did. First, they announced plans to change their cooking oil, promising to reduce the trans-fat content of their french fries and breaded chicken products. Then they did some name-dropping, in a manner of speaking, announcing that they would drop their signature *Biggie* and *Great Biggie* sizes. Henceforth, their sizes for drinks and french fries would be, simply, *small*, *medium*, and *large*.

Here's where it got interesting: following the change, those order-

169

ing *small* fries from Wendy's received what used to be called *medium*. Those ordering a *medium* drink got what used to be called a *Biggie*.

Those ordering "large" got what was once known as a *Great Biggie*. Caught between public relations pressure from health-conscious boomers and the steady demand from millions of customers, Wendy's devised an ingenious solution: they changed their language. Portions remained about the same, but the names were slimmed down. Health-conscious customers could order the same old large portion of fries and still feel as if they could sleep tight, knowing they had ordered *small*.

> Actually, National Public Radio reported that Wendy's smallest size grew 25 percent *after* the name change.

"Big" is even getting the squeeze in the upscale coffee category, where Starbucks has laboured so hard to stomp out "small." In the summer of 2008, Intelligentsia Coffee of Chicago, whose brews are served in more than nine hundred restaurants and outlets, announced it would phase out its twenty-ounce coffee and espresso beverages. "Drinking our coffee," professed the company's founder, Doug Zell, "is not like drinking jug wine." He went on to argue that highly concentrated flavours are best enjoyed in smaller quantities.

Okay, let's check the scoreboard. To recap: "big" used to be better as a rule. During the seventies oil crisis (and again more recently) "big" became bad in automobiles. "Big" then made a comeback with the SUV boom of the 1990s but was beaten back by the forces of "small" during the oil crisis sequel a decade later. "Small," meanwhile, was bad in upscale coffee but good in fast food. At press time, the jury is still deliberating on "Grande" coffees.

If "small" has been squeezed out of the fancy coffee category and is struggling for a place in fast food, it's still got plenty of room in women's clothing. In dress sizes, as with Wendy's drinks and fries, small is big business or to borrow the old copywriter's maxim, "Less is more." Depending on where you look, what was a size 8 in the fifties

170

had shrunk to a size 4 by the seventies. Today, it's a size "zero" or even—wait for it—"double zero," and the *Boston Globe* has quoted industry experts as predicting negative integers were coming. I don't think they were kidding. While the clothing stays the same, the size numbers shrink. One can imagine a customer lined up at Wendy's in a size 6 dress that used to be a 12, ordering *medium* fries that used to be a *Biggie* and eating them in her *intimate kitchen*.

Now, the advertising industry can't take all the flak for this nomen-clatural shell game. The adversarial system is alive and well in mar-keting, and within it, the "language" requires a brand to show itself in the best possible light. When "supersize" becomes a problem instead of a boast, when trans fat is named public enemy number 1, or when animal rights become a popular cause, marketers adapt as quickly as they can but rarely fast enough to escape pointing fingers and the pop-ular voice shouting, "Aha!"

DOOZIES: AD TERMS ENTER THE LANGUAGE

Advertisers constantly struggle to adopt the latest words and catch-phrases in the surrounding culture, though in rare, magical moments, a slogan, catchphrase, or marketing icon gnaws through its leash and becomes part of popular language. It's a dream few marketers ever achieve, but it does happen. One of the earliest legends about such a phenomenon dates back to 1926.

That year entrepreneur E.L. Cord bought the rights to a failed automaker. Previously run by brothers Fred and August Duesenberg, it wasn't the automobile he was after: it was the engineering genius of the brothers themselves. Cord promptly put them to work on the most opulent, most powerful, best-engineered vehicle the world had ever seen. When the Model J Duesenberg was unveiled at the New York car show of 1928, the automotive world swallowed its gum. With an unheard-of 265 horsepower straight-8 engine with dual overhead camshafts, the Duesenberg J could hit 151 kilometres per hour—in

171

second gear. In 1931 a custom-made Duesenberg might cost you upwards of $20,000—about a quarter million of today's dollars. Even as the Great Depression cut an ugly swath through the Western world, the Duesenberg thrived. After all, it was the conveyance of choice for Clark Gable and the Prince of Wales.

But the Duesenberg J wasn't just a car. It was a "doozy." The word *doozy* existed prior to the appearance of this monumental vehicle, but it found new life moments after the first J model rolled off the line and became a popular term for anything extraordinary or exceptional. Long after the 1937 collapse of Cord's empire, the word lingers and remains an example of how marketing influences modern language.

> Also spelled *doozie*, it's said to have derived from *daisy*, as in "She's a real daisy." Don't ask me why, I just work here.

> The language has been similarly infiltrated by the metaphorical superlative "the Cadillac of. . . ."

It wasn't the first time something like this had happened. By the late 1800s, New York was building its natural gas infrastructure, and utility companies needed to sway consumers. Marketing campaigns were launched to promote the superiority of gas stoves, and so came the slogan "Now You're Cooking with Gas." Perhaps by design—or simply by happy accident—the phrase fit neatly into any situation involving superior performance, and soon the slogan became part of the mainstream vernacular.

Fast-forward now, to January 1984. The Wendy's Restaurant chain—yes, them again—was about to debut a creatively daring TV spot. They were in good hands: the director was the great Joe Sedelmaier. The ad itself, titled *Fluffy Bun*, featured an older actress, Miss Clara Peller. According to legend, Ms. Peller had a respiratory condition and had trouble uttering her scripted line "Where is all the beef?" So the line was shortened to "Where's the beef?" and a catchphrase was born.

> I shot my first major TV campaign with Joe.

172

In his book *The Tipping Point*, Malcolm Gladwell opined that if an idea is to resonate, it must posses a "stickiness factor"—some quality that causes it to linger in your imagination. "Where's the beef?" stuck as few buzz phrases ever have and became an everyday expression denoting a lack of substance. And it was fully inserted into common parlance months later, when U.S. presidential hopeful Walter Mondale used it to trash Democratic rival Gary Hart in a televised debate. Some even suggested that Mondale's use of that line finished Gary Hart and helped Mondale win the presidential nomination. Okay, that *and* Gary Hart's sex scandal.

> The moment is preserved on YouTube. Search: 1984 Democratic Debate: "Where's the beef?"

Advertising buzz phrases have infiltrated popular usage before, from the direct-marketing staple "I've fallen, and I can't get up," to Budweiser's once-ubiquitous "Whassup?" From Braniff Airlines in the sixties came the line "If you've got it, flaunt it!," and in the late sixties, Virginia Slims cigarettes ran ads featuring the phrase "You've come a long way, baby," which has since been abused, re-used, parodied, retrofitted, and customized. Decades later, in the summer of 2004, the *Canadian Oxford Dictionary* defined the phrase *double-double* in its second edition—one small step for popular culture, perhaps, but for the Tim Hortons coffee chain, that was a doozy.

> **Dou·ble-dou·ble** *(noun)* esp. *Cdn* A cup of coffee with a double serving of both sugar and cream.

MEDIA CHOICES AS A LANGUAGE

There's no avoiding Marshall McLuhan's über-classic phrase *The medium is the message*. Media are languages unto themselves, and when you decide to run an ad in a particular medium, you're choosing the conventions of language that go with it. Newspaper ads, for instance, evolved into a predictable combination of headlines, illustrations, and a terse description, traditionally used for retail sales. Magazines adopted the convention of a headline and usually an

173

illustration, with longer-form information or copy. And as "reason why" advertising was popularized, the copy became longer and more elaborate. In time, ambitious magazine ads provided a "good read"—and advertisers hoped to lure readers by, say, telling a story in 750 words. Magazines offered another important benefit: they hung around the house for a month or more. Radio traditionally filled 60 seconds with some 185 words, and the copy for billboards was even more parsimonious. According to an old rule of thumb, billboards had to tell their story in seven words or fewer. I stress that these are conventions, not rules: in fact, they're meant to be broken, often producing spectacular results.

Here are but two of so many great examples: in London, a chocolatier called Thornton's erected a street-level billboard made of real chocolate as an Easter promotion. It lasted three hours. The buzz (sugar-induced and otherwise) lasted much longer. Elsewhere, a billboard just above a sidewalk featured a large, three-dimensional lightbulb and a small logo in the corner for the *Economist.* A sensor lit up the bulb each time someone walked beneath it.

Expect no impartiality here. Radio is, was, and will always remain my first love among media.

These conventional "languages" have been built on the perceived strengths and weaknesses of each medium. Newspaper is usually regarded as an information medium, good for dispensing details on relatively short notice. Magazines are regarded as less immediate but often more stylish, their themes more special-ized and their readers less time stressed. Radio is the most personal, the most intimate of media, offering the triple-whammy of the human voice, music, and the vastly superior imagery of the listener's imagination. Billboards and outdoor ads can inspire through a single, brief, strik-ing idea. Television, for its first half-century at least, was the medium best able to generate water cooler talk. It is traditionally considered a high-impact, "top of mind" (a.k.a. "in your face") medium, and it's more expensive. Just being on TV gives an advertiser an air of importance. Understanding the language of each medium (or not) has

174

resulted in the mightiest triumphs and nastiest belly flops of marketing.

Even within a given medium, context is king. Scheduling an ad during the Super Bowl trumpets a message about a brand long before the spot airs; it implies big production values and shows that the advertiser swims among the biggest of fish. But with great media power comes great responsibility: audiences expect high production values and superior entertainment from Super Bowl ads. These commercials are critiqued, dissected, and reviewed by both the press and viewers, sometimes even before they reach the air. An impressive broadcast campaign or expensive magazine ad can imbue a brand with credibility as quickly as a fading, photocopied flyer ("Earn $500 a week at home!") lashed to a corner lamppost with packing tape screams "small time."

Consider the range of choices in print media and what they say about advertisers. On the "ordinary" end, household flyers have become the domain of ads from local merchants and chain stores, while a full page in *Vanity Fair*, well, your photo shoot will probably cost many times the entire budget of most ads in household flyers. And that's before you pay for the space in the magazine. But a *Vanity Fair* ad says you are big, important, part of the "in" crowd, and fashion savvy. Just *being* in VF says you're hip—never mind that you'll probably be one of fifty-plus pages of ads that run before the editorial begins. The key is that the *Vanity Fair* brand is about being *exclusive*, a cachet that rubs off on its advertisers. Different media, with their hierarchies, speak volumes about the advertisers who buy them. But the perennial king of the marketing jungle—television—doesn't roar quite as loud as it once did.

> It's a rookie mistake among marketers to try to "convert" a detailed print ad to radio—or to "translate" some TV ads to print, where the nuance of an actor's voice and performance are lost.

> In his hilarious book *How to Lose Friends and Alienate People*, Toby Young describes how he once tried, in vain, to get into the prestigious *Vanity Fair* Oscar party: and he *worked* for them.

A strong sign of television's slow fall from media supremacy came in 2005, when I was honoured to represent Canada on the first-ever Radio Lions jury. There we were told of two interesting trends: that entries in the TV ad category were down and that entries for the "Cyber Lions" category—that's for online marketing—were up. To put this in perspective, the Cannes Lions International Advertising Festival was founded on television and film in 1959, and those two media have been the flagships ever since. Until now.

> Three things I'd like you to know about Cannes: (1) Wow, it's humid; (2) Wow, there are a lot of naked octogenarians; and (3) Wow, my hotel charged me 10 euros just to *sit* by the pool.

To register what that means in my business, consider this: a generation ago, television was the top ad medium, and a major brand wouldn't dare exclude it from their media buy. Today, major brands are shifting their annual marketing budgets out of TV. Billboards, too, have lost the status they once enjoyed and are coming to be regarded as the "smokers" among advertisers—reviled, marginalized, and in some jurisdictions, restricted or even banned. Yet no major brand can afford *not* to have a website. The shift has begun.

STRANGE NEW TONGUES: STRANGE NEW MEDIA

As marketers discover new forms of ad media, they quickly learn—as they're still learning on the Internet—that each one has a language of its own. Take *ambient media*, for instance. This substrain of guerrilla marketing (see Chapter 7) is fast rewriting the language of persuasion. Flying into some major airports a few years back, you couldn't have missed the ads on the grass beside the runway as you were about to land. "Hey, you in the window seat," it read. "Bored? Uncomfortable? Next time, fly Virgin." Marketers working for the *Economist* came up with a brilliant idea (in addition to their billboard lightbulb campaign): they put ads on buses—not on the sides but right on top, with the headline, "Hello to our readers in high office." They reasoned that

176

many of their readers would have earned cushy, windowed offices in the upper floors of downtown buildings, and that those execs would appreciate the humour when they looked down.

When BMW re-launched the Mini in 2001, ambient campaigns effectively leveraged the oddball appearance of the tiny car. In some cities, a Mini was installed on top of an SUV, which would drive along city streets with a sign reading, "What are you doing for fun this weekend?" A Canadian campaign enclosed a Mini in a cage on a sidewalk, with a sign reading, "Do Not Feed the Mini."

In another ambient ad, a paint brand created a sign in the shape of a giant paint swatch, and through its empty panels pedestrians saw the colours of the sky beyond. A fitness company rigged the horizontal grip bars in city buses to resemble barbells. A cellular network provider's giant billboard over a downtown building said, "Hate dropped"—and part of the sign bearing the word "calls?" was embedded in the sidewalk below, as though it had crashed down. In another campaign, most of the white stripes in one downtown crosswalk were dirty, but one was brilliantly white, and it bore the image of the detergent icon Mr. Clean. A "quit smoking" product on the back panel of a bus showed a man's face positioned so the bus exhaust seemed to be coming out of his mouth. In another campaign, small crosses of yellow caution tape were placed around cracks in brick buildings and potential burrows in sidewalks and openings in walls, and the tape was emblazoned with the name and number of an exterminator. In yet another dramatic display, a giant razor rested well back in a field, blade down, against a billboard, which was blank except for the razor's brand name in a corner. A long, even swath of close-cut grass led right up to the blade.

At its best, ambient advertising is creative and eye catching, conveying a loud, clear message about a brand. The downside is that messages like these fill what used to be ad-free spaces and contribute conspicuously to ad clutter.

177

There's a story about Alfred Hitchcock that provides a great example of how to leave the circle incomplete. In his early days, Hitchcock made a living drawing caption cards for silent pictures. Legend has it that once, when charged to write a caption about a man cheating on his wife, he simply drew a candle burning at both ends.

I'm a firm believer in not completing the circle, in letting the listener place the last piece of the puzzle. Or as ad great Howard Gossage used to say, "When baiting the trap, don't forget to leave room for the mouse." Gossage wasn't talking about entrapping someone; he was talking about storytelling. Following this principle, ambient media can be both simple and memorable. For instance, when you receive a rubberized business card for a personal trainer, readable only when you grasp one hand on each side and stretch it, you're no longer just an audience: you become an active participant in the ad, you've just had a "conversation" with a brand. Great ambient ads are the buskers and performance artists of marketing, inspiring and entertaining. The "how" of their messages routinely trumps the "what." Stretching that business card creates a more interesting and memorable connection with the personal trainer's brand than the information printed on it.

THE TAP PROJECT: THE LANGUAGE OF ACTION

The language of persuasion has expanded beyond words, images, and icons; beyond the tone of a message; and beyond non-traditional methods like ambient advertising. Ideas themselves have become a new language of persuasion, as New York learned from the unorthodox marketing minds of Droga5.

In 2006, when *Esquire* magazine chose to consider Dave Droga for its "Best and Brightest" issue, they asked him to strut his stuff: conceive a campaign that would demonstrate what he and his company were about and what set them apart. That's when Droga's team set about creating something meaningful . . . out of nothing. The inspiration would come one night as Droga was served the routine glass of water in a restaurant. As he put it: "I remember thinking, We have to make

178

people aware of the luxury we have and help others who don't have it."
A month later the team returned with a plan: they called it The Tap
Project. In the theoretical jargon of the marketing boardroom, their
goal was to "turn a ubiquitous product into a global brand."

Here's how it worked: on March 22 that year (coinciding with the
United Nations "World Water Day"), participating New York restaurants invited their customers to pay $1 for the tap water normally
served with their meal. One hundred percent of the proceeds were
directed to UNICEF.

To begin at the beginning, The Tap Project was more about spread-
ing an idea virally than advertising or marketing in the traditional
sense. As Droga told *Esquire*, "People tolerate advertising to get to the
content. I don't see why advertising can't become the destination *and*
the content."

So how do you get thousands—millions—excited about an idea,
even a great one? Given that he's helping trash more than a century of
marketing convention, Droga's modus operandi is worth breaking down.

First, the hardest part: *start with a great idea.* Like many such
concepts, Droga's was apparently simple. Water is so universal, so
essential. Everyone can immediately grasp its importance, yet so many
of us can be caught taking it for granted. Twenty percent of the world's
population lacks access to clean drinking water, and every day more
than five thousand children die as a result. Those are terrible figures,
but they are easy to understand.

Second: *recruit leaders.* Rather than standing at street level and
shouting up at people, The Tap Project started at the top, using
UNICEF as a calling card, enticing leading New York restaurants
and high-profile chefs to join up. The Tap Project board and is high-
profile supporters made up a who's who of Gotham, from actors Mary-
Louise Parker and Rosario Dawson to musician-composer Pharrell
Williams, as well as UNICEF goodwill ambassadors Lucy Liu and
Sarah Jessica Parker.

179

On the strength of the idea, and the clout of its celebrity base, the *New York Times* donated a full page for an ad created *pro bono* by Droga5. As simple, clear, and blue as the idea of water, those ads showed water presented as wine in clear bottles labelled "NY Tap," with the simple headline "NOW WITH ADDED KARMA."

As the campaign grew, cities plugged their own names into the ad.

Third: *find a focal point.* This focal point was "World Water Day" (which overflowed into "World Water Week" a year later). Limiting an annual campaign to a finite time period invites people to help, and then in effect gives people permission to disengage until next year. Animal trainers—if you'll pardon the metaphor—call this a "release" command: granting the animal permission to stop obeying a command to sit or stay.

Fourth: *keep it simple.* In the same way that some insist you can fake sincerity, simplicity can end up being quite complicated. So it's often the first casualty when a great idea is being executed. But not in Droga's Tap Project. It was simple and effective: Dine at a participating restaurant and donate $1 to UNICEF for the tap water you're served. That was it.

The first year, nearly three hundred New York restaurants participated, raising enough to provide a year's worth of clean water to children whose need was greatest. Moreover, word spread—as Droga's viral ideas are wont to do. Within a year the campaign had expanded to major cities across the country, and a new who's who (of ad creative this time) donated their time and talent—among them, Goodby, Silverstein & Partners of San Francisco (the agency that created Got Milk?) and Portland's Wieden & Kennedy (the agency behind Nike). Picture the Yankees and the Mets working elbow-to-elbow at a barn raising. The secret to this cooperative network was letting each local agency put its own stamp on their Tap Project work, without a central power (Droga, for instance) overseeing the work.

The goal is for every restaurant worldwide to join the annual cause. Even in its infancy, this campaign was UNICEF's largest in more than a half century (with potential to eclipse its famous Hallowe'en drives). And it's growing fast. The Tap Project trashed generations of advertising convention, which operated on the principle that a campaign's effectiveness is tied to the cost of its media. This is the school of advertising that believed that if they threw enough $20 bills against the wall, eventually it will fall down.

When Abraham Lincoln occupied the White House, the public had access to the building—even to the upper floor where the president lived. As he emerged each morning from his bedroom, Lincoln was besieged by swarms of office-seekers, who filled the halls, day and night, competing for his attention. The more there were, the less attention he could offer them. Today you as a potential consumer get to play Lincoln, running a daily gauntlet of marketers who want just a few moments of your day, and ultimately, to take up lodging in some corner of your mind. Meanwhile, a new breed of communications pioneers, Dave Droga among them, is changing the language and flow of messages. Rather than besieging or pleading, they're inspiring, entertaining, drawing *you* to *them*, and causing ideas to flow like, well, water. Using new media and revolutionary new ideas—in some cases, using ideas *as* a medium—they're rewriting the language of persuasion.

> A popular Lincoln story tells of a time when the president was sick with the pox. "Tell the office-seekers to come and see me," he told an usher, "for now I have something I can give them."

Marketers do not, by nature, take the lead in opinion and attitude, yet they are innovators in effective communication and in the art of persuasion beyond words. When self-help books appear on "dressing for success," using body language, and making yourself memorable in a job interview, they describe techniques advertisers have long since gleaned through years of trial and error and research and testing.

181

THE LANGUAGE OF PERSUASION

In the age of persuasion, there's a distinct scent, and touch and feel, of change in the air.

RICHIE CUNNINGHAM-ITIS

Creative Director Doug Linton told me one of my favourite market research stories: years ago, as Honda was establishing itself in the motorcycle business, it assembled a focus group of motorbike owners and potential buyers and invited them to test Honda's bikes. Then they asked questions: Do you like the design? (Answer: yes.) Does it handle well? Good speed, cornering, and such? (Answers: yes.) Is the price reasonable? (Answer: not bad.) Would you consider buying one? (Answer: No. We like Kawasaki.)

Honda's researchers wrung their hands and paced some floors until they had a brainstorm. That's when they changed the language of the question: If Kawasaki were a celebrity, who would it be? (Answer: Clint Eastwood.)

If Honda motorcycles were a celebrity, who would they be? (Answer: Richie Cunningham of *Happy Days*.)

Bingo. Honda's problem wasn't its product; it was people's perception of its brand. Only clever research could reveal what was ailing Honda: its bikes weren't viewed as *macho*.

THE "ADVERTISING WORKS *BUT NOT ON ME*" MYTH

When I'm introduced to someone at a social gathering and I tell them my profession, I'm amazed at how often I'm told that, yes, advertising works, "but it doesn't work on *me*." From that I infer that the rest of us—the great unwashed who are influenced by ads—must be a pack of weak-willed idiots.

This is denial.

It's based on the false (if imaginative) assumption that advertising has some magical power over the masses.

Think of it thus: you're the customer, seated at a comfy table in a restaurant where you're offered ice water and sourdough rolls. And a menu.

On that menu are all the ad messages you're exposed to in a day. (Granted, given the volume of daily ad clutter, it may run several volumes.) You are at complete liberty to pick and choose, to ask questions or to ignore. Your waiter, meanwhile, might offer a pitch for the day's special, (roast venison and rosemary in a lingonberry reduction). You may have water and rolls; you might opt for the chateaubriand for two. All choices seeming equal, it could be the personality of the waiter that tips the balance.

Did the ads—the menu items and the waiter's pitch—*work* on you? Or did they simply help you choose things you want (or need, depending on how peckish you are)?

Yes, Virginia, advertising works, but only in advocating a given choice or decision. That choice, in the end, is always yours.

Love is of all passions the strongest,
for it attacks simultaneously the head,
the heart and the senses.
LAO TZU

A SENSE OF
PERSUASION

Smell is a potent wizard that transports
you across thousands of miles and all the
years you have lived.
HELLEN KELLER

Considering the long, storied relationship between athletic shoes and smells, the experiment was a natural. In the late 1980s, Dr. Alan R. Hirsch, the self-described "Jacques Cousteau of the nose"—a neurologist studying the ways smells influence retail shopping habits—asked thirty-one shoppers to examine identical pairs of new Nike shoes in identical rooms. The only discernible difference between the two locations was the air: purified air was pumped into one space, while the other was treated with a mixed floral scent. Questionnaires distributed to the shoppers later revealed that 84 percent preferred the shoes in the scented room. What's more, those shoppers estimated the value of the shoes in the scented room at more than $10 above the pair in the unscented room. One famous study concluded that 75 percent of emotions are generated by what people smell and that 99 percent of all those marketing messages churning around you are directed at the eye and ear—an imbalance that advertisers have yet to address.

Sight and sound can also work to contrary purposes. A celebrated example is the first Kennedy-Nixon debate during the presidential campaign of 1960. Nixon had a low, confident voice and smooth oratory, where Kennedy had a high nasal tone and a speaking style better suited to grand, written pieces than to conversational ad libs. Radio listeners favoured Nixon's performance, but visually, Kennedy won. His eyes were calmly fixed on the camera; he was tanned and relaxed from a few days' rest; his crisp, dark suit looked formal and presidential; his expression was kind and winning. Nixon, still recovering from the flu, and from a knee injury, was underweight and pallid and perspired during the broadcast. He refused makeup, which made him appear paler still under the harsh television lights, and his grey suit appeared dull on black-and-white TV. He hadn't learned to see the camera as his audience, just as he had difficulty looking people in the eye. TV viewers gave Kennedy the nod. In this battle of eye versus ear, the eyes had it.

George Lois created an iconic cover for *Esquire* magazine in May 1968, showing Nixon getting makeup applied by four different hands, with the headline "Nixon's last chance. (This time he'd better look right!)."

Food manufacturers and distributors have also known for years that it's vital to appeal to the right senses. That's why free samples in supermarkets increase the likelihood of sales. These aren't just taste tests. They're sensory experiences of sight, touch, smell, and taste. The "tryer" (as a friend's eight-year-old calls them) delivers a bite-sized pitch for the product. The other magical ingredient is time. A sample monopolizes a customer's attention for as many as twenty or thirty seconds. That's gold to a supermarket brand. Procter & Gamble reckons that shoppers make up their minds about most products in just three seconds.

WHERE A BRAND RESIDES

A brand is more than an abstract idea, a slogan, or a logo. It's an experience that appeals to the senses and the emotions. John Wayne's brand is about being tough, honest, and durable but with a soft heart. Switzerland's brand is embodied in chocolate, precise timepieces, and pristine villages amid snow-capped mountains. Albert Einstein's brand is that of a gentle, dishevelled, childlike genius. It doesn't matter whether or not these images are real because brands aren't about what you know; they're about what you feel.

I've sat in on focus groups where male beer drinkers declare their undying love for a particular brand, insisting that others are "crap," yet moments later, they can't identify their beloved brand among others in a labels-off taste test. People attach themselves emotionally to brands, though they often don't realize it. That's especially useful in

187

a product category—such as beer—where differences among major brands can be difficult to discern.

Perhaps you favour a certain breed of dog, breath mint, or automobile on its merits. You may memorize a tangible product benefit: that it has a kids-friendly temperament, that it's specially formulated with chlorophyll and retsin, that its V6 offers 275 pound-feet of torque. In most cases, though, tangibles are translated into emotions before they're stored in the brain. The dog is cute. You have confidence in the breath mint. The vehicle suits your style.

Holdup King Willie Sutton was quoted as saying he robbed banks because "that's where the money is." Willie Sutton probably never uttered the famous line. It's believed that a newspaper reporter put the words in Mr. Sutton's mouth for the sake of a story, after an interview yielded only curt, one-word answers. Likewise, advertisers often forgo arguments and tangibles and set about creating an emotional impression—and they'll use all of your senses to do it. But they can't do that until they've unclenched their fingers from around some ancient marketing assumptions.

STRANDED IN A TYPOGRAPHIC AGE

The modern ad industry was built on print. Ad copywriting was developed in newspapers, flyers, magazines, and posters. So it's not too surprising that today the entire ad trade is too often stranded in a print mentality. Media philosopher Neil Postman called this the "typographic mind," the result of an entire culture conditioned to communicate through the printed word.

Advertising is restlessly exploring new ways of connecting with consumers, yet so much of the industry is stuck in Postman's print mentality. Campaigns most often begin in boardrooms where creative teams are presented with words, in the form of taglines and mission statements. Although great radio ads use the power of characters and the tone and nuances of the human voice, many of the bad ones are

188

little more than print ads read aloud. To avoid this problem, one of the radio giants, Dick Orkin, approaches a campaign by asking the client: "How do you want me to make people *feel?*" Dick isn't just a pretty face.

The business of persuasion was built on print because print is tangible. It allows for pondering, re-reading, and slow reconsiderations. Brands understand the power of written and spoken words and arguments and promises and benefits. And they favour traditional media, whose costs are predictable, and whose audiences can be quantified and measured.

Marketing to the senses isn't logical. Neither is appealing to people's emotions in order to sell them spaghetti sauce. Marketing is such a time-stressed, results-hungry business where advertisers are none too comfortable sailing their brands into the uncharted waters of sensory persuasion. Yet confining a relationship with customers to television and the printed word is like building a romantic relationship on going to the movies and handshakes. A romance is multifaceted, and that includes flowers, chocolates, perfume, walks in the park, promises, and nice dinners. In a world where the competition can easily match your offerings, marketers need to create an experience, an emotional connection.

The move toward sensory advertising is being made ever so cautiously, as centuries-old habits are hard to break. But when advertisers remember those thirty-one shoppers in the scented room, fawning over that pair of shoes, you can just hear the tumblers clicking between their ears.

Or they could take a lesson from Walt Disney. In the fifties, Disney took the brand he'd created through his many animated screen triumphs and translated them into his own world. Disneyland is more than an idea; it's a holistic brand experience with its own music, its own look, and its own sounds and smells. Disney succeeded in creating a place that feels magical; it's safe, high quality, and family appropriate. The attention to detail is relentless, and every aspect faithful

189

to Disney's brand vision. Yet the sensory aspect of the Disney brand experience merely scratched the surface. It would be years before mainstream marketing would take seriously the link between the sensations of colour and music and mood—a science championed a century ago by a quirky Russian composer.

SYNESTHESIA: A NEW/OLD IDEA COMES OF AGE

In 1915 a New York audience was treated to a performance of Alexander Scriabin's Symphony no. 5 in F-sharp Major for piano, organ, chorus, and orchestra (Prometheus, Poem of Fire, opus 60). What they also experienced was a Scriabin innovation: the *clavier à lumières*—a keyboard of lights. Playing various sounds produced lights of corresponding colours: F major, for instance, representing Hell, produced a blood-red light. The composition called for the entire concert hall to be flooded with colours, but in the end Scriabin had to settle for lights projected on a screen.

The Greeks called these sensory relationships *synesthesia*, from the roots *syn*, meaning "union," and *aesthesis*, meaning "sensation." The word is often used to describe an unconscious linking of two or more senses. Some people, for instance, involuntarily assign colours to certain numbers or to days of the week. Others might "see" a year in a three-dimensional shape or link specific colours to different types of sounds.

Tied in with these corresponding sights and sounds are moods. It's no secret that "happy" music is the domain of major keys, while "sad" music tends to reside in minor keys. Synesthesia tends to add a visual element to the mix; the key of D minor, for instance, might be seen as brown or purple and carrying a mood of "melancholy womanliness." Stellar musicians who likely were or are synesthetes include Leonard Bernstein, Franz Liszt, and Tori Amos. Duke Ellington was also among their number; he once said: "I hear a note by one of the fellows in the band and it's one colour. I hear the same note played by someone else and it's a different colour. When I hear sustained musical tones, I see just about the same colours that you do, but I see them in textures. If Harry Carney is playing, D is dark blue burlap. If Johnny Hodges is playing, G becomes light blue satin."

As advertisers come to understand these connections, they are changing the ways they infiltrate your imagination, and none approach your senses more systematically than the marketing minds behind Singapore Airlines.

SINGAPORE AIRLINES: COME SEE, TOUCH, SMELL, TASTE, AND HEAR WITH US

Since the 1970s Singapore Airlines has deviated from the conventional flight plan of airline marketing. They decided not to compete on the basis of the traditional *unique selling proposition* (or USP—a marketing term for that one special something that distinguishes a brand from all others). They chose not to promise more flights or more comfort or better economy. Instead, they set about building a flying experience.

First, the airline personified its brand with the "Singapore Girl," distinguished by a colourful sarong kebaya uniform designed by French couturier Pierre Balmain. The airline's cabin decor uses similar patterns, and the Singapore Girl's makeup was even conceived to mesh with the overall colour scheme. Nowadays, few major marketers this side of the Playboy Mansion would dare market anything by way of "girls," but the icon still thrives. In 1994, the year the Singapore Girl turned twenty-one, she was immortalized with her own wax figure at Madame Tussaud's in London—the first brand figure to be thus distinguished.

Singapore "boys" do exist, though, no, they aren't called that. And they wear light blue business jackets and grey pants.

But that's just the beginning of the experience. Over the years, every aspect of its flights were painstakingly choreographed and the menu carefully chosen to complement the brand; even the captain's in-flight announcements were scripted by its ad agency. Then, in the 1990s, they added a new

191

dimension: "Stefan Floridian Waters," a fragrance created specifically for the Singapore Airlines brand. It was worn by flight attendants and gently infused into the hot towels issued before takeoff. Are customers expected to be conscious of all this? Probably not. But when they next board a Singapore flight, the aroma of that perfume is meant to bring warm, happy memories of all previous Singapore Airlines experiences . . . well . . . wafting back. Working together, the design, the sound of its flight announcements, the "feel" of its fabrics, the taste of its menu, and the on-board fragrance form the "sixth" sense of Singapore Airlines' brand. That's according to the Buddhist meaning of the term, where the sixth sense is related to mind and thought. Which raises a question:

HOW MANY SENSES ARE THERE?

It's a stinky question. Neither marketers nor scientists nor philosophers nor theologians agree on precisely how many senses humans possess. While Buddhists believe there's a sixth sense, biologists, neurologists, and other scientists argue that there are several additional senses, including ones that register heat, cold, pressure, pain, hunger, thirst, balance, and body awareness. Make yourself comfortable. This debate could take awhile. These are the same types who took seventy years to decide that Pluto isn't a planet.

Meanwhile, the issue creates many a new frontier for marketers to explore. Food and restaurant brands can play on your sense of hunger—hence the conventional wisdom that if you do your grocery shopping while hungry you'll buy more food. Cynical insurance and security brands can play on your sense of fear, offering protection from possible threats. Pharmaceutical brands provide relief from the sensation of pain. Others offer to protect you from the sense of embarrassment you may feel if your breath smells bad, your clothes are out of style, or heaven help you, your spouse suffers from ring-around-the-collar.

192

As brands such as Singapore Airlines learn to reach beyond the two-dimensional, typographic world of flat images and words, they are just beginning to understand the powerful possibilities of appealing to the senses.

CHURCHES, BASEBALL, AND DINNER PARTIES

Does this idea of sensory experiences seem familiar? It ought to. Religious groups—notably, the Roman Catholic Church—have practised it for centuries. The world's great cathedrals are literally works of art, designed by some of history's greatest creative minds, their interiors adorned with frescoes, sculptures, and paintings by the masters. Sanctuaries are acoustically designed to accentuate the human voice, and spectacular organs are installed specifically to suit the space. Walking in, a parishioner is struck by the visual splendour; the smell of old wood; and the unique, sweetish odour of incense. Then there's the tactile sensation of the pews and "kneelers," the soft rests where parishioners kneel and pray. There's the taste of wafer and wine during communion. A televised mass can capture only a fraction of this holistic "brand" experience.

Speaking of religion, Hollywood has been fond of worshipping baseball, whose divine properties are rooted in a similar combination of sensory inputs. In *Field of Dreams*, the ghost of Shoeless Joe Jackson, played by Ray Liotta, waxes nostalgic about the spiritual ache caused by the smell of a leather and grass, the sounds and sensations of train travel, the ornate trappings of downtown hotels, and the roar of the crowd. In literature, it was the sensation of a familiar smell— that of a biscuit dipped in tea—that caused novelist Marcel Proust to pour forth his seven-volume epic *Remembrance of Things Past*.

When you play a sport, visit a country, or even attend a dinner party, a number of sensations are combined to form one memorable experience. At my house, when guests arrive for dinner, you can bet my family has slaved for hours to make our home look "normal"—meaning

193

that it's been scrubbed and tidied, with flowers and coffee table books strategically placed and showing no signs that it's actually inhabited by humans. The air is filled with the scent of various perfumes, aftershaves, breath mints, scented candles, the smell of dinner cooking. You feel the soft fabric of the couch, the wineglass in your hand, and the warmth of the fire. You taste the crab puffs and crudités, dinner, dessert, and maybe some brandy. Now sit tight, and I'll call you a cab.

A vivid, sensory-rich experience can also stem from a simple camping trip. What could evoke stronger memories than forsaking a roof, floor, and windows for the sounds of a breeze whisking through the leaves and the crackling of a campfire, the feel of a sleeping bag, the smell of the woods, the smoke, the taste of s'mores, and the tingle down your spine at 2 a.m. when you hear some scavenging quadruped playing tetherball with the garbage bag you tied to a branch before bed. Add the smoky smell of your clothes on the way home.

You get the idea. Marketers aren't inventing the multisensory experience; they're simply tapping into the powerful emotions and memories they stir, going back thousands of years. A simple whiff of perfume on an elevator can send you reeling back through time to when you were on a date with a certain girl in a Plymouth Scamp in 1976, and a multitude of associations like that are filed in your mind. During the relatively recent age of persuasion, some marketers are labouring to unlock the secrets of triggering those associations, while others have already lodged themselves in our imaginations. Their ads and the products that go with them can bring back memories with a single sound— or in the case of Kellogg's, an orchestrated series of noises.

SNAP, CRACKLE, AND POP

194   Where's the logic in selling a breakfast cereal on the strength of "snap, crackle, and pop"? Kellogg's Rice Krispies (known to Australians as "Kellogg's Rice *Bubbles*") were launched in 1928, just as network radio

swept across North America. Advertisers seized upon the cereal's most conspicuous attribute: the distinct sounds it makes when mixed with milk. It was a natural audio device for radio and easily translated into print with the characters Snap, Crackle, and Pop, as originally created by children's illustrator Vernon Grant. A 1930s print ad interpreted the sounds as meaning "Listen! Get Hungry!," adding, "And it's a joy to see children heed this appeal."

There's something deliciously proactive about the Rice Krispies campaign. What if Kellogg's hadn't seized on the distinctive sound as a marketing tool? It's entirely possible that a noisy cereal might have been considered somehow flawed. Yet Kellogg's effectively converted this potential problem into a strength. In fact, consumers consider Rice Krispies to be stale if they *don't* snap, crackle, and pop.

As a matter of fact, Kellogg's has spent years honing the texture and crunch of its cereals in pursuit of the ideal sensory combination. According to Martin Lindstrom, author of *BRAND sense: Build Powerful Brands through Touch, Taste, Smell, Sight and Sound*, Kellogg's has gone so far as to have a Danish laboratory specializing in breakfast cereal crunch—yeah, I laughed too—develop a distinctive crunch and appearance to distinguish Rice Krispies from knock-off brands. In the end, the cereal maker has created a brand that works with the movement of broadcast and the static nature of print. All told, that may be one reason the brand has endured for over eighty years.

SMELL IT LIKE BECKHAM

If food and dry-goods makers and airlines use sounds and sights and smells and touch and taste to sell their brands, what does a fragrance brand do? Selling a specific scent—such as good ol'-fashioned lavender or "fresh surf" or lilac—might help sell deodorants, but it's not enough to inspire brand loyalty in the rough-and-tumble (if sweet-smelling) personal fragrance category. There, emotion is the persuasive currency of choice.

In January 2003, Céline Dion launched her own fragrance line in cahoots with Coty Inc., a New York–based fragrance and cosmetics firm. What exactly does Céline Dion's brand smell like? If you're prepared to roll up your sleeves and do some serious digging, you'll learn that her fragrance, "Enchanting" (as opposed to its sister fragrance, "Belong"), is composed of the scents of icy pear, crisp apple, freesia, plum, mimosa, transparent jasmine, rose, orris, muguet, violet, amber, and musk. Few can imagine, based on that list, what the fragrance actually smells like. Yet most have a strong impression of Ms. Dion. By translating her formidable celebrity brand into a perfume, Coty Inc. is using emotional shorthand with its shoppers, who are informed that "Like the artist herself, it speaks directly to the heart . . . Romantic notes blend with memorable bouquets, stirring palpable emotions." In case you were wondering, that is what Céline Dion smells like.

Major fragrance lines don't sell scents. They sell emotion and ideas, so many of which are tied to celebrity brands. Your dad might have splashed on Aqua Velva or Hai Karate, but this generation can "wear" Jennifer Lopez, Isabella Rossellini, Beyoncé, Britney Spears, and Shania Twain. And Coty launched a David Beckham brand in the late spring of 2006, just in time for both Father's Day and the World Cup.

> David Beckham, just so you know, is all about Italian bergamot and grapefruit, with a heart of herbaceous star anis, cardamom, and red pimento— and a bottom of rich Haiti vetyver, patchouli, and white amber, exuding confidence, masculinity, and glamour.

These fragrances aren't just a cross-promotion between a fragrance company and a celebrity brand—though they are that too. They allow customers to make a statement about who they are. When you "wear" Vera Wang or the Olsen Twins or, yes, even Donald Trump, you're branding yourself. And if you don't find a celebrity fit, you can always wear the branded scents of Adidas, Desperate Housewives, or Chupa Chups.

196

VANILLA ON A COOKIE SHEET

There's an old real estate trick for the day of an open house: bake bread. Or better yet, cookies, which potential customers can enjoy while inspecting your curling trophies. Some simmer potpourri on the stove or simply splash a few drops of vanilla on a cookie sheet in a slow oven or even dab some on selected lightbulbs. In time, your home will fill with an aroma that suggests fresh baking. Mmm. Comfort. Family. Grandma in her apron.

Retail stores also understand the importance of scent as a calling card. Many pay thousands for systems that spray specially tailored scents in the air, and though the results are anecdotal, they're impressive. In the early nineties, the *New York Times* reported that when environmental psychologist Dr. Susan Knasko introduced a scent into a Philadelphia jewellery store, customers lingered, on average, for several seconds longer. As we learned from supermarket samples, that extra time can easily be translated into sales.

The report adds, however, that these few extra seconds did not translate into sales. Dr. Knasko suggested that this was because consumers don't purchase jewellery impulsively and that in a store selling cheaper items, there may have been more sales.

The same report cited a case where the aforementioned Dr. Alan Hirsch introduced different scents—their composition evidently being a carefully guarded secret—into different slot machine zones at a Las Vegas casino. One scented zone did about the same business as an unscented area, but in a second scented area, Hirsch reported gambling increased by 45 percent. And the stronger the scent became, the more money people spent. Hirsch's results prompted many salvos of criticism, and Hirsch himself admitted he had no idea why it worked: "Actually, I thought the other odour was going to work too." Some retailers, of course, begin with a natural advantage in aroma marketing. It's impossible to travel in the same postal code as a Cinnabon store without being aware of their distinctive scent. And the smell of a KFC franchise can reach ravenous consumers long before its sign is visible. Of course, those retailers are fully

197

aware of what they're doing. According to Rachel Herz, a psychologist at Brown University, both franchises have explored ways to enhance their natural smell by pumping it out into the air, even in synthetic form, to attract customers' attention. Cinnabon has also extended its brand through cinnamon-flavoured candles in jars capped with a generously large logo.

It's no secret to the hotel business that the way to a consumer's heart is through her nose. Which explains magazine ads for Westin Hotels offering a sample of their signature fragrance, "White Tea." It's a calming scent that characterizes every hotel in their chain. They'll even sell you some for your home, as potpourri or in candle form. A Minnesota company, AromaSys, Inc., markets scents for hotels, casinos, and spas, including a lovely floral-citrus smell for the Miami Marriott Dadeland Hotel, the hope being that a pleasant scent might prompt a pleasant experience and longer stays. Or when you smell that scent while back home in the snow of February, it will induce a warm flood of Miami memories and yearnings to return.

COFFEE AND THE PERFECT MAN

The experiments extend beyond food and the lifestyle environments of hotels. America's Exxon on the Run experimented with injecting a strong coffee smell in the area of its brewing kiosks and reported a sales spike of 55 percent. The Knot Shop, a Chicago retail chain specializing in men's ties, tried and then abandoned an aroma experiment. Experience taught them that a majority of men's ties were purchased by women, so they sought to fill the store with a scent of "the perfect man." Already this sounds like trouble. What does the perfect man smell like? We may never know: in five stores they dispersed the scent of leather, oak, and pipe tobacco with no appreciable change in sales either during the time the scent was used or after the experiment was abandoned.

Despite lofty projections in the 1990s, aroma marketing hasn't overtaken the industry quite as vigorously as some had predicted. The first reason is that its science remains elusive. Research provides boatloads of anecdotes about emotional associations between smells and feelings, such as Dr. Hirsch's assertion that men are sexually aroused by the scents of pumpkin and lavender. (And Dr. Rachel Herz doubts this theory, claiming that smell associations are based on past experiences and not on any inherent association.) The second reason is cost: it could set a hotel back tens of thousands of dollars to pump a customized smell through its corridors, making for a mighty expensive air freshener, especially if there's no hard science tying the scent to happier customers and longer visits.

The third reason is a nagging fear that adding a scent might actually drive customers away. In 1945 producers of the play *The French Touch* couldn't resist an aroma marketing experiment of their own. First, they scented the programs with French perfume. Usherettes were then liberally doused in the same scent. As if that weren't enough, producers arranged to have the same smell blown through the theatre's ventilation system. The audience, overcome with sleep, struggled for the exits as the actors somehow persevered to the curtain call. The hugely successful Got Milk? campaign ran into a similar problem in San Francisco. Milk ads in five bus shelters were covered with adhesive strips, giving off the strong smell of chocolate chip cookies. Strategically, they were designed to give commuters the urge for one of those snacks—and the mandatory glass of milk that goes with it. But complaints poured in to the transit authority (which managed the billboards), with irate commuters saying the strips represented a danger to those prone to asthma and allergic reactions. The removal of the posters was heralded as a triumph for the environmental illness community. And that brings us to the fourth reason why aroma marketing is slow to catch on: retailers and marketers fear it could expose them to lawsuits because of the threat that certain smells could present to customers. For now, most retailers and hotels remain content to fill their spaces with Muzak. It's hard to imagine someone launching a class-action suit against the makers of ambient in-store music, though if anybody launches such a cause, someone, please, put me down for $50.

PORTABILITY

Despite the rapid growth of new media, sight and sound remain the two easiest sensations to convey to a mass audience. That's partly because taste, touch, and smell are difficult, and expensive, to convey to a vast audience. Those samples of snack foods and detergents that are tucked in flyers and dropped in your mailbox appear at great expense to the management. Flyers and card ads with scratch 'n'sniff features are a bit less cumbersome to deliver, but they're still pricey to produce.

At one low ebb in the human story, some wise guy created a means of infusing fragrance samples in magazines. While appreciated by the thrifty who use them to line dresser drawers, they cause many others (me included) to sneeze their way through their favourite publications. Smell is also a hard thing to communicate effectively over great distances. Or it was, at least. A tech outfit called DigiScents has worked for years to find a way to digitize smell, allowing you to, say, pop by your favourite coffee emporium and email the heavenly scent to a friend across the continent. An immediate application might be to enhance gaming experiences, where a whiff of cordite might accompany gunfire or burning rubber would enhance the cyber sensation of a car chase.

CAUTIONARY TALES: ROLLS-ROYCE AND COCA-COLA

Many popular brands practise sensory marketing without being fully aware of it, and this can create some unique marketing problems. For instance, when car fanciers complained to Rolls-Royce that their newer models lacked the *je ne sais quoi* of its older models, they were stumped. The design hadn't undergone any significant changes, and customers couldn't quite place the difference.

200

The problem, the Rolls-Royce people learned, was the smell of the car. As newer materials had replaced old, the Rolls had lost the distinct smell its customers had unconsciously come to love. The older models smelled of woods and leathers and wools, which were later replaced by foams and polymers. So the ever-meticulous folks at Rolls-Royce set about recreating that original sensation. Using their 1965 Silver Cloud as a reference point, they identified eight hundred elements that contributed to the former beloved smell. Hence, just before a new Rolls-Royce leaves the plant, the underside of its seats are treated with a special scent harkening back to the Rolls of old.

The lure of "new car smell" has turned into a real push-me-pull-you for the auto industry. On one side is the near consumer-aphrodisiac effect the scent has on consumers. On the other side is the environmental illness community, puffed up a little from their victory in the San Francisco bus shelter incident, who note that in most cars, the scent consumers adore actually emanates from various paints, adhesives, and sealers. One automotive writer equated the enjoyment customers derive from their whiffs of same to "glue sniffing." To make amends, some Japanese carmakers had vowed to eliminate the smell.

Yet so strong is the emotion connected with "new car smell" that many brands—including Cadillac, Mercedes-Benz, and, yes, Rolls-Royce, have created and patented the scent they add to vehicles as they come off the production line. If you must know, Cadillac calls its scent "Nuance."

Sound is no less important to makers of upscale cars. Mercedes-Benz, for one, has assembled a department—a *department*—to oversee the "sound" their car door makes when it closes. The result is a kind of live-action audio ad for Mercedes, a sound that says "craftsmanship" every time you close the door.

Like Rolls-Royce, Coca-Cola tried an innovation that didn't go over so well with some customers. It was the 1950s, and the company decided to put its famous drink in cans. For most companies, that would not be earth-shattering news, yet the gradual replacement of the original glass Coke bottle would forever change the world's most familiar brand. Sure, Coke tasted the same. But as Lindstrom observed, Coke underestimated—or ignored—the importance of the look and feel of its bottle. That famous contoured bottle was introduced in 1916, when Coke was seeking a unique design to distinguish it from upstart competitors. Today that shape is still recognized worldwide and coveted by collectors. The rarest might cost an eBay buyer several thousand dollars.

After Coke began dropping its glass bottle, so to speak, in favour of cans and plastic containers, surveys showed that consumers believed Coke tasted better from a glass bottle than from a can. And Coke in glass remains a hot commodity in U.S. border states. Some stores in that vicinity are stocked with bottles that found their way across the border from Mexico, where glass remains the real thing. Coca-Cola spokes-folk call this "bottlelegging," and they can't understand why thousands would go to such trouble and expense to drink the exact same product from a bottle instead of a can. Some argue that people are attracted to a different sweetener used in the Mexican product, while others insist the difference really does lie in the tactile quality of the old-style bottle and its role in the Coke brand "experience."

Those new to the marketing business quickly learn an important truth: a product is just a product, but a brand has value. One is a packaged thing that sits on a shelf in a store. The other is an idea—a "feeling" tucked somewhere in your imagination. That is where you keep your own private supermarket, with favourite brands stored neatly up front; brands you don't like stored in dark, distant aisles you'll never visit; and the rest either forgotten or never invited in. This mental shelf space is limited. That, at least, was the view of fifties ad giant Rosser Reeves, who preached the law of displacement: when a consumer finds a new soap she likes, he believed the previous favourite slowly loses its place on the cranial shelf.

202

A new generation of marketers is coming to regard sensory marketing as a means of Krazy-Glueing a brand to a prominent spot in your mind. By appealing to your eyes, ears, touch, nose, and taste, it nestles deep enough in your imagination—goes the theory—not to be dislodged by a competitor who appeals merely to your eyes and ears. But this kind of thinking is new—brand new, if you don't mind my saying so.

The smartest marketers are now learning what churches and revellers and real estate people have known for years and what Alexander Scriabin preached a century ago: that a combination of sensory experiences has a powerful influence on the imagination. So you can count on the world of persuasion to look, sound, feel, taste, and smell a lot different in days to come.

THE CONSPIRACY MYTH

The myth that advertisers conspire to manipulate the unsuspecting public rose to prominence in the 1950s as the Cold War was intensifying, as respectable people rooted (or ratted) out real and imagined communists, and as the word *brainwash* was imported from China. In this climate, James Vicary coined the phrase *subliminal advertising* and claimed that visual messages planted at 1/3000th of a second during a film enticed theatregoers to buy more food and drinks from the concession. Few remember that attempts by others to duplicate those results were fruitless and that Vicary later admitted his "findings" were fabricated. Does subliminal advertising work? I doubt it.

Are there, in the unsavoury alleys of my business, miscreants who slip images of naked women into ice cubes and inject "I buried Paul"—type backwards messages into their audio, hoping to hypnotize you into reaching for your debit card? Maybe. But not on my watch. In some thirty years in the ad business, having dealt with thousands of the world's top ad people, the subjects of subliminal seduction, secret schemes, and mind manipulation have never come up. Not once.

Of course, that's what we *want* you to believe . . .

10

THE HUMAN FACE OF PERSUASION

In general, my children refused to eat anything that hadn't danced on TV.
ERMA BOMBECK

n 1889 Missouri newspapermen Chris Rutt and Charles Underwood purchased the Pearl Milling Company. Milling was a tough, competitive business, but the two entrepreneurs had an edge. They'd invented a new product for time-stressed nineteenth-century housewives: ready-mixed, self-rising pancake flour. Add some water, some milk, and—Bob's your uncle—you'd have pancakes on the grill.

What Rutt and Underwood lacked was a marketing device worthy of their innovation. But one night, when Rutt was attending a vaudeville show, he found inspiration in the form of a blackface minstrel performer who wowed the audience with the popular ditty "Aunt Jemima." Ping! That was it. They had their product and their marketing angle, but just as destiny began to knock, the two went broke. So they sold their mill, their formula, and their marketing idea to fellow miller R.T. Davis, who made some clever additions of his own. He included powdered milk in the pancake mix, which meant all housewives had to do was add water. He also threw in some rice and corn sugar to tweak the flavour.

That's when Davis demonstrated some marketing genius of his own. He found a woman to personify the brand: fifty-nine-year-old Nancy Green, who assumed the identity of Aunt Jemima. Green, born a Kentucky slave, was "discovered" while working as a domestic servant for a Chicago judge. She was the ideal spokesperson: pleasant, outgoing, and confident. And so it was that Green and the new pancake mix came to be launched with considerable fanfare on one of the greatest stages in the world.

The Chicago World's Fair of 1893 introduced the world to George Ferris' enormous wheel, on which people were lifted eighty metres

206

above the ground. Eadweard Muybridge thrilled the crowds by show-ing moving pictures on his zoopraxiscope, and John Philip Sousa's band gave daily concerts, as did ragtime legend Scott Joplin. It was also at this fair that the term *midway* was introduced. And then there were the new brands which first appeared that year in Chicago—great, lasting ones, including Juicy Fruit gum, Shredded Wheat, and Quaker Oats. At one point Milton Hershey came to the fair and was suffi-ciently impressed by a European chocolate maker's display to buy his equipment, allowing the confectioner to add chocolate to his line of caramel treats.

CHICAGO, OZ, AND DISNEYLAND

The Chicago World's Fair was formally known as "The World's Columbian Exhibition," a moniker that marked four centuries and a year from the time Columbus had stumbled upon the Americas in search of a trade route to Asia. The look and feel of the fair's archi-tecture gave it the nickname "the white city," and this (some say) inspired the look of the Emerald City in L. Frank Baum's classic, *The Wizard of Oz.* Among the labourers who helped construct the fair's buildings was Canadian-born Elias Disney, whose son Walt would reflect their look and feel in his iconic theme parks.

Against this backdrop, R.T. Davis introduced the world to Aunt Jemima. Dressed in a costume inspired by the slave era, Nancy Green made pancakes for hours on end, regaling passersby with songs, conversation, and tales of plantation life. The predominantly white audience (many African-Americans were prohibited from attending) literally and figuratively ate it up. Green was a favourite at the fair, receiving a medal and certificate for her appearance, and from that one event, Davis received fifty thousand orders for his pan-cake mix.

207

THE HUMAN FACE OF PERSUASION

The abstract idea of an easy-to-use pancake mix satisfies one hemisphere of the brain but inspires little emotional connection between the shopper and the brand. The true secret ingredient of Aunt Jemima and of so many other brands is the human element: Aunt Jemima herself—a personality with an engaging story who can easily find a cushy place in the consumer's imagination. But like so many other brands, Aunt Jemima's pancake mix also succeeded because of luck and timing: the marketing power of the Chicago World's Fair, creative innovations in brand marketing, and a growing excitement about new consumer brands.

SURROGATE SALESFOLK

"Advertising," wrote the legendary adman Fairfax Cone, "is what you do when you can't go see somebody. That's all it is." Advertising, then, is not a selling tool; it's a surrogate salesperson, representing the genuine article to a wide audience. It doesn't sell shoes, but it tweaks people's curiosity enough to send them to a shoe store where they'll meet a human being. And there the selling begins.

This is why, as "Aunt Jemima" was charming thousands at fairs and exhibitions, Alfred C. Fuller chose to zig, where the marketing world zagged. At the turn of the twentieth century, the Nova Scotia–born entrepreneur plunked down $375 to start a brush-manufacturing company and immediately parted company with the deep thinkers of marketing. Even in those days, marketing was about "big." A company made as much product as possible, advertised on a grand scale, and operated in volume. Fuller chose a different route. In 1906 he advertised all right—but for salespeople, to take his product door to door, literally into people's homes. He believed that a one-on-one sales pitch was the most effective way of convincing people of the merits of his brushes. Rather than spending money on mass media, Fuller invested in people—good old-fashioned, commission-driven sales reps, running on road food and shoe leather. It was a gold mine. By

1919 the Fuller Brush Company was making a million dollars a year. By 1960 it was making $109 million a year.

FAMOUS FULLER BRUSH MEN

Red Skelton's film *The Fuller Brush Man* helped ingrain Fuller's business in popular culture, and he was not the only high-profile personality to connect with the enterprise. Over the years, real-life Fuller Brush men included New York Yankee Joe DiMaggio, *American Bandstand*'s Dick Clark, and actor Dennis Quaid. In 1952, *Time* magazine reported that evangelist-to-be Billy Graham had sold the highest number of Fuller brushes in his area of North Carolina because "he was convinced that there are no finer brushes than Fuller brushes, and his conviction was contagious."

This lesson isn't entirely lost on twenty-first-century marketers. Even today's high-tech online marketing incorporates the low-tech human touch. One major computer company, for example, has streamlined its Internet shopping portal, allowing its thousands of customers to build a custom computer with all its cyber bells and cyber whistles, right to the point where the order is ready to package and ship.

Ah, but there's one more step: before the deal is completed, the customer is to call a number and speak to a customer service rep. The procedure is presented as a safeguard, a final check to make sure the customer is ordering exactly what she wants. And so it probably is, though it serves a vital marketing function as well. The customer service reps are part of a "Profit Recovery Team," whose mission it is to up-sell the consumer, pointing out peripherals, and other extras that might add a few more dollars to the transaction. Automated selling might be easy, convenient, and cost efficient, but in the end, it's the human touch that persuades the most.

209

RADIO AND THE POWER OF THE HUMAN VOICE

The rise of radio in the 1920s altered the business of persuasion because of its reach, immediacy, and popularity, but it also exposed the advertiser-customer relationship to the tone, personality, and nuance of the human voice. Ads were no longer just flat words passively printed in newspapers and magazines; they were presented by human beings in a conversation—albeit one way—in a tone and manner a visitor might use if they were sitting right there at your kitchen table. Many advertisers and their products became household fixtures: Don Wilson for Jell-O desserts, Ernest Chappell for Campbell's Soup, Harlow Wilcox for Autolite, and Pierre André for Ovaltine.

So many top producers have said that 90 percent of directing is casting and in radio, where I live, it's true that casting makes or breaks a commercial. Period. When an actor is right—absolutely right—for a part, you could hear that spot read by a thousand others, and I promise that like a homing pigeon, a boomerang, or a house cat in a Disney picture, you'd return to that one person. Every time. It's more than a question of "voice"; it's about personality, and impressing a particular personality against a script is a defining feature of great radio. Above all, top radio writers come to understand that everyone has a unique sound.

Even Stephen Hawking. Well, actually, *especially* Stephen Hawking. The renowned physicist and mathematician is actually British, yet his voice synthesizer has an American accent. Asked why he continues to use it, Hawking said he hasn't yet found a voice he likes better.

Me, I'm obsessed with the human voice. I am in awe of its ability to soothe, to distress, to lead, and to break your heart. It's magical, it's compelling, it's mysterious, and every human being has been blessed with a sound they can call their own.

BETTY CROCKER, AUNT JEMIMA, AND ELEANOR ROOSEVELT

Brand icon Betty Crocker was invented in 1921 by the Washburn Crosby Company, to give the enterprise a human face and to answer the company's mail. In the early 1920s Betty had her own radio show, *The Betty Crocker Cooking School of the Air,* and by 1945 she was voted the second most famous woman in America—second only to Eleanor Roosevelt. Like Aunt Jemima's, the face of Betty Crocker has been updated over the years; today's version is a computerized amalgam of seventy-five women's faces.

SILLY RABBIT: CARTOON ICONS AREN'T JUST FOR KIDS

It was broadcast that breached the psychological wall between marketers and children, and broadcasters who created characters—including Snap, Crackle, and Pop—as brand ambassadors to young listeners. And by the time television had plucked a new generation of young viewers away from radio, cartoon brand icons were flooding the airwaves, most conspicuously in the breakfast cereal category. The Trix Rabbit ("Silly Rabbit. Trix are for kids!") and Tony the Tiger were products of the 1950s. In the 1960s came Lucky the Leprechaun for Lucky Charms, The Honeycomb Kid, and Captain Crunch. Post launched its TV-stars-cum-cereal icons Sugar Bear and Linus the Lionhearted (whom we met in Chapter 4), and the Flintstones introduced their own cereal line. By then kids were already on a first-name basis with Popsicle Pete and Bazooka Joe, and took safety advice from Smokey the Bear.

When you realize that many famous cartoons—from the Warner Bros./Bugs Bunny classics to *The Flintstones*—were actually created for adult audiences, it's easier to understand why cartoon icons can be used to appeal to adults in advertising. Alka-Seltzer created Speedy, in the shape of one of its tablets, to introduce the famous phrase "Plop,

211

plop, fizz fizz. (Oh, what a relief it is.)," and a White Knight rescued homemakers with Ajax detergent if he could get his horse past the muscle-bound Mr. Clean. The Jolly Green Giant provided the veggies once the Michelin Man got you home.

Cartoon icons are especially useful to advertisers because they can be created to personify the benefit of a brand in a way that few live spokespeople can. When Michelin wanted to convey the idea of "safety" in their tires, they created the Michelin Man to embody that virtue. Over the years, you are trained to make that association automatically, and a shorthand is created: see the chubby Michelin guy; think safe. Animated characters are non-threatening, they hark back to our childhoods, they give us warm feelings, and as imagery, they are infinitely controlled by the advertiser. This is the other necessary element: animated characters make no outrageous contract demands or get their mug shots, front and profile, on the covers of supermarket tabloids. And sometimes animated characters are chosen simply for the creative opportunities they offer. Two wisecracking lizards (Frank and Louis, for Budweiser) give copywriters lots of comic opportunities.

REAL OR NOT REAL?

We know that Aunt Jemima and Betty Crocker are not real, but the advertising world is filled with non-existent brand icons. Here are a few famous ones:

- *Mrs. Olson (Folgers coffee)*. Actress Virginia Christine was no more Scandinavian than Fernando Lamas. The Los Angeles–born actress was a classically trained pianist and soprano and had appeared in such big-screen and TV classics as *High Noon*, *Judgment at Nuremberg*, the original *Invasion of the Body Snatchers*, and *The Adventures of Superman*.
- *Madge the Manicurist (Palmolive dishwashing liquid)*. Shakespearean actress Jan Miner played Madge, the

wise-cracking manicurist who presoaked her client's fingers in dish soap. She also performed the ads in French, German, Danish, and Italian. Miner's association with her alter ego left her virtually uncastable in TV and film (though she did play the mother of Dustin Hoffman's character in Bob Fosse's *Lenny*), but she relished the freedom her ad income gave her to pick and choose stage roles.

- *Cora the Coffee Lady (Maxwell House coffee)* was a late-career role for Wicked Witch of the West actress Margaret Hamilton.
- *Frank Bartles and Ed Jaymes (Bartles & Jaymes wine coolers).* Ever on the front porch, actors David Joseph Rufkahr and Dick Maugg spent six years thanking you "for your support."

Meanwhile an impressive group of major brands were built on the images of real people:

- *Duncan Hines* was an American food critic who sold the rights to his name. The brand was subsequently licensed to Nebraska Consolidated Mills, and in the mid-fifties, Duncan Hines cake mixes were launched.
- *Chef Boyardee* was the late, great, and very real Hector Boiardi. Italian born, he was later a short-order cook in Cleveland. As a restaurateur, he bottled and sold his spaghetti sauce to grateful customers. When he died in the 1980s, Chef Boyardee products were grossing a reported half-billion dollars a year.
- *"Wendy" of Wendy's Restaurants* was a nickname for Melinda Thomas, daughter of Wendy's co-founder Dave Thomas.
- *Sara Lee* was the daughter of Charles Lubin, owner of a chain of bakeries. He named his first product—a cream cheesecake—in her honour. As his company expanded, it adopted her name.

213

THE PROBLEM WITH REAL PEOPLE

One problem with living, breathing brand icons is that they're mortal. The death of Wendy's boss Dave Thomas in 2002 shook the company in two ways. The fast-food giant lost both its corporate leader and its public face. Thomas's onscreen image of non-actor rigidity and aw-shucks likeability, combined with his off-screen reputation as a philanthropist, brought an instant, positive association with the Wendy's brand. But his death brought the long, successful campaign to an abrupt halt.

Other brand icons move on. Victor Kiam enjoyed instant fame in his Remington commercials, telling the story of his wife buying him a shaver: "I was so impressed," he said in many an ad, "I bought the company!" In 1992 Kiam semi-retired, and so ended a highly resonant campaign. By the time Lee Iacocca left Chrysler in the early 1990s, he was seen as the man who almost single-handedly rescued the automaker from ruin. His absence deprived the brand of the warmth and personality it knew in the eighties.

Some brands have even attempted to exhume famous icons. Kentucky Fried Chicken has twice tried to resurrect its long-deceased founder, Colonel Harland Sanders—first with a look-alike actor then as a cartoon character (voiced by veteran character actor Randy Quaid). Both attempts fell flat and were quickly shelved. In 1997 two years after popcorn icon Orville Redenbacher drowned in his condo hot tub, he was resurrected in a live-action TV spot through computer-generated imaging (CGI) and a sound-alike actor was chosen from an audition pool of hundreds. Early reviews ranked the ad "creepy" or "eerie" before someone coined the phrase "Deadenbacher." The campaign was quietly laid to rest.

Actors who portray brand icons present unique perils. One American

> Tougher still for Chrysler, after Iacocca supported a failed hostile takeover of Chrysler in 1995, a court order prohibited him from speaking publicly about the company.

actor who played Ronald McDonald in Canada during the 1980s later denounced the burger chain and its marketing practices. Thornier still was the story of former Marlboro Man actors Wayne McLaren and David McLean. McLaren, a pack-and-a-half-per-day man, was a professional rodeo rider and actor who took modelling jobs between gigs. In the late 1980s, he was diagnosed with lung cancer and launched a public service campaign, trading on his Marlboro connection, smacking tobacco companies for their lifestyle advertising. David McLean appeared in print and television ads as the Marlboro Man during the 1960s and 1970s. A smoker from the age of twelve, he died of cancer in 1995. His widow and son filed a wrongful death suit against Philip Morris.

TOP AD ICONS OF THE TWENTIETH CENTURY

In 2000 *Advertising Age* magazine had ranked the Marlboro Man as the top advertising icon of the twentieth century. Ronald McDonald placed second on the list. Also among the top ten were Betty Crocker and Aunt Jemima.

LONGEVITY IS GOOD, LONGEVITY IS BAD

When the marketing clicks, brand personalities come to feel like old friends or at least old acquaintances. The longer, the better. Jan Miner played Madge the Manicurist for twenty-seven years. The Budweiser Clydesdales have been hauling wagons since the thirties. The Coppertone girl has bared her tan line since 1944. And that pleased-looking chap in the black hat has been selling Quaker Oats since 1877.

But changes in social attitudes create no end of problems for marketers whose brand icons fall out of step with the times. By the 1950s Aunt Jemima, still portrayed in slave-era headgear, became a symbol of racial injustice. So began a series of brand makeovers. By 1968 she had been emancipated. She became thinner and her skin became

215

lighter—a far cry from the coal-black cartoonish caricature of the early twentieth century. The kerchief disappeared, and a white blouse replaced the nineteenth-century print dress. She was given a modern hairstyle and pearl earrings. By the twenty-first century, she would look more like a younger, working grandmother than matronly kitchen help.

It took almost as long for Uncle Ben to make his way from the kitchen to the penthouse. In the spring of 2007, Masterfoods, the division of the Mars empire that had taken over the Uncle Ben's Rice brand, announced that Uncle Ben was changing. A new portrait was revealed, and an Uncle Ben website launched. The man has done all right for himself: he's been trans-formed from "Uncle Ben" to "Ben" and now chairs the board of Uncle Ben's Rice. Mind you, it's a fictitious title for a semi-fictional charac-ter in a nonexistent corporation. The ceremonial gesture didn't cost the company a dime.

> Traditionally, "Uncle" and "Aunt" were honorific titles given older African-Americans by white Southerners, in place of the more formal and more respectful "Mr." and "Mrs."

BRAND ANACHRONISMS

It's often the case that changing tastes and sensibilities drive brand icons off the cultural landscape:

> Another product from a similar mindset, "Nigger Hair Tobacco," was sold in North America in the early twentieth century. Though long since discontinued, its empty tins still surface at auctions and flea markets.

- For more than sixty years, "Darkie" brand toothpaste was among the category leaders in Southeast Asia. Their trade-mark logo was a bulging-eyed, black-face minstrel. Though Colgate Palmolive bought a 50 percent share of the brand's parent company in 1985, it was three years before the name was changed to "Darlie" and the logo altered to look racially ambiguous.

216

- In 1967 the Frito Bandito ran afoul of consumers in a campaign designed to sell Fritos Corn Chips. The cartoon character—voiced by the great Mel Blanc—showed the dishevelled, six-gun-packing, greedy, covetous stereotypical Mexican outlaw. After protests by a group called the Mexican-American Anti-Defamation Committee, the Bandito was cleaned up: his hair was shaved and his teeth were straightened. Only when the Bandito was called out by a U.S. congressional committee investigating ethnic stereotyping on TV was the character retired.
- In the 1970s public pressure forced America's "Sambo Restaurants" to change its name, which conjured up the racist imagery of the English children's book *Little Black Sambo*. Unlike the images in the book (which a century after publication remained on the American Library Association's list of Top 100 challenged books), the restaurant's cartoon icon was a light-skinned child. In 1981 the chain changed the name of its stores in America's Northeast to "No Place Like Sam's." A year later all but the original store in California were closed.
- Pillsbury once marketed a line of "Funny Face" powdered kids' drink mixes using cartoon icons "Injun Orange"—complete with feathers and paint—and "Chinese Cherry," who had slit eyes and buckteeth.

The jury is still out on the Cleveland Indians and the Washington Redskins.

ATHLETES AND ENDORSEMENTS

Some of the most valuable faces in marketing belong to heroes, and nowhere are heroes more ready-made than in the world of sport. Today it's hard to imagine there was ever a time when sports and marketing slept in separate beds: when owners *informed* players of their salaries,

217

when endorsement money really was chump change, and when Nike was a half-remembered answer on a Grade 12 Greek mythology exam. That would all begin to change in the 1920s, at the same time that radio began to revolutionize mass marketing.

It wasn't advertisers—but an athlete—who came a-courtin'. In 1925 American football was agog over one Harold Edward "Red" Grange of Forksville, Pennsylvania. An All-American running back at Illinois State, Grange had led his college team to an undefeated season two years earlier. He achieved the status of legend during a game in October 1924, when he returned the opening kick-off 95 yards for a touchdown, then scored three more touchdowns within the first twelve minutes. When the gun sounded, Grange had scored five touchdowns and covered 402 yards. A nickname was inevitable: his was "The Galloping Ghost."

Among his admirers was entrepreneur C.C. "Cash & Carry" Pyle, a theatre owner and promoter from Champaign, Illinois. While Grange attracted large crowds and almost single-handedly revived the game, Pyle made them pay. In 1925 Grange signed with the Chicago Bears for a minimum $100,000 per season—seventy-five times the average American salary that year. And for Grange and his manager, it was just the beginning. Pyle arranged starring roles for the football player in Hollywood "B" pictures and set up tours of exhibition games, earning him hundreds of thousands of dollars beyond his pro football salary. Pyle became the great alchemist: transforming fan adoration into money. He created a new climate for sports superstars, where showers of adoration mixed with showers of cash and where Babe Ruth could make $80,000 a year. (When told he made more than the president of the United States, Ruth scoffed: "I had a better year.") But Pyle's formula didn't tap the full potential of the star athlete as an advertising front man. That game would play out on a different pitch a few decades later.

By late 1960 Arnold Palmer was on top of the golf world. He had won the U.S. Open and had twice won the Masters. Given that millions studied his grip, it's remarkable that so few seemed to notice the handshake he offered Mark McCormack, who was about to pick up where C.C. Pyle had left off. When McCormack found him, Palmer had a $5,000-a-year deal with a sporting goods firm. Within four decades, with McCormack's help, Palmer's fortune would be estimated at upwards of $200 million. From clothing lines, corporate holdings, branded merchandising, and TV endorsements.

Two years before his famous handshake, Mark McCormack was a promising golfer himself. He'd qualified for the 1958 U.S. Open, but unlike Arnold Palmer, he didn't make the cut. As the very model of a modern sports agent, he pioneered the tactic of refusing to speak first in negotiations. His silence, of course, intimidated others into talking, and the more they talked, the more money they'd shovel into the pockets of McCormack's clients. "Mark the Shark" founded International Management Group (IMG) and, as S.L. Price wrote in *Sports Illustrated*, this king of the eighteen-hour day scheduled playtime with his children and planned casual phone calls months in advance.

By the 1970s *Sports Illustrated* had crowned McCormack the most powerful man in golf. By the 1980s he was known as the most powerful man in tennis. By the turn of the century, they gave up on pigeonholing and declared him simply "the most powerful man in sports." McCormack, more than anyone, built a bridge linking pro athletes to major brand marketers.

There's a good reason why star athletes are so attractive to marketers compared to, say, actors, writers, and artists. Sport is the last great unscripted entertainment left on the planet. It provides real-time spontaneity long since pasteurized out of television (even reality TV); long since removed from popular music, film, and the Internet; and long, long gone from politics. Sport writes its own stories on its own schedule, culminating in moments even the greatest creative mind couldn't conceive. It has a unique ability to produce those "Where were you and what were you doing when . . . ?" events. It drew

219

Canadians together on occasions known simply as "the Henderson goal" and "the Carter homer." Others were wowed by the Fog Bowl, the "Immaculate Reception," Joe Louis defeating Max Schmeling, and the Rocket on—well, *any* night. Sport offers the *chance* of failure, elation, and the unexpected, including once-in-a-lifetime plays that can elevate an athlete from "good" to "god." For marketers, these moments can't be manufactured or bought.

But they can be rented.

SUPERSTARS AND THE BRANDS THAT LOVE THEM

McCormack was instrumental in helping define different classes of athletes. Those who perform amazingly make the news. Those with celebrity appeal make *People* magazine. The rare few who combine those qualities appear in both. They are the superstars, many of them prepared to reign in their chosen sport but not always prepared for life as a sports celebrity. "It's just amazing," mused Wayne Gretzky, "how many companies suddenly want you to hold up their product after you've held up the Stanley Cup."

When *Forbes* magazine published its 2007 list of the twenty-five best-paid athletes, no one was surprised that one Eldrick "Tiger" Woods topped the list. Granted, he has never hoisted the Stanley Cup, though it might require three elite athletes to lift his bank book. According to *Forbes*, Woods made $100 million, just $13 million of which was earned playing golf. The balance came from endorsements and appearance fees, and most of that was from Nike, so personifying Nike Golf has been far more lucrative for Woods than the game itself. And Woods' value to Nike isn't hard to quantify: the shoe company had also signed a contract to pay the golfer some $25 million a year. *Forbes*, meanwhile, puts Nike Golf's annual revenue at $600 million.

Soon after renewing his vows with Nike, Woods signed a deal with PepsiCo to endorse Gatorade, reportedly worth more than $25 million a year. Note the symbiosis: rival sponsors dream of having Tiger Woods endorse their brands; rival golfers dream of attracting such high-end sponsors—especially when that sponsor falls within the coveted "big four" product categories: shoes, cars, a clothing line, or a major soft drink. On the other end, athletes who find themselves hawking kitchen gadgets or endorsing a local plumbing firm might be seen as riding the buses in the bush leagues of persuasion.

Sports superstars—in the marketing sense of the word—are themselves powerful brands, whose influence lasts well beyond their playing careers. Four years after his retirement from basketball (after being gracelessly dumped by the Washington Wizards), Michael Jordan still ranked among the top ten highest-paid athletes, with an income that year topping $31 million. *Forbes* reported that Jordan's Nike brand brought in a half-billion dollars in annual sales. And what of Arnold Palmer, the dean of modern sports marketers? He appeared in the "Top 25" list, with an income of $25 million, none of it from tournaments—he'd retired the year before—but rather from sponsors such as Callaway golf equipment, Rayovac batteries, and Rolex watches.

Marketers have come to understand the bond between star athletes and adoring fans, and they know that attaching themselves to a sports hero can help buy them a place in people's hearts. As for the athletes, whose unscripted, near-superhuman skills help them dominate their game, they must learn to read the script and adopt the role created for them by agents, advertisers, and ultimately the fans if they ever hope to graduate from stardom to nobility.

For their part marketers learn the hard way about the dangers of pinning their brand to dynamic, fragile, and often volatile human beings. The journey from hero to zero is as short as the press conference announcing the positive doping test of soon-to-be-ex–gold medallist Ben Johnson. In an instant an injury might deflate the marketability of a superstar, as it did with Bo Jackson in 1991. And a fast track to the

221

Hall of Fame might be blocked by a betting scandal, as it was with baseball's Pete "Charlie Hustle" Rose.

They, and a long list of others, prove that it's the people who giveth celebrity and the people who taketh it away.

STAR POWER: CELEBRITY ENDORSEMENTS

King Edward VII was called many things, but "huckster" wasn't prominent among them. This despite a print ad circulated in 1910 showing a large portrait of His Majesty, surrounded by an ornate border and the royal crest, beneath the headline "HIS MAJESTY KING EDWARD VII CHOOSES AN ANGELUS PLAYER-PIANO." It reported with great excitement the contents of a telegram—a photo of which was imposed over the monarch's feet. The copy dripped of self-congratulation: "Although this is by no means the first time a King, or member of royalty, has purchased an ANGELUS, nevertheless this most recent royal tribute is doubly impressive and particularly significant. In view of the fact that all the leading piano-players, both American and foreign, are sold in London." It's unlikely that the ad was run with the consent of His Highness. To the impudent rascals of Wilcox and White, makers of Angelus player pianos, it was an irresistible opportunity to cash in on the royal persona and an early-twentieth-century example of the power of the celebrity endorsement.

> I tell my writers always to put the client's name in UPPER CASE in scripts. At one quick glance, this automatically eliminates a client's first question: How many times am I mentioned?

Among the emerging stars of music, film, and stage in the early part of the twentieth century, a caste system of sorts was forged. Low- and mid-level stars and—*pshaw*—radio celebrities might endorse products. But those at a higher level of celebrity—the biggest film stars (the so-called Hollywood Royalty)—placed themselves above the need to hawk products to the masses. Not needing to do endorsements was in itself a sign of prestige.

222

But that imaginary wall separating the "star" classes began to buckle in 1980, when legendary Japanese director Akira Kurosawa took a break from shooting his epic *Kagemusha* to shoot a series of art-house TV ads for Suntory whiskey. The commercials showed him at work behind the camera alongside another legendary director (and *Kagemusha* executive producer) Francis Ford Coppola. The two are then seen poring over production stills while cordially sipping glasses of Suntory. (The experience would, twenty-three years later, inspire Coppola's daughter Sophia to make *Lost in Translation*.)

That campaign seemed to open a door through which Hollywood celebrities, most of whom wouldn't be caught dead in a North American ad, crossed the Pacific to make Japanese ads.

MADE FOR JAPAN: HOLLYWOOD STARS GO ASIAN

In the eighties, at the height of his Rocky-dom, Sylvester Stallone appeared in a Japanese ad for ham. Arnold Schwarzenegger hawked instant noodles. This and other endorsements of products from the Asian archipelago were part of an underground ripple spread through North American culture: it was cool for major film stars to make Japanese commercials. The trend declined some in the nineties, though even the commercially aloof Harrison Ford made ads for Kirin beer and Madonna endorsed Shochu liquor. And in the past few years, big names have returned to Japan, among them Scarlett Johansson, Brad Pitt and Angelina Jolie, and Kiefer Sutherland.

Oddly enough, throughout the eighties, some high-ranking celebrities were already working on ads in North America—anonymously, doing uncredited radio ads and off-camera work on TV commercials. Throughout the 1990s, hundreds of thousands heard but didn't see— and probably didn't recognize—the voices of Demi Moore (for Oscar Mayer or Keds), Lauren Bacall (for Spray 'n' Wash or Fancy Feast cat

223

food), and Michael Douglas or Donald Sutherland selling cars. Ben Kingsley's and Sam Waterston's voices were also for sale. Advertisers who in the 1970s might have sought an actor who sounded "a little like" Gene Hackman could suddenly hire . . . Gene Hackman.

Stars are protective of their own brands. They know what enhances it and what doesn't. That's why stars will refuse to do anything that's not in their brand character. Bob Newhart, for one, has often said, "My character wouldn't do that," and he knows whereof he speaks, with what may be one of the longest-running brands around. Some celebs even refer to their brands in the third person. Take Howie Mandel, for instance. When I was working with him on a car campaign, interviewing him about his career and using his responses as part of the commercial, his answers to my questions were hilariously bizarre. He could see it was throwing me. My first question was: "As a kid, what did you want to be when you grew up?" Howie's answer: "A pair of pants." He then leaned over and said to me, "You know, 'Howie' will never give you a straight answer."

The lure of making Japanese ads helped major celebrities see opportunities to build their brands through advertising, and soon, this attitude spread to North America, where advertisers had come to regard Hollywood agents as the nabobs of "No." I experienced this "thanks but no thanks" approach once, when on a lark, I called to see if Bob Newhart would be willing to voice a campaign I was writing. I could almost hear his agent hold the phone away from his ear, so as not to get advertising cooties. "Mr. Newhart," he informed me, "does not do commercials. Thank you for calling." As far as his agent was concerned, I might as well have been a vacuum cleaner salesman, or worse, a telemarketer.

MY CLOSE, PERSONAL FRIEND, BOB

A decade after being rejected by his agent, I had the joy of directing Bob Newhart in a series of radio ads for Bell Mobility. We used a voice patch—I was in our Toronto studio talking to Bob in a Los Angeles studio: we "met" many times, without ever making visual contact. When Bob appeared at a Toronto benefit, my wife and I were escorted backstage, where I introduced myself. He smiled that familiar smile and we shook hands, and while he was polite, I found him a little standoff-ish and it took me awhile to realize why. He had been a welcome guest in my living room for so many years, but *I* had never spent any time in *his* living room. It demonstrated to me, once again, that the "relation-ship" between a celebrity and an audience flows one way.

Nevertheless, there has been a real shift in the willingness of Hollywood icons to endorse products. To see it, you need simply flip through an edition of *Vanity Fair* magazine. In a single issue, you might find P. Diddy for "I Am King" fragrance, Sean Connery for Louis Vuitton, and Penelope Cruz for L'Oréal. This warming of major celebrities to advertising owes something to the wave of commercialism that swept through the culture during the Reagan years. Here, after all, was an actor who'd hosted *Death Valley Days* and who'd appeared in ads for soap and shirts. Film merchandising dollars were rolling in, and the siren call of advertisers' dollars worked their magic on major celebrities, and perhaps more significantly, on their agents, who came to realize that the more exposure their clients got, the more popular they became.

EXTENDING THE CELEBRITY BRAND

A few years back, my wife and I spent a lovely day touring the Niebaum-Coppola Estate Winery, owned by Francis Ford Coppola. Also on the tour were Maria Shriver and her yet-to-be-governor hubby, Arnold

Schwarzenegger. (Go figure: even celebrities are suckers for the celebrity brand.) Coppola's winery is actually just one of many extensions of the Coppola brand. The name that has graced classic films, a Suntory ad, and several wine labels also appears on packaged pasta, jars of spaghetti sauce, and—wait for it—resorts in Belize and Guatemala.

And Coppola is but one example. Before she was eighteen, Hilary Duff had forged a brand empire, with a TV show, feature films, a recording contract, and her own clothing line. And she has plenty of A-list company: hundreds of celebrities have launched apparel lines of their own, from Wayne Gretzky to P. Diddy, to say nothing of Bono's earth fashions and Janet Jackson's lingerie. But if asked to choose a queen mother of extended celebrity brands, Martha Stewart would get my vote. The woman is a living, breathing brand if ever one existed. With or without its association with the ankle bracelet, her name resonates a feeling of home and hospitality.

Is there any limit to how far a celebrity brand might be leveraged? Former *Mercury* astronaut Frank Borman went on to the presidency of Eastern Airlines, and the list of celebrities-turned-politicians grows each year. Hockey Hall of Fame inductees Red Kelly and Ken Dryden ran successfully for Parliament, and their fellow inductee Frank Mahovlich was appointed to the Senate. South of the border and across the pond, celebrities have also gravitated to politics, including British actor Glenda Jackson, astronaut John Glenn, "B" movie actor Ronald Reagan, and my wine-tour buddy Arnold Schwarzenegger.

BREAKFAST WITH FRANK

During the mid-eighties, I was doing the advertising for Eastern Airlines, and once, while at the Miami head office, I noticed the company president, Frank Borman, having breakfast across from me in the cafeteria. There were two burly bodyguards on each side of him, watching the man eat his cereal. Later, I asked the director of marketing why

> Frank had bodyguards. "If you want to hijack a plane," he said, "you take the plane. If you want to hijack the airline, you take Frank."

The more titanic a brand becomes, the harder it is to steer, and the more it's subject to the currents, eddies, and prevailing winds of public opinion. Celebrity brands are no different. Just as a national brand of spaghetti sauce might have a team to manage it, celebrities surround themselves with an entourage of lawyers, publicists, managers, stylists, astrologers, spiritual advisers, shrinks, bodyguards, and assistants, all charged with protecting, sculpting, maintaining, and repairing the brand. Add to that a threat unique to those in the realms of stardom: an army of reporters, photographers, and gossip press who stand to profit from their successes and especially from their failures.

I have often wondered if a fallen celebrity has more interest to the general public than a squeaky-clean one—like the way an undefeated heavyweight boxer is just boring but a champion who is avenging a loss is fascinating. Rocky Marciano was the only heavyweight star in history to retire undefeated. Yawn. No biopic was ever made about him. But Muhammad Ali, after his loss to Joe Frazier, became a human-interest story of epic proportions.

In all facets of celebrity there lies a fascination, a magnetic drawing card that keeps us watching. That allure is powerful. And power is persuasive.

THE "AD DOESN'T WORK BECAUSE I DON'T REMEMBER THE BRAND" MYTH

When friends discuss ads they like, there's often an aha moment when somebody says, "But can you remember what the ad is for?" Sure enough, people often remember the ad but not the product. Or do they?

I see it this way: so many great ads don't alter opinions; they plant seeds, which you take in willingly, then happily allow them to settle in below your conscious topsoil. For example, suppose you see an ad you enjoy for, say, a brand of frozen pizza. You love, love . . . *love* the ad and describe it in great detail to friends—though you can't remember the brand. But next time you're at the supermarket, staring down at a half-dozen brands of frozen pizza and seeing no discernible difference between them, I'll bet you a nickel your eye will gravitate toward the brand whose ad you loved. The "happy association" between the name of the product and the wonderful commercial could be all it takes to make that brand first among equals in your mind.

But what if it's a really lousy product? You'll remember that too. Hence the marketing axiom "Nothing makes a bad product fail faster than a great ad."

We find that advertising works the
way the grass grows. You can
never see it, but every week you
have to mow the lawn.
ANDY TARSHIS

THE LONG
AND SHORT OF IT

Myself and time
against any two men.
SIR JOHN A. MACDONALD

The Master Lock Company of Milwaukee, Wisconsin, launched a TV ad in July 1998 that quickly sent ripples throughout the advertising and media industries. If you had blinked, you might easily have missed it. The ad was one second long, ever so briefly showing a bullet striking a padlock but not breaking it. The cost of running the ad wasn't disclosed; because broadcasters hadn't run ads that short until then, a rate would have been negotiated specially.

Fans of the TV series *Mythbusters* will know that bullets very rarely destroy padlocks. In one episode they laid waste to the old movie myth about shooting locks off treasure chests and impromptu jail cells. Who knew?

No less astonishing than the ad itself was the positive reaction it received from some factions of the marketing business. Richard Kirshenbaum of the New York ad agency Kirshenbaum Bond & Partners declared, "It's a great idea." Some praised the one-second ad as an antidote to ad-zapping (treating commercial breaks as an opportunity to make a sandwich and/or powder one's nose). A few years later, Honda would introduce a series of five-second ads, which would be lauded as an antidote to the ad-avoidance technology of TiVo. Media companies, of course, love shorter, smaller ads. They're almost always proportionally more expensive than larger ones.

The über-short TV ad, dubbed a "blink," is symptomatic of the trend toward pithier advertising. An industry that once cultivated long, meaningful courtships with prospective customers has turned to the marketing equivalent of speed dating, replacing long-form prose with snappy one-liners. Yet the move to shorter ads is also a symptom of a bigger condition: the rapidly shrinking attention

230

span of a media-saturated, real-time, instant-messaging, fibre-optic-connected, time-stressed society.

Advertisers know that the popular attention span is shrinking and that too many messengers are competing for your attention. The "long-copy" print ads of a generation ago have all but vanished in the wake of "drive-by" advertising, with its pithy lines: *Think Different. Intel Inside. Drivers Wanted. Just Do It.* There may be only a few copywriters in the business trained to write the elegant, engaging long-form ads of what my kids call the "olden days."

The time and space we use for communication are both diminishing. Along with one-second ads come phones and portable gadgets that cram feature films onto 1.5-inch screens. *Reader's Digest* condensed books have given way to talking books, popular with commuters. We can cook meals, surf the web, and chat hands free in this 24/7 age in which comedian Steven Wright reports: "I put instant coffee in the microwave and nearly went back in time."

Among marketers, the siren call of expediency and the hyperactive desire to save a buck are shrinking time and space in the age of persuasion, allowing for less quality time between advertisers and customers.

And that's a problem.

THE MORE YOU TELL, THE MORE YOU SELL

The expression has a 1950s, cigar-smoked, loud-checked-jacket, hankie-in-the-breast-pocket tone to it, but it's true. Salespeople have known for years that more time spent with prospective clients typically increases the chance of making a sale. And the more quality time spent, the more lucrative the transaction is likely to be. One of my favourite books is *You Can Negotiate Anything* by master negotiator Herb Cohen. He's a guy who's called in when major corporations are merging or even in hostage situations; the man could have sold British clothes to Gandhi. A key precept he keeps coming back to is the importance of time.

231

Most ads for retail stores aren't designed to sell products; instead, they're contrived to get you into the store. Once you're there, the salespeople go to work. All smart marketers know that a transaction is not an event; it's a process. At an appliance store, for instance, an experienced sales rep knows that the longer he can keep you in conversation, the better his chance of selling you a stove. Something happens as the minutes pass. He asks you questions, you answer; you ask him questions, he answers. He cracks a joke, you laugh. He offers you a coffee and asks you how you take it. You say one sugar with cream. He says, "Me, too." He casually asks you what you're looking for and when you need it. An important exchange of information takes place. And information is power. The salesman, armed with that information, also becomes less generic and more human. A relationship (however superficial) forms. As the minutes pass, they become an investment made by both sides, and the conversation becomes increasingly difficult to break off. Time is precious, and when it is invested, we are all reluctant to walk away without a dividend.

Did you ever wonder why telemarketers talk for so long without letting you get a word in? Some are so good you've got to believe they take breathing tips from pearl divers. Barely have you uttered a one-syllable acknowledgment that, yes, you are the man-or-woman-of-the-house than they're out of the gate, reciting their script (which cannot possibly contain punctuation), designed to go on and on until it plays you out like a brook trout. Telemarketers know from statistics and experience that the longer you're on the line, the likelier they are to make a sale. Why? I'm neither a telemarketer nor a psychologist, but I'd give you six, two, and even that the power of guilt is involved: *the telemarketer has invested all this time and attention and energy making a case for me to buy something. After all that, she'll be disappointed if I say, "No."*

But as Herb Cohen points out, you can use this to your advantage. Come back to the appliance store with me for a moment. Suppose you've been on the floor with the salesman, chatting about a particular

232

model of refrigerator. You chat for ten minutes . . . twenty . . . a half hour . . . forty minutes. By then, it's hard to say "No" because the salesperson has invested so much time in you. That's exactly why you should walk away. Or at least *start* to walk away. The more time a sales rep spends with you, the more leverage swings over to your side. Why? A salesperson does a quick cost-benefit analysis and calculates how many other sales he may have lost while spending so much time with you. He'll then be extremely reluctant to let you walk away without a sale. The very moment you turn to leave is when a shift of power will occur. The power moves to you, the need for concessions shifts to him, and that moment is the best time to strike a deal.

BORN TO TALK

Civilization—for want of a better word—has long been based on two magic ingredients: talk and time. Some twenty-five hundred years ago, Greek philosophers engaged in rhetoric, a form of speech designed to convey an idea persuasively. Similar techniques were used in thirteenth-century England, when King Henry III summoned local muckety-mucks to form a "Parliament": a place of talk, where representatives of various shires could hash out advice to pass on to the king, which, to no one's surprise, almost always had something to do with taxes.

Parliamentary persuasion has always been vitally linked to the time spent speaking. Where Canada's Parliament now fixes a guideline of ten to fifteen minutes for most speeches, the tradition a century ago was for a major speech to go on for hours. John Diefenbaker, Canada's thirteenth prime minister and one of the country's great populist speakers, loved to tell a story about one David Lafortune, a member of Parliament who, in 1912, spoke for fourteen hours and ten minutes before stopping to say, "I believe I have now laid the foundation for the case I am about to present." That was after the earliest days of Canada's House of Commons, when Liberal leader

233

Edward Blake routinely spoke for five hours at a stretch and when Prime Minister John A. Macdonald spoke five hours during the Pacific Railway scandal.

Politicians south of the forty-ninth parallel during that time were no strangers to protracted oratory. When Abraham Lincoln ran for the U.S. Senate in 1858, he engaged the incumbent, Stephen Douglas, in a series of now-legendary public debates. One October afternoon in Peoria, Douglas spoke for three hours according to a mutually agreed-upon format. When Lincoln's turn came, he noted that it was 5 p.m. and suggested that the crowd pop home for a bite of dinner and then reconvene that evening for another four hours of debate. Today, in stark contrast, it's impossible to imagine a politician speaking—and an audience listening—for more than an hour.

> Lincoln blazed a new trail in rhetoric with his famous Gettysburg Address, which in just over two minutes, helped revive the spirits of a war-ravaged Union. The hapless lug who had to follow Lincoln was Edward Everett, a Unitarian clergyman and statesman, who later told the president: "I should be glad if I could flatter myself that I came as near to the central idea of the occasion, in two hours, as you did in two minutes."

> One of the authors, who will remain nameless (though his initials are "T O'R") is one of those shameless BlackBerry addicts you read about in the Lifestyle pages and in medical journals. It is said his thumbs can crush walnuts.

The Herculean attention spans of those nineteenth-century audiences aside, one reason for the lengthy speeches was this: they fit the medium of the open-air public meeting. Neither candidate had to concern himself with how many pages the text would consume or how much precious airtime they would chew up. Or how their remarks could be made to fit on a BlackBerry. What's more, long speeches suited an era unlike our own, with its predilection for condensing and compacting life experiences.

ADVERTISING DISCOVERS TIME

Despite the circumlocutory habits of the nineteenth century, in the early days of print ads, the conversation between advertisers and prospective customers was terse and formal. "Consumption, surely cured!" declared a box ad in the Regina *Leader*, although there was a longer postscript, which read: "To the Editor: Please inform your readers that I have a positive remedy for the above-named disease!" If consumption wasn't your problem, there was "Burdock Blood Bitters! Acts upon the bowels, liver, kidneys and the blood." Household items were itemized, priced, and synopsized with prehistoric slogans: "White Rose toilet soaps: three cakes for twenty-five cents. The King of Toilet soaps *for the money.*" (Those are my italics: I love the way that little qualifier completely deflates the boast.)

However, in the 1920s, as radio began breaking advertising into tiny increments of time, a copywriter named John Caples revolutionized the persuasive power of print advertising. As a copywriter for the ad agency Ruthrauff & Ryan, Caples was assigned, in 1925, to write a print ad for a musical correspondence program. He took on the task and ran with it—but in an entirely new direction. Caples chose to swim against the current of advertising's high-rent copy style. He fashioned a story around his product: correspondence courses from the U.S. School of Music. The ad incorporated text with line-art drawing beneath the now-famous headline "They Laughed When I Sat Down at the Piano. But When I Started to Play!" A nod first to a great headline: the reader has a good idea of the storyline and is drawn in. But Caples' skill doesn't end there. His text goes on to tell the story of Arthur, who, yes, sits down at the piano at a party, and, yes, people laugh. Ah, but when he started to play . . . Beethoven's *Moonlight Sonata* flowed lovingly from his fictional fingertips. He was the hit of the party. The women wanted to be with him, the men wanted to *be* him (I paraphrase), and he owed it all to the U.S. School of Music.

The story unfolded in one thousand words, parcelled off with five sub-headlines. Consider for a moment that lesser mortals writing the same ad might have crashed clumsily through the front door

235

of the reader's imagination with an opening like: "Want to learn to play music in your spare time?" or "Learn your choice of instrument, at your pace, on your schedule!" Instead, Caples dropped bread crumbs, attracting the reader with a very human story. The key word here is "story" because the power of that ad is in the storytelling, which drew readers in and convinced them to spend precious time with the ad, greatly increasing their chances of retaining its message.

Caples, who served as a U.S. Navy seaman in the First World War and as a Navy commander in the Second World War, became an instructor at Columbia University, wrote several books on advertising, spent much of his career at the firm of Batten, Barton, Durstine & Osborne, Inc., and became one of the great advertising philosophers. In his book *Tested Advertising Methods*, he wrote:

> I have seen one advertisement actually sell not twice as much, not three times as much, but 19½ times as much as another. Both advertisements run in the same publication. Both had photographic illustrations. Both had carefully written copy. The difference was that one used the right appeal, and the other used the wrong appeal.

A new generation of ad copywriters would learn to master the "good read" at the heart of great long-form print ads. David Ogilvy wasn't talking through his fedora when he said, "On the average, five times as many people read the headline as read the body copy. When you have written your headline, you have spent eighty cents out of your dollar." And he's right. Though any great ad writer understands the power of that remaining twenty cents—the body copy.

Within the marketing world, the crown jewel of Ogilvy's legendary works is the print ad for Rolls-Royce we encountered in

236

Chapter One—the one with the famous headline "At 60 miles an hour the loudest noise in this new Rolls-Royce comes from the electric clock." But it's the treasure chest of Rolls-Royce fun facts in the following five hundred words of copy that interest us here. There are thirteen in all, each with its own paragraph. Number 5 reads: "The finished car spends a week in the final test-shop, being finely tuned. Here it is subjected to 98 separate ordeals. For example, the engineers use a *stethoscope* to listen for axle-whine." Number 8 goes like this: "The coachwork is given five coats of primer paint, and hand rubbed between each coat, before *nine* coats of finishing paint go on." And each morsel becomes more delicious. Here's Number 11: "You can get such optional extras as an Espresso coffee-making machine, a bed, hot and cold water for washing, an electric razor or a telephone." The details are jaw dropping, even a half-century later. Ogilvy believed devoutly in the value of homework and information in ad copy, and through his careful research and thoughtful, elegant choice of words he left the reader feeling that she had just spent five very charming minutes with a top-notch salesman.

Doyle Dane Bernbach's famous "Lemon" ad for Volkswagen was just as masterful as the Rolls-Royce pitch—and for the same reason. Yes, the headline "Lemon" was an eye grabber, but it was the 164 words of sterling body copy that lifted the ad over the fence. People don't spend time with curt headlines, and DDB knew it. So they supported their print

There is evidence that the famous headline had been used decades earlier in an ad for the Pierce Arrow. Granted: the copy in the Rolls-Royce ad attributes the line to the editor of a British trade magazine, who might have had the earlier version of the line rattling around in his brain.

This ad by DDB is exceptional not only for its originality but also for the fact that it was self-deprecating. Canadians love self-deprecating humour and respond to it in advertising. Americans, on the other hand, do not as a rule. Whenever I've written self-deprecating ads for U.S. agencies, they've been turned down—which speaks to the vast tribal differences on either side of the forty-ninth parallel.

ads with copy that attached a warm, witty humanity to each brand. Similarly, DDB's ad for Avis, famous as the car rental brand that confessed it was no. 2 (But We Try Harder) featured warm, witty copy beneath the headline "So why go with us?" It read:

> We try harder.
> (When you're not the biggest, you have to.)
> We just can't afford dirty ash-trays. Or half-empty gas tanks. Or worn wipers. Or unwashed cars. Or low tires. Or anything less than seat-adjusters that adjust. Heaters that heat. Defrosters that defrost.
> Obviously the thing we try hardest for is just to be nice. To start you out right with a new car, like a lively, super-torque Ford, and a pleasant smile. To know, say, where to get a good pastrami sandwich in Duluth.
> Why?
> Because we can't afford to take you for granted.
> Go with us next time.
> The line at our counter is shorter.

Again, the writing has become a destination. By tacking 107 lovingly crafted, self-deprecating words onto their familiar catchphrase, Avis won more quality time with its customers, allowing its brand to nestle just a little deeper in their minds.

Great print ads have used hundreds of words to engage millions of readers over the years, for many precious minutes, but in keeping with Caples' legendary piano ad, the long copy always starts off with a "fast," intriguing line. That hook needs to grab the reader as quickly as the average billboard message, which is designed to be written in seven words or less and read in under three seconds. A fantastic Zippo cigarette lighter ad from the early sixties, for instance, contained plenty of well-written copy, but its headline was

238

the eye-catcher: "The amazing story of a Zippo that worked after being taken from the belly of a fish." A series of ads for *Reader's Digest*, in a format designed by John Caples, would lure the reader with a bold headline such as "You can't buy a Congressman for $5000. But you can rent him." The copy would then describe an upcoming *Reader's Digest* article about how a "political action committee" can influence a congressman's vote with a maximum-allowable $5,000 donation. A similar technique was used by a company called Albany Life, which coaxed readers into spending some time answering a brief survey under the headline "Answer these ten questions and work out the date of your own death." The emotional hook was the anxiety adults inevitably feel about their own mortality. All such ads might make a worthy anthology. The time readers spend with them are a richly deserved reward for the advertiser and a testament to a great sense of concept, shrewd marketing strategy, and especially brilliant writing.

During the quarter century I've spent writing ads, including many for print, I've seen the long-form ad rapidly disappear as clients lose confidence in their ability to sequester time-stressed readers for more than a few seconds. As I look over coffee table books of the notable print ads of the past decades, the trend is unmistakable: brief headlines and grabby visuals have displaced elegant prose and storytelling. The art of long, persuasive copywriting is being lost. Especially storytelling.

ONCE UPON A TIME

The power of stories to influence is probably as old as communication itself, and persuasive tales have punctuated every culture through the ages. Once upon a time, for instance, in the kingdom of Persia, lived a mighty king, Schahriar. Enraged to learn of his wife's faithlessness, the king resolved never to trust a woman again. So every day he would take a new bride, and each morning after, the new bride was beheaded. And so it went for three years, until the king married Scheherazade, the beautiful daughter of his top adviser. Knowing what the king planned, Scheherazade ordered a trusted servant to wake her before dawn. She, in turn, woke the king and told him a story. Not just *any* story: a story so compelling the king sat completely transfixed, and just as the tale reached its height of suspense, Scheherazade stopped and promised to finish the story the next night. The next night, of course, she finished the story and told him another, leaving its conclusion to the following day. For a thousand and one nights, Scheherazade spun these tales, including "Aladdin and the Magic Lamp," "Ali Baba and the Forty Thieves," and "The Seven Voyages of Sinbad the Sailor."

That's the power of storytelling. For the king the tales were enthralling and irresistible. For Scheherazade they were life saving. In the age of persuasion, they became the bread and butter of the great agencies of the twentieth century: vehicles to engage, involve, and build relationships with audience members.

Early radio soaps used the power of episodic storytelling—later dubbed the "cliffhanger" (in the days of movie serials). In 1935, for example, Lifebuoy created illustrated print ads around original characters. The only constant was that the soap, invariably, was the hero. Adapting the idea for radio, Lifebuoy created five-minute "mini-dramas"—heart-wrenching sagas of woe, featuring the wise, down-home papa Ethan Whittier. As one episode unfolds, Ethan is telling his wife about his visit with their daughter and her husband in New York City, where he suspects the marriage is in trouble. Is there another woman? No! insists the daughter. Hmmm. Cross off "skirt chasing." Money trouble? Nope, husband Henry is doing just fine on Wall Street. Finally, when the tearful daughter sat on Ethan's knee, just as she did as a child, the ever-perceptive dad puts his nostrils to the problem. As he explained later to his wife:

240

ETHAN: I don't mean nuthin' more
          nor less than just plain B.O. Yup,
          that daughter of ours, she's filled
          her bathroom up with a lot of fancy
          perfume soaps that ain't worth a
          dime-a-dozen, and not a cake of
          Lifebuoy in the place!

> *B.O.* is usually meant to stand for "body odour," though the lab-coat set might insist it stands for "bromhidrosis," the clinical term for the smell of bacteria growing on the body.

Ain't that the way? One minute he's bouncing you on his knee, and next thing you know, B.O. is wreaking—or "reeking"—havoc on your marriage.

Even in the very limited context of a broadcast ad, storytelling is a potent tool. Now and then, great "storytelling" ads even imprint themselves on an entire culture. No kidding: in Great Britain, a 1980s ad for the Yellow Pages did just that. It told the story of an older, frail but gentle man searching in one bookstore after another, in vain, for a copy of *Fly Fishing* by J.R. Hartley. He visits store after store in hopes of finding the book. But not one shop carries it. He then returns home to his daughter, where she senses his disappointment and his weariness. She sits him down and steers him to the Yellow Pages. Within moments the gentleman is on the phone to a bookseller who, to his joy, *does* have a copy. Then the twist. Into the phone he says, "My name? J.R. Hartley." *He's* the author. The ad went for heartwarming, rather than funny, and the spot won an enormous cult following in Britain, to the point where "My name? J.R. Hartley" became a popular catchphrase. It gets better: today there actually is a book called *Fly Fishing* by J.R. Hartley. It was published after the ad appeared: the author used a pseudonym to cash in on the popularity of the commercial. Life sometimes imitates ads.

> Actor Norman Lumsden, who played the elderly man and who actually took up fly fishing several years after making the ad, died in 2001, at the age of ninety-five.

For its Seventy-Fifth Anniversary, Canadian Tire opted for some storytelling of its own, creating an infectious TV ad called "Bicycle." Bathed in Canadiana and heritage, the commercial features an older-sounding man narrating the story of his boyhood on the farm and his dream of owning the shiny new red bike he saw in a Canadian Tire catalogue. The art direction was beautiful and simple, and the voiceover—a W.O. Mitchell homage—blanketed the ad in nostalgia. When the boy seems ready to give up on his dream, his father surprises him with the shiny new bike. It's a simple, three-beat story: Boy wants bike. Boy loses hope. Boy gets bike. "Boy, what I'd give," concludes the voiceover, "to have seen my face that day." What made it an especially effective bit of storytelling is the fact that it isn't about seventy-five years of Canadian Tire. It's about the part Canadian Tire has played in the lives of Canadians. Viewers can relate because so many of them have childhood memories of flipping through a Canadian Tire catalogue. This helps explain why I always ask new clients about their "brand story." I want to know the tale they've been weaving as a company to this point in time. I want to get a sense of the tonality, the history of the brand over the years, the quality of their storytelling. Because a brand is a kind of character, and every character has a story. And stories are irresistible.

In 1969 Thomas Murray of the ad agency Campbell-Ewald wrote an incredible print ad for client North American Rockwell. The company was a manufacturer of such things as missiles, avionics equipment, semiconductors, and space exploration navigations systems. How do you endear a firm with that product line to the American public? Murray wrote an ad, a long-copy ad, of just under five hundred words. The headline was "America is about to put men on the moon. Please read this before they go." The copy begins:

Perhaps the best way for anyone to try to understand the size of such an undertaking is not for us to list the thousands of problems that had to be overcome, but for you to simply go out in your backyard some night, and try to imagine how you'd begin, if it were up to you.

And it concludes with:

> We ask you, in the days ahead, as we wait for the big one to begin, to understand this fantastic feat for what it is and to put it in the proper perspective, a triumph of men, of individuals, of truly great human beings. For our touchdown on the moon will not be the product of magic, but the gift of men.

It was more than corporate branding; it was master storytelling. It captured the momentous occasion that was about to occur and it perfectly communicated Rockwell's part in the incredible feat without once having to mention a laundry list of the company's contributions. As a matter of fact, Rockwell's only presence was a logo at the bottom of the print ad. Not only did the general public respond to that piece of writing with letters and requests for reprints; the ad was also read into the Congressional Record on July 15, 1969, the day before the moon landing.

It is widely known in our industry that people who have already purchased a high-ticket item such as a car are among those most likely to read car ads because they are looking for reassurance that they made the right decision. The ad acts as a balm for that slight post-spend dip in enthusiasm, ultimately arming them as roving emissaries for the product.

THE MAN BEHIND THE CURTAIN

There's a lovely story about journalist and writer L. Frank Baum: one evening in his Chicago home, he was telling a story to a group of children, including his own four sons. He spun a tale of a Kansas farm girl named Dorothy, whose house was caught in a cyclone,

243

touching down in a faraway land. When one of the children asked the name of that strange country, Baum looked about the room for inspiration. Then he spotted a drawer on a filing cabinet labelled "O-Z." "Why, Dorothy landed in OZ," he explained. Of course, Baum didn't say he'd found the name on his office furniture. That would have spoiled the moment. Likewise, the Wizard of Oz never wanted anyone to discover him manipulating the machinery that controlled the sound, smoke, and mirrors that sustained the facade of his powerful magic. "Pay no attention to that man behind the curtain!" he bellowed when he was found out. The Wizard didn't want people to notice the inner workings of his brand. But in the age of persuasion, marketers are taking the opposite view: inviting people behind the curtain to see what makes their image tick has become a powerful marketing device.

Since the 1970s there's been an explosion of a whole new genre of storytelling—"behind-the-scenes" accounts of how, for instance, a feature film was made. In fact, these "making of" clips have become a staple in the feature-film industry. Many appear online, tweaking audience interest, even as a movie is being shot. Typically, they surface just before the film is released to theatres, and they are excerpted on entertainment magazine shows such as *Entertainment Tonight*. Some "making of" features have even ranked their own hour of prime-time television. Ultimately, most are tacked onto DVDs as bonus features.

So great is the public appetite for tales of the "man behind the curtain" that "making of" documentaries have spread beyond film, TV, and music to advertising. YouTube is becoming a storehouse of short documentaries about "how we made this commercial." Try searching "making of" and "commercial" on YouTube and you'll see what I mean. Some tell the story of an interesting ad concept. Some tell of shooting a celebrity within an ad—such as Beyoncé for

Emporio Armani Diamonds—or of George Clooney for the Nespresso brand coffee machine. An American Express card documentary shows M. Night Shyamalan making an American Express commercial starring, yes, M. Night Shyamalan.

Many advertisers, like filmmakers, now have two crews on the set: the "A" crew to shoot the commercial and a "B" crew to shoot the "A" crew shooting the commercial. The value of taking the audience behind the camera, and into the minds of writers and art directors and filmmakers, can eclipse that of the ad itself. When these "making of" stories are told well, they feel like mini-dramas, where the marketers and the brand itself become the heroes. If you like them, you find yourself invested in their mission and quietly cheering for their success. Put clinically, these features encourage consumers to spend more time with a marketer—and the more time they spend together, the greater the marketer's chance of gaining a sale.

There's no doubt that the human brain is wired to communicate through stories and has been for centuries. Judeo-Christian tradition is preserved in stories and parables, and Abraham Lincoln used stories to entertain, enlighten, and win people over. Kenneth Burke, the writer and literary theorist, called literature and stories "equipment for living." Balladeers and entertainers such as Harry Chapin and Shel Silverstein carved out great careers for themselves by putting stories to music. There is visceral appeal in those four simple words: "Once Upon a Time." Yet the time available to marketers to tell tales—and for people to hear them—is shrinking. As a result, long-form storytelling is disappearing from print ads, but it's finding new life in broadcast in the form of

Here's one of my favourite Lincoln stories: he used to speak of a client who asked him to bring a suit against a man who owed him $2.50. But the debtor was poor and couldn't pay. Lincoln tried to dissuade his client, but the man insisted. So Lincoln agreed to take on the case and charged the man $10 to resolve the matter. Lincoln kept $5 for himself and gave $5 to the defendant, who paid off his debt and came out $2.50 ahead.

Storytelling remains a staple in broadcast ads. One of my favourites was a five-second radio spot made many years ago, advertising the classified section of a British newspaper. It featured a sobbing woman reading her ad: "Wedding dress. Never worn!" I have always admired how much story was packed into those four words.

branded entertainment and online at sites like YouTube and Metacafe.

THE MTV EFFECT

On Saturday, August 1, 1981, New York's MTV was launched as a platform for music videos—but the idea was not new. The Beatles are actually credited with creating the first music videos. Because their touring schedule was so demanding, they weren't always available to make appearances on, say, *The Ed Sullivan Show* to promote a new song. But they understood how important those appearances were. So they decided to make films of themselves performing the songs and sent them to Ed. Short films for the songs "Paperback Writer" and "Rain" were shot and distributed, making them the first music videos to come into being. Film of Elvis Presley's "Jailhouse Rock" had previously been shown on television, but it was just lifted from the movie. The Beatles' films were made especially for TV.

Those music videos are easy to find online. Watch Paul McCartney closely, and you'll see he has a chipped front tooth that day, the result of a tipsy moped accident.

So MTV wasn't there for the very first videos, but when it did come on the scene, it changed the style of television almost overnight. Its videos and its "host" segments used jittery, oscillating, hand-held cameras, and some videos packed thirty edits into thirty seconds. All of this made for speed-limit storytelling—television with attention deficit disorder—but the fashion caught on and soon set the pace for advertising and film.

But at what cost? For starters, it trained audiences to become impatient with long-form storytelling. According to the *Washington Times*, early research suggests that the intense stimulation of "flash-cut" television might be rewiring the brains of children. One study of

246

2,600 kids aged one to three suggests that children exposed to higher levels of TV are more likely to develop an attention-span deficit by the age of seven. Some scientists argue that attention-deficit problems are genetic and not related to television habits. But others, like those who performed the study of the two-thousand-plus kids, seem to suggest that TV watching plays a big role. Visual broadcasts may be helping rewire young minds, not so much through *Sesame Street* or *Teletubbies* as through the high-intensity TV that children see their parents watching—MTV, for instance. As the *Washington Times* observed, you might need to brace yourself for a new media malady: second-hand TV.

The MTV style, meanwhile, pervades entertainment television, documentaries, feature films, and certainly advertising. In addition to faster edits and pacing, MTV-style music is more intrusive. Hand-held cameras create a sense of constant movement and swaying. As result, a new generation of filmmakers is moving seamlessly from television to advertising to feature films.

MTV'S BRAVE NEW STYLE—WITH TONY AND RIDLEY SCOTT

Brothers Tony and Ridley Scott embody this new MTV production style, and the generation of artists moving seamlessly from advertising to feature films and back again. One of Tony's first big breaks was directing a TV ad for DIM, the French lingerie maker. The MTV influence was evident in his hit 1986 film *Top Gun*. Part of that movie's soundtrack was the song "Danger Zone" by Kenny Loggins, and when it came time to shoot the music video, Tony directed that too. His brother, Ridley, is renowned for directing such feature films as *Alien, Blade Runner, Thelma and Louise,* and *Gladiator.* He also directed *1984,* the landmark TV spot that launched the Apple Macintosh. He'd been a camera operator on thousands of commercials and regarded advertising as his "film school."

ORATORY

Nearly a century after Abe Lincoln and Stephen Douglas logged all those hours debating before the open-air crowds of Illinois, political oratory found new life on the air. In January 1933, barely moments after being sworn into office, Franklin D. Roosevelt was using radio to help find the words a desperate people needed to hear. "First of all let me assert my firm belief," he told thousands at his inauguration and countless more listening at home, "that the only thing we have to fear is fear itself." Barely three weeks later, as a banking crisis loomed, the new president returned to radio, launching the first of his now-famous "fireside chats."

Just as the Vietnam conflict would be dubbed the first war "on TV," the late 1930s begat the first war "on radio." For the first time, leading statesmen were using radio to unify their citizens. In 1941, Roosevelt used his now-undisputed mastery of radio to find the words, the feel, and the tone his people needed to hear: "Yesterday, December 7th, 1941— a date which will live in infamy. . ." On the other side of the Atlantic, Adolph Hitler's rise to power was fuelled in part by his oratory as he sold visions of hope to a berated nation. In Great Britain, Winston Churchill invested a huge amount of his time using radio to rally, fortify, and inspire a nation in very real danger of defeat. His key speeches from the floor of the House of Commons were re-read later for a radio audience (by actor and Churchill sound-alike Norman Shelley, according to some historians). Generations later, fragments of his remarks still resonate—from "We shall never surrender," "The end of the beginning," and "Some chicken! Some neck!," to "This was their finest hour." Churchill held up a mirror to the British people: one that reflected their best qualities and everything they wanted themselves to be. With an actor's gift, he made his speeches sound effortless, yet Churchill greatly valued the time he took with radio listeners,

Roosevelt had earlier dictated the line to a secretary, as "a date which will live in history."

When she returned with the speech typed out, Roosevelt, while busy chatting with someone else, made just one change, crossing out "history" and writing "infamy."

and few outside his immediate circle would know how hard he agonized over the text of his speeches. Hence the comment from one F. E. Smith that "Winston spent the best years of his life preparing his 'impromptu' speeches."

Before radio, only the smallest percentage of a country could actually hear their president or prime minister or king, but by the time Franklin Roosevelt died, there were few in America or in the Western world who hadn't. It wasn't all about oratory; it was about intimacy and time spent with listeners. England's King George VI also knew the importance of this new method of communication and forged a strong bond with his subjects, battling a lifelong stammering problem to speak to them on radio.

Where Roosevelt and Churchill introduced the persuasive power of oratory to radio, twenty years later a former American naval officer named Kennedy would do the same for television. His speeches, many the work of writer-adviser Ted Sorensen, contained perfectly measured oratory that still swirls in the ether today—from "Ask not what your country can do for you . . ." to "There are some who say that Communism is the wave of the future. *Let them come to Berlin.*" A generation later, former actor and TV host Ronald Reagan would build on that lesson, using TV oratory to reach audiences as none had before. When the shuttle *Challenger* exploded, it was Reagan who went on screen to offer the right words, as crafted by speechwriter Peggy Noonan. Borrowing from a sonnet by a Royal Canadian Air Force pilot John Gillespie Magee, he recalled that just that morning the *Challenger* crew had "waved goodbye and slipped the surly bonds of earth to touch the face of God."

There's a trend here: many of the great twentieth-century orators may not have made up their most famous lines. Variations of Churchill's phrase "blood, toil, tears, and sweat" date back to writings of the seventeenth century, and feminist politician Ethel Snowden had used the term *iron curtain* with reference to the Soviet Union in 1920, decades before Churchill made it famous. Antecedent phrases that likely inspired JFK's "Ask not what your country can do for you . . ." date back at least to the late nineteenth century.

Reagan was by all measures a TV president. By the time he was elected, oratory had been compressed and compacted into shorter, punchier pieces. The era of the sound bite had begun.

Today's sound bite is yesterday's oratory left in the dryer too long, shrunken into terse one-liners and made to fit the tiniest news capsules. Walter Cronkite once noted that during the 1968 U.S. presidential election, TV news clips of major candidates averaged 42.3 seconds in length. By 1988—seven years into the MTV era—they were reduced to just 9.8 seconds, and by 1992 they were down to 8.2 seconds. Political persuasion had gone from half-hour fireside chats to six-word buzz phrases.

No wonder "Friends, Romans, Countrymen, lend me your ears!" has given way to George H.W. Bush's "Read my lips: no new taxes." Long before voting began, the major nominees in the 2008 presidential election were packed neatly into one-word synopses: "Maverick" vs. "Change." Steamed away during that reduction were long-term, meaningful relationships between politicians and voters. In a beautifully written (no, the irony is not lost on me) article by adman Maurice Saatchi titled "The Strange Death of Modern Advertising," a new strategy is put forth for the twenty-first century: "One Word Equity." Saatchi argues that under today's bombardment of advertising, only brutally simple ideas break through. They travel lighter, they travel faster. In each category of business, he says, it will only be possible for one brand to own one particular word—and for each word to be owned by only one brand in the sense that the brand and the word are inextricably linked in the consumer's mind. "It is the modern equivalent of the best location on the best street," explains Saatchi, "except the location is in the mind." In this sense, the word *search* is owned by Google. Sony used to own *innovation* but let it go, and now Apple owns it. *Safety* is owned by Volvo. It's a fascinating strategy, but it further underlines the trend toward Exocet-missile brevity. And like a missile, the

250

result is destruction—in this case, the demise of eloquence and persuasion.

I mentioned earlier the longevity of brand icons, from Aunt Jemima to Palmolive's Madge the Manicurist to Mr. Clean. Today plenty of advertisers live on the brand equity amassed by campaigns created many years ago, such as the Budweiser Clydesdales (1933), the Jolly Green Giant (1928), the Columbia Pictures torch lady (1924), Smokey the Bear (1944), and even *Mad* magazine's Alfred E. Neuman (1954). However, many marketers don't dare invest the time necessary to properly court customers and build relationships, although they spend a fortune on campaigns. Instead, campaigns are rarely, if ever, designed for more than a few months at a time. Brands with the courage to spend vast amounts of money on advertising are terrified of investing time. The casualty is the relationship between a brand and a customer: if the pitch is fleeting, so is the loyalty.

Stop for a moment and analyze yourself. Are you as loyal to brands as you once were? I suspect not. And you probably ignore advertisers more now then ever, because the relationship you have with what they are selling is tenuous, built on price and sales, not the value and inherent appreciation of the problem it solves in your life. Most consumers now have a "What have you done for me lately?" response instead of the former "I wouldn't use any other product" attitude. That's the risk: the shorter and more abbreviated we become, the less we as an industry resonate. We become a shot glass of communication, rather than a big round glass of red wine to be savoured. It also feeds the popular refrain that advertising is shallow, meaningless, and just an annoyance. It's calories without any protein.

All the same, there are some bright spots. Take the long-running HBO series *The Sopranos*, for example. We got to know the characters intimately because the storylines played out in such long acts, continuing from one episode to the next, and viewers found themselves dreading the very final episode. They never wanted it to end—because they'd spent real time with characters who had become almost-real people to them.

Imagine feeling that way about a product. I think there once was a time when you did.

THE MYTH OF THE SPONTANEOUS IDEA

As a kid I loved to watch the TV sitcom *Bewitched*. Its co-protagonist Darrin Stephens zipped off each day to work at his ad agency, McMann and Tate, where he'd glad-hand his client, agonize over an easel, and then (late in the second act) in a "eureka" moment, conceive the "big idea" (invariably a slogan). With or without witchcraft.

It's true that great ad campaigns are rife with wonderful, spontaneous ideas, but the real-life process isn't nearly so pretty.

Even the greatest concepts die quickly if they don't fit the brief—the blueprint of the client's objectives. So during a campaign's gestation period, an idea is challenged, tweaked, and second-guessed. It must defeat rival ideas presented to the client, and it has to translate neatly into its intended medium. A great radio concept, for instance, might not work in print. It must run a brutal gauntlet of approvals, tests, and focus groups—both within the ad agency and at the client's head office. To understand this ordeal is to develop a whole new appreciation for those all-too-rare ad campaigns that inspire and delight—and more importantly—work.

I promise you: almost no one this side of Darrin Stephens suddenly comes up with an idea and walks straight into a studio to record it.

A great ad idea is like a sperm swimming alone in hostile territory and facing millions-to-one odds against reaching its destination. To depart from the simile for a brief moment, even the most brilliant ad ideas are likely to be hunted down, bullyragged, beaten up, mutated, and committeed beyond recognition.

All else being equal, my money's on the sperm.

THE WALL OF CYNICISM

12

History will see advertising as one of the real evil things of our time. It is stimulating people constantly to want things, want this, want that.
MALCOLM MUGGERIDGE

Advertising is only evil when it advertises evil things.
DAVID OGILVY

All of us who professionally use the mass media are the shapers of society. We can vulgarize that society. We can brutalize it. Or we can help lift it onto a higher level."
BILL BERNBACH

Duthe Chicago World's Fair of 1893, the thousands who were introduced to Aunt Jemima and electric light and Juicy Fruit Gum and the Ferris wheel couldn't have missed Clark Stanley, a.k.a. "The Rattlesnake King." He was a travelling cowboy who sold a miracle cure-all. His product was snake oil, purportedly from a recipe passed on from a Moki Pueblo medicine man. Before astonished crowds, Clark would reach into a bag and retrieve a rattlesnake, cut it open, and toss it into boiling water. As its fat rose to the top, Stanley skimmed it off and set it aside, calling it "Stanley's Snake Oil."

It was nothing of the kind, and the bottles of elixir Stanley sold had nothing to do with snakes apart from the name on the label. Still, hundreds of rattlesnakes were dispatched at the fair for the sake of spectacle. Advertisements at the time billed Stanley's Snake Oil as a "wonderful pain-destroying compound. The strongest and best liniment known for the cure of all pain and lameness." Evidently, it did not cure hyperbole. The medicine, which was to be taken externally, supposedly healed people of "rheumatism, neuralgia, sciatica, lame back, lumbago, contracted muscles, toothache, sprains, and swellings." But wait—there was more! The remedy was also purported to cure "frost bites, chill blains, bruises, sore throat, and bites of animals, insects and reptiles." Even better, it could be yours for a paltry fifty cents a bottle. And that is why "snake oil" would become a metaphor for a worthless product sold on a mountain of exaggeration.

The "snake oil" era of the late 1800s was a high-water mark in the growth of "patent medicines"—a term that came to refer to remedies sold without prescription, a practice dating back nearly two centuries, when British monarchs began issuing patents for various panaceas.

Over time, "patent medicine" became something of a misnomer, as the term came to refer to concoctions that had *no* patent. This meant that their manufacturers were not required to divulge the products' ingredients. The new medicines were aggressively marketed, with fancy illustrations, designs, and typefaces—and ultimately dubious claims—on their labels to distinguish them from their competitors' wares.

Some popular British brands were shipped across the Atlantic, where they found favour with American colonists. Among them were Turlington's Balsam of Life, Bateman's Pectoral Drops, and Hooper's Female Pills. Following the U.S. Civil War, as railways allowed for mass distribution and the telegraph led to mass marketing, popular new brands sprang up, including such elixirs as Swamp Root Kidney and Liver Medicine, produced by the Kilmer brothers of Binghamton, New York.

It wasn't until 1917 that the U.S. government seized a shipment of a brand of snake oil sold at that time and had it analyzed, only to discover what generations of disillusioned customers must already have suspected: the concoction. It was a mixture of mineral oil, beef fat, *turpentine*, camphor, and red pepper. Lydia Pinkham's formula—meant to be taken internally—was a blend of "black cohosh, life root, unicorn root, pleurisy root, and fenugreek seed" and one magic ingredient: 19 percent alcohol.

The era of patent medicines had peaked long before John E. Kennedy and Albert Lasker had their fateful meeting in Chicago, which led to the foundation on which modern advertising philosophies are built. By then, the like-minded cynics had delivered a blow to advertisers everywhere.

And we're still smarting.

FOOL ME ONCE

In the first years of the twentieth century, as advertising became big business, voices of reason appealed for ethical grounding within the industry. Lying and cheating in advertising "are commercial suicide," wrote author Daniel Starch in 1923. "Dishonesty in advertising destroys not only confidence in advertising, but also in the medium which carries the dishonest advertisement. . . . No one can be ill in a community without endangering others; no advertiser can be dishonest without casting suspicion upon others." In other words, advertisers might compete against each other, but people see them as tethered together. If one sinks, it could drag others under with it.

People were learning to be wary of what they read in newspapers, many of them created to trumpet one political party and disparage others. This skepticism had been fuelled by the 1880s newspaper war between Joseph Pulitzer's *New York World* and William Randolph Hearst's *New York Journal*, which begat the phrase "yellow journalism" (reporting that favoured sensationalism over substance). Case in point: in 1897, when artist Frederick Remington asked Hearst to let him return home from Cuba, insisting there was no war, and his boss reputedly replied, "Please remain. You furnish the pictures and I will furnish the war." U.S. president Theodore Roosevelt lashed out at muckraking journalists who launched outrageous attacks with no basis in fact.

> Both Hearst and Pulitzer ran a cartoon strip featuring a character called "the Yellow Kid." Critics seized on this to refer to the style of both papers as "Yellow Kid journalism," which later became simply "yellow journalism."

When radio introduced the human voice to a mass audience, a very different relationship began, with a greater sense of intimacy. If this led to a sense of trust among listeners, it was to be severely tested by two men. Many today have heard the legend of Orson Welles' *War of the Worlds* broadcast. Relatively few may know of a strikingly similar radio hoax created by Britain's Ronald Knox a

258

dozen years earlier. Knox was a radio pioneer with an unlikely CV. He was a Catholic priest, biblical scholar, evangelist, author of crime fiction, and satirist.

On Saturday, January 16, 1926, in the letter-perfect style already established by announcers of the British Broadcasting Corporation, Knox began routinely announcing cricket results. Then he notified listeners of a labour strike brewing in London's Trafalgar Square. Between bulletins, music was played, and with each announcement the audience was given generous clues that Mr. Knox was having them on:

KNOX: Mr. Poppelberry, the secretary for the national movement for abolishing theatre queues, has been urging the crowd to sack the National Gallery.

Over the next several minutes, the reports became increasingly disturbing, with Knox's cheerful "newsreader" disinterest adding a strange counterpoint:

KNOX: One minute please . . . from reports that have just come to hand, it appears that Theophilus Gootch, who was on his way to this station, has been intercepted by the remnants of the crowd still collected in Trafalgar Square, and is being roasted alive.

Throughout the brief broadcast, Knox cheerfully reported that the houses of Parliament and Big Ben had been demolished with trench mortars, the Savoy Hotel had been blown up, and the minister of traffic had been hanged from a tramway post. He concluded the broadcast with Mr. Poppelberry and his fictitious mob heading his way:

259

KNOX: The more unruly members of the crowd are now approaching the British Broadcasting Company's

London station with a threatening demeanour.
One moment please . . . Mr. Poppelberry, the secretary for the national movement for abolishing
theatre queues, with several other members of the
crowd is now in the waiting room. They are reading copies of the *Radio Times*. Good night everybody . . . good night.

In the hours following the Knox broadcast, Greater London would experience a smaller-scale version of the panic North Americans would feel a dozen years later. Newspapers were late reaching outlying areas, leaving the four-year-old BBC as the main source of information for many. During a few uncertain hours, calls poured into the BBC. There were reports of people fainting. One insistent listener called the Admiralty to demand that the fleet be moved up the Thames to control the mob.

It was a foolhardy satire, given the context of the time. The Russian Revolution less than a decade earlier had left the Western world in jitters. Listeners would have been well aware of the worldwide labour unrest that followed the First World War (including the Winnipeg General Strike of 1919). Few had any reason to imagine that an announcer on the BBC, which brought them news of real events, would be the source of a hoax. The Knox satire had strained the credibility of the new medium.

FOOL ME TWICE

On October 30, 1938, North American listeners were already on edge as war loomed in Europe, and that was the evening Orson Welles presented his mischievously realistic-sounding radio adaptation of H.G. Wells' *War of the Worlds*. At 8 p.m., with the dishes done, some six million tuned in to hear Welles' erudite *Mercury Theatre*, many of them no doubt already familiar with Welles in his role as

260

Lamont Cranston in *The Shadow*. But Cranston would soon be far from their minds as they were drawn into the vortex of Welles' you-are-there account of a failed Martian invasion of Earth, starting at the initial landing site of Grover's Mill, New Jersey.

Mercury Theatre wasn't the most popular radio show at that hour. As Welles' broadcast began, some thirty million listeners had tuned in to Sunday night's top offering: NBC's *Chase & Sanborn Hour,* with Don Ameche, Edgar Bergen, and Charlie McCarthy.

While most took the broadcast for what it was—an intriguing radio adaptation of H.G. Wells' story—a surprising number of listeners thought it was genuine news coverage of an alien invasion. It was later claimed that one million of the show's six million listeners believed Martians were invading. And as a result laws were passed prohibiting broadcasters from presenting fiction in the form of live news events. Some thought Welles' innovation might end his career, but the opposite happened. Now that *Mercury Theatre* had exploded its way into the national psyche, it soon attracted a major sponsor—Campbell's Soup—and Welles won a major Hollywood contract.

BOGUS WAR—REAL PANIC

Orson Welles' *War of the Worlds* trick caused some real, distressing fallout:

- Hundreds of nurses and physicians converged on a Newark, New Jersey, hospital to offer their services.
- A man in Pittsburgh discovered his wife in her room, holding a bottle of poison and saying, "I'd rather die this way than that."
- One New Jersey hospital treated fifteen people for shock and hysteria, some requiring sedation.

People would react to Welles' infamous "Martian broadcast" the way they remember being on the business end of any practical joke: some with a laugh and a shrug; some with relief; some with outrage;

261

Let me rise to the defence of my industry for a moment: few outside the business realize how unbelievably difficult it is to create good advertising. As early as 1923, novelist Aldous Huxley wrote: "I have discovered the most exciting, the most arduous literary form of all, the most difficult to master, the most pregnant in curious possibilities. I mean the advertisement . . . It is far easier to write ten passably effective Sonnets . . . than one effective advertisement."

The word *huckster* is likely Danish or Dutch in origin and refers to a street peddler (a.k.a. *hawker*). Originally, the term meant "low" or "stooped" because peddlers were often weighed down by the heavy sacks of goods they carried on their backs.

and nearly all with their trust eroded in what they hear, see and read.

At the same time, radio ads, so many of them clumsily executed and intrusive, had come to be regarded as a growing nuisance. And since radio and the advertising that powered it had saturated popular culture, the annoyance was pervasive. William J. Cameron, director of public relations for the Ford Motor Company, put it this way in 1938: "Never before the advent of radio did advertising have such a golden opportunity to make an ass out of itself. Never before could advertising be so insistent and so unmannerly and so affront its audience." By the 1940s it had become fashionable to call advertising people *hucksters*, a word with a pejorative tone that only increased with the release of the wonderful Clark Gable–Deborah Kerr film *The Hucksters*, based on Frederick Wakeman's novel of the same name.

THE 1/3,000TH-OF-A-SECOND CON JOB

Stop me if you've heard this one:

> Fort Lee, New Jersey, 1957: unsuspecting filmgoers are enjoying *Picnic*, with William Holden and Kim Novak. In the projection room, an important marketing experiment is being staged. Researcher James Vicary has installed a tachistoscope: a machine that can project subliminal images of tiny fractions of a second, far below the person's conscious threshold of perception. Every five

262

seconds, and for a duration of just 1/3000th of a second, Vicary injected two alternating messages: "Drink Coca-Cola" and "Hungry? Eat popcorn." The results were spectacular: Coca-Cola sales jumped 18.1 percent, and popcorn sales jumped 57.8 percent. Vicary dubbed his method "subliminal advertising," the practice of manipulating consumers to make purchases they might not otherwise make. He declared it a "new brand of human perception" and said his device was capable of prompting people to buy something even if they didn't want to.

And if you believe that, I've got a bottle of cure-all I'd like to sell you. Turns out the great "popcorn" experiment was a fraud. Vicary refused to divulge the mechanics of his gizmo and its effect until patents were approved. Meanwhile, he received retainers and consulting fees from ad agencies. But when a motion-picture trade magazine divulged the location of the theatre where the experiment was said to have happened, the manager insisted that no such experiment had been staged in his theatre. When Vicary suggested the new technology would revolutionize television, an engineer at RCA refuted him, insisting that TV technology was incapable of carrying images that brief.

In 1959, not long after the great subliminal "experiment" became a *cause célèbre*, James Vicary dropped off the public's radar. Years later no one in the patent office could find any evidence of an application from Vicary or any reference to a subliminal advertising device. Another researcher, Dr. Henry Link, later duplicated Vicary's experiment and found no evidence that people reacted to the messages. Behavioural studies before and since have confirmed the principle that "zero perception" equals "zero response," meaning subliminal messages have no known effect on human behaviour.

263

It's interesting to note that with Vicary's "discovery"—as with the Knox hoax in the 1920s and the Welles trick in the 1930s—social

The term *brainwashing* is said to have originated a half-century ago, with author and former U.S. State Department worker John Marks. It's derived from a Chinese word, meaning literally "to wash the brain."

The subject of yet another classic film, John Frankenheimer's *The Manchurian Candidate* (1962), with Frank Sinatra.

In my quarter-century in the marketing business, the subject of subliminal advertising has never come up. Not once. Advertising is completely transparent. It is completely upfront in its desire, and the assault is head-on.

conditions were ripe for a conspiracy theory. Vicary's hoax came during the heyday of the Cold War: when "Reds under every bed" and *brainwashing* were popular watchwords. Brainwashing referred to communist mind-control techniques (while the CIA was secretly performing mind-control experiments of its own). Advertising, meanwhile, was enjoying a spectacular postwar surge, and as it was being transformed into a conspicuous cultural force, it also became a ripe target for suspicion.

The irony, of course, is that Vicary's claim—that the multibillion-dollar marketing industry was engaged in massive deceit—was *itself* revealed as bunkum.

THE SIXTIES

Advertising also got the short end of the stick during the "great disillusionment" of the 1960s, when marketing messages came to be perceived as a voice of the Establishment—communications from "The Man," the very one hippies were trying to bring down. Then, just when it seemed that advertising's stock couldn't drop any more, a story leaked about dubious goings-on relating to an advertising photo shoot. A team with the ad agency BBDO New York was trying to get a product shot of Campbell's vegetable soup, but the soup wasn't cooperating: the vegetables, however plentiful, were hiding beneath a tiny, glassy sea of red broth. It looked as if the soup contained no vegetables at all. So the team dropped in some marbles, which raised the vegetables to the top. The stunt resulted in a probe by the U.S. Federal Trade Commission, much to the delight of Campbell's

264

archrivals at the H.J. Heinz Company, who had launched the complaint with the U.S. Federal Trade Commission in the first place.

Advertisers mustn't dare forget Marshall McLuhan's observation that "all advertising advertises advertising." The marble incident (which would have been dubbed "marblegate" had it happened just a few years later) cast a pall on all advertising. And two lessons emerged from the incident that are well worth noting: the first is that Campbell's—and its ad agency—didn't get away with the deception. I believe that few advertisers—if any—do. "If you tell lies about a product, you will be found out," warned David Ogilvy, "either by the Government, which will prosecute you, or by the consumer, who will punish you by not buying your product a second time."

Which leads to lesson 2: I doubt that any discipline this side of national politics is subject to more rigorous checks and balances than advertising—not by governments or industry regulators (who tend to constrict the honest brokers and leave loopholes for transgressors) but by the advertiser's competition. Rival brands watch one another constantly—as Heinz watched Campbell's—tracking their opponents' every move and ready to pounce on anyone foolish enough to cut corners or make a false claim. Blowing the whistle on an adversary can hobble a brand's enemy and give the watchdog competitor a bigger share of the market. As ad giant Leo Burnett said, "Regardless of the moral issue, dishonesty in advertising has proved very unprofitable."

SCRUTINY

There's no evidence that P.T. Barnum ever said, "There's a sucker born every minute," though he was fond of remarking that people liked to be fooled (literally: "humbugged"). And it's true that most people love to lose themselves in movies and books and songs and to allow illusionists and magicians to suspend their belief. But they don't like to be deceived.

Research has turned up some interesting points about our ability

265

to deceive and to detect a lie. According to psychologist Richard Wiseman of England's University of Hertfordshire, people have what he calls a "truth bias"—a natural inclination to believe what they're told. It's especially strong when it involves someone close to us: for instance, when someone says something, their spouse or partner is more likely to believe them than a perfect stranger would.

Advertising enjoys no such intimacy. Quite the opposite: people are constantly on the prowl for fakes and phonies in the age of persuasion. As much as I dislike busting up a good rhyme, I don't believe advertisers can "fake it 'til they make it." Over the past century, savvy consumers have developed a healthy resistance to the hollow sales pitch. Maybe all that snake oil did some good after all.

Further studies have revealed some fascinating differences in people's ability to detect lies in some media as opposed to others. Britain's MegaLab Truth Test of 1994, supervised by Dr. Wiseman, tested some hundred thousand respondents on their ability to spot a fib, using three different media. It worked this way: British broadcaster Sir Robin Day was interviewed twice about his favourite films. In one interview he told the truth, but in the other he lied. The survey revealed that 73 percent of listeners correctly identified the lie when the interviews were broadcast on radio, 64 percent got it right when they were published in a newspaper, and just 52 percent spotted the deception when it was broadcast on television. Pardon me if my radio bias is showing: I love radio for its ability to separate the authentic from the inauthentic.

The eyes can so easily deceive. In another experiment, Dr. Wiseman conducted a mock trial in which all facts and conditions were the same except for one vital component: the appearance of the defendant. Just 25 percent of a mock jury convicted a good-looking man, while 40 percent of another mock jury convicted an ugly man. Score a point to Michael Deaver, whose visually driven imagery of the Reagan presidency brought politics once and for all into the television age.

266

Does this mean that advertisers should flock to television to foist substandard junk on a perception-challenged public? It might work— if and only if

- they can afford to have people buy their product just once,
- sales are made quickly before word of mouth inevitably kills the product, and
- the advertiser doesn't mind rail travel (not the train, mind you; I mean "rail" as in "being ridden out of town on a—").

And where does that leave the Internet? So many online sources are anonymous or dubious. Humanity, warmth, and authenticity are so hard to establish. Jef I. Richards of the University of Texas put it this way: "I believe 'credibility' is one of the biggest issues yet to be addressed by Internet advertisers," adding, "[It] no longer is strictly a brick-and-mortar issue. I can't judge someone by their place of business, when I conduct that business on the Internet. I can't grasp a hand and look into their eyes to judge their veracity."

HUMANIZING THE INTERNET

As social networking sites such as Twitter gain popularity, an interesting trend has emerged. Where in the past, people would post comments under pseudonyms such as "WunderLord" and "Dancing Cow," many are now choosing to sign their real names. This gives comments a potency and personality they lacked when posted anonymously.

AUTHENTICITY, AGAIN

Even brands that strayed from authenticity over the years are finding their way back. By this I mean brands that are built on a strong set of core values; which are conveyed clearly and well understood; and which remain constant.

267

When Nike took on hockey, it brought in the most knowledgeable hockey people and tied itself to the game's elite. Their philosophy, as they get bigger, is to dig deeper and to develop genuine expertise and meaningful ties to a sport and to those who play it. Only by embracing the giants of the game could Nike achieve the authenticity it needed to move, as it has, from a standing start to a place where it can challenge the game's long-established brand giants.

The thread running through the entire age of persuasion is the growth of technology—from Morse code to marketing goods by rail to mass marketing to broadcast to the Internet. In their haste to seize each "advance" in technology, marketers tend to embrace the shortcuts and savings but overlook the hidden cost: the distance added between a brand and its audience. The greater the distance, the more a brand sacrifices intimacy, humanity, and with it, authenticity. Rather than correcting this, many marketers have fixed their eyes on short-term profit, as opposed to long-term brand building. The desire for transactions has displaced the need for relationships. Customers, spotting the phonies, turn away.

Only by recognizing this cost can marketers scale the wall of cynicism they have helped build and turn their attention back to forging genuine, long-term relationships. To do this, they must invest time, finding meaningful ways to engage customers with something more than one-off guerrilla stunts and pithy, three-word catchphrases. They must invest genuine personality in their brand, respect their customers, and above all, honour the Great Unwritten Contract, which requires them to give something back in exchange for the interruption caused by their advertising.

My job as marketer is to coax my clients into investing in their own authenticity. Your job as consumer is to become ad literate to the point where you can discern the sheep from the goats.

FURTHERMORE

I'm often asked about what's ahead—about the future of persuasion. I'm somewhat wary of taking on the challenge because so many who've snapped at the same bait have been hooked, played, landed, stuffed, and mounted as monuments to humankind's inability to look forward.

Lord Kelvin, for instance, was clever enough to devise a scale to measure absolute temperature. But he wasn't much of a prognosticator. More than a century ago, he proclaimed that "heavier-than-air flying machines are impossible." He would find a place in history's comic relief file, alongside Emperor Joseph II, who scolded Mozart for stuffing "too many notes" into *The Marriage of Figaro.* They'd later be joined by the hapless Decca Records executive who passed on the Beatles, warning: "Guitar bands are on their way out."

That said, there are hints as to what's ahead. Especially regarding new technologies. In preparation for the 2002 picture *Minority Report,* Steven Spielberg held a three-day summit of futurists, urban planners, Internet gurus, designers, and MIT eggheads to help brainstorm the year 2054. Spielberg wanted a complete technological and social view of the future. And his future included advertising. Brass at Lexus, Reebok, Nokia, Guinness, Bulgari, Pepsi, and Aquafina were also consulted, and included in the film, partly to give the future a realistic feel and possibly also to give Mr. Spielberg's production budget some fast product-placement cash.

What emerged was a technological look at the future of advertising, beginning with high-tech databasing. The film portrayed a culture of ubiquitous retina-scanning devices, combined with databases containing consumer histories. Not only would machines detect any individual's location; they could also customize on-the-spot sales pitches. Chattering, moving characters would adorn cereal boxes. On the subway, people would read "electronic ink" newspapers: stories transmitted through constantly updated moving pictures.

As customers entered a store, they would be scanned and identified and reference made to their previous purchases, allowing an automated voice to offer a customized welcome.

> I shudder to imagine a store full of people hearing: "Welcome back, Mr. O'Reilly. Did that industrial-strength laxative do the trick for you? We've got a two-for-one today on the spray-on hair you like." Brrr.

THINGS I'D LIKE TO CHANGE ABOUT ADVERTISING AND MARKETING

1. Ban advertising from the boards at NHL hockey games. Leave the playing area pristine.

2. Let people drink beer in beer ads. Who are we fooling?

3. No more junk mail. Just think of the chiropractic bills our letter carriers are racking up.

4. Stop turning great songs into jingles. When the Beatles' song "Hello Goodbye" gets turned into "Hello Good Buy" for a retail store, it's time for a spanking.

270

5. No more bodily functions in ads. 'Nuff said.

6. No more telemarketing. 1–800 has become a toxic readout on my home phone.

7. Banish commercials from movie theatres. Sorry, this breaks the contract. All ads should give you something in return. These don't.

8. No more hard-sell ads that yell at you. I think advertising is intrusive enough without this going on. Gives all advertising a black eye.

9. No more perfume samplers in magazines. Gesundheit.

10. No more odious overrepetition in advertising. We get it. We get it. We get it.

11. No more being put on hold for forty-five minutes by companies we pay. "Your call is important to us. Sort of. Actually, not really. Please go away."

What amazed one of Spielberg's prognosticators was that the future of persuasion—as depicted in the movie—was based largely on technology that's available today. Airports are now experimenting with facial recognition technology. Retina scanning has been adopted for use in government agencies, at some banks, and in prisons. The location of anyone with a cellphone can be triangulated with unnerving accuracy. If their purchase history were referenced, they could be emailed a coupon for a favourite brand of crackers, right there in front of them, in the supermarket aisle. An industry insider once told me the average cellphone user takes advantage of only about 10 percent of the functions their phones are capable of. Through credit and debit cards, purchase histories are also easy to database, and on sites like Amazon when you search for one book, they're quick to suggest that if you like this title, you might like these other three.

What are we waiting for? Experience has taught us that a march into higher tech tends to get stuck in the gumbo of the human equation. Older consumers, for instance, are traditionally reluctant to adopt new technologies. Witness the older relatives most of us can quote, complaining that "computers are just glorified typewriters" or that "I won't do my banking with a machine." Call it the "one generation" theory or what you will: technology is often ready long before people are ready to wrap their minds around it. Sometimes it needs to sit out a generation before it's widely accepted.

What can and must change is that advertisers must constantly realize the consumers they court are growing smarter and more media literate. These customers understand that their attention is a commodity and when they spend it, they deserve something in return. Marketers who ignore this principle, do so at their peril.

In 1787 Thomas Jefferson wrote to James Madison: "I hold it, that a little rebellion, now and then, is a good thing, as necessary in the political world as storms in the physical." A rebellion is taking shape in marketing, and in these times of flux, amazing changes can be muscled in. As Rahm Emanuel, President Barack Obama's chief of staff, said, "Why waste a crisis?" You can see it in some of the brightest, most innovative new ad shops to emerge over the past few years. And best of all: the manifesto has already been written.

In the late 1960s, the people at Time, Incorporated, had an idea. They decided to hold a contest in which ad agencies would be invited to create an ad in the public interest. The stakes were attractive: the winning team would receive $25,000 and a bust of Johannes Gutenberg and the winning entry would run on a full page in the *New York Times*.

272

The winning ad was all text: two columns of large bold type under an enormous black headline sandwiched between two thick red lines. The ad had been conceived by Bob Levenson, a legendary creative director at Doyle Dane Bernbach. The headline read: "Do This or Die." Then came the two columns. The left column read:

Is this ad some kind of trick?

No. But it could have been.

And at exactly that point rests a do or die decision for American business.

We in advertising, together with our clients, have all the power and skill to trick people. Or so we think.

But we're wrong. We can't fool any of the people any of the time.

There is indeed a twelve-year-old mentality in this country; every six-year-old has one.

We are a nation of smart people.

And most smart people ignore most advertising because most advertising ignores smart people.

Instead we talk to each other.

We debate endlessly about the medium and the message. Nonsense. In advertising, the message *itself* is the message.

A blank page and a blank television screen are one and the same.

And above all, the messages we put on those pages and on those television screens must be the truth. For if we play tricks with the truth, we die.

So ended the first column. The second column took careful aim at the hand that feeds ad agencies:

Now. The other side of the coin.

Telling the truth about a product demands a product that's worth telling the truth about.

Sadly, so many products aren't.

So many products don't do anything better. Or anything different.

So many don't work quite right. Or don't last. Or simply don't matter.

If we also play this trick, we also die.

Because advertising only helps a bad product fail faster.

No donkey chases the carrot forever. He catches on. And quits.

That's the lesson to remember.

Unless we do, we die.

Unless we change, the tidal wave of consumer indifference will wallop into the mountain of advertising and manufacturing drivel.

That day we die.

We'll die in *our* marketplace. On *our* shelves. In *our* gleaming packages of empty promises.

Not with a bang. Not with a whimper.

But by our own skilled hands.

> Doyle Dane Bernbach Incorporated.

All marketers and advertising people need to read the sentiment,

The full text is reprinted here with the kind permission of its author. I asked Bob about the ceremony that Time, Incorporated, threw to honour the winning ad back in 1969. He said it was a lovely dinner with excellent speeches and a choice of chicken or fish. When I asked if the ad could just as easily run today, he said it could. And then, with too much modesty, he said it would undoubtedly make as little difference as it had the first time, adding: "Maybe this time I'd opt for the fish."

the honesty, and the searing articulation of that message at least once in their careers. It's also something they should tape to their walls. It's about treating the audience with respect. And behaving with honour in an industry with virtually unlimited access to the public airwaves and print pages. "Do This or Die" is indeed a manifesto that can't be read too many times.

While working on the *Age of Persuasion* radio series, I once had the happy fortune of coming across a striking, and little-remembered, quote that appeared in the trade publication *Printers Ink*. Dated 1915, it suggested that when the historian has finished his narrative of the coming century . . .

> . . . and comes searching for a subtitle which shall best express the spirit of the period, we think it not at all unlikely that he may select "The Age of Advertising" for the purpose.

That short observation was prophetic in its understanding of the decades to come. But given the new forms of persuasion the people at *Printers Ink* couldn't have foreseen—Internet marketing, ambient marketing, guerrilla marketing, branded entertainment—the phrase "age of advertising" doesn't have quite the right ring to it.

FURTHERMORE

ACKNOWLEDGMENTS

MUSIC: END CREDITS THEME

ANNCR: Say, folks, a few heartfelt words from the authors. *The Age of Persuasion: How Marketing Ate Our Culture* has been made possible in part by these wonderful folks:

Diane Martin of Knopf Canada—

SFX: EMAIL MESSAGE ARRIVES
—for sending that first email.

Angelika Glover, the authors' infinitely patient editor at Knopf Canada, for her struggle to break the authors of three decades' worth of bad writing habits.

Kathryn Dean, copy editor—the left brain the authors never had—whose enthusiasm and attention to detail saved the authors from stepping in many a metaphorical cow-pie.

277

Beverley Slopen, the authors' literary agent, for calmly piloting the authors through the rocks and shoals of publishing.

At CBC—

SFX: CBC I.D. MUSIC
The chronically likeable Chris Boyce, Director of Programming at CBC Radio, for believing that a show about advertising might be just crazy enough to work.

And back at the ranch:

MUSIC: LONELY, DRAWLING TRAIL-RIDING MUSIC, W. HARMONICA:

Tyna Maerzke, producer extraordinaire at Pirate Toronto, for making sure *The Age of Persuasion* radio series got to air each week.

Debbie Kitts for tirelessly answering listener emails, and for making sure the emails addressed to Mike or Terry personally, get answered by Mike or Terry, personally.

And—

MUSIC: SWEDISH NATIONAL ANTHEM

278

This book marks the first *Age of Persuasion* venture without the authors' resident "fifth Beatle," and valued colleague, engineer Keith Ohman. If any passages within these pages don't "sound" clean, crisp, and impeccably paced (flaws for which the authors are solely responsible), well, *that's* the sound of Ohman-less-ness.

ACKNOWLEDGMENTS

NOTES

INTRODUCTION: WHAT HATH GOD WROUGHT

xii One bracing December day: Hicks, Brian. *Ghost Ship : The Mysterious True Story Of The Mary Celeste And Her Missing Crew* (New York : Ballantine Books, 2004).

xiii Way back in 1917, novelist Norman Douglas: Andrews, Robert. *The Routledge Dictionary of Quotations* (London: Routledge and Kegan Paul, 1987), 5.

xiii Worldwide advertisers now spend upwards of $600 billion: Elliott, Stuart. "The Media Business: Advertising; Forecaster Cuts Estimate for Growth in Ad Spending," *The New York Times*, 29 June 2006.

xiv It took the United States four years to spend that much: "Cost of U.S. War surpasses $600 billion," *United Press International*, 24 October 2007.

xiv Statistics suggest that people spend more time exposed to advertising: "Americans Not Making Time for Making Love," U.S. *Bureau of Labour Statistics online*, 25 September 2007, www.bls.gov/news.release/atus.t01.htm, http://www.medicalnewstoday.com/articles/91086.php.

xiv Marketing (possibly from the Latin word mercari: Chantrell, Glynnis, ed. *The Oxford Dictionary of Word Histories* (Toronto: Oxford University Press, 2002).

xiv Advertising (from the Latin word word advertere: Ibid.

xvii Six years earlier, Lasker: Gunther, *Taken at the Flood*, and McDonald, David "The Man Who Invented Modern Advertising" *The Beaver magazine*, August/September 2004.

xxiv The first, of course, is ransom notes: Clark, Eric, *The Want Makers: Inside the World of Advertising* (New York: Penguin Books, 1988).

xxiv Since the early twentieth century, advertising: "U.S. Annual Advertising Spending Since 1919" *Galbi Think!*, 14 September 2008, http://www.galbithink.org/ad-spending.htm.

CHAPTER 1: CLUTTER

3 People chose Coke: Walker, Rob *Buying In: The Secret Dialogue Between What We Buy and Who We Are* (New York: Random House, 2008).

4 And it's not just physical space advertisers covet: "Brooks Boyer, Vice President and Chief Marketing Officer," *Chicago White Sox: Front Office*, http://chicago.whitesox.mlb.com/cws/team/exe_bios/boyer_brooks.html.

4 More recently, a number of sources, including: "How Many Advertisements is a Person Exposed to in a Day?" *American Association of Advertising Agencies*, March 2004 http://www.aaaa.org/eweb/upload/FAQs/adexposures.pdf.

4 This game probably began in 1957 with a speech: ibid.

6 Research reveals that advertising in elevators generates: "Elevate Your Business with Elevator Advertising," *Hi-Rise Communications Ltd.*, http://www.elevatorads.com.

7 At least one church, in Munster, Indiana: "About Steve Munsey," http://www.stevemunsey.org.

7 Some have built compounds on large acreages: de Vries, Lloyd, "Some Churches Closed on Christmas," *CBS News Online*, 7 December 2005, http://www.cbsnews.com/stories/2005/12/07/national/main1103153.shtml.

11 That itself was bold talk for a great broadsheet: *The Times*, 8 June 1891.

¹² Newspapers themselves would soon become: Walkom, Thomas, "Newspapers," *The Canadian Encyclopedia, Vol. II* (Edmonton: Hurtig Publishers Ltd., 1985).

¹⁶ I am supposed to be one of the more fertile inventors: Ogilvy, David. *Ogilvy on Advertising.* (New York: Vintage, 1985), 16.

²⁰ For the first two years of TV: Getz, Matt, "Public Responsibility of Broadcasters," "Drowned in Advertising Chatter," "The Case for Regulating Ad Time on Television," *Georgetown Law Journal, Vol. 94, Issue 4*, April 2006.

²⁰ It's up to the Canadian consumer: McArthur, Keith and Robertson, Grant, "CRTC Bows out of Ad Controls," *Globe and Mail Online*, 17 May 2007, http://tdw4.globeinvestor.com/servlet/ArticleNews/story/RTGAM/20070517/wrcrtc0518/stocks/home.

²² TV advertising will have lost: McKinsey & Co., quoted by Frank Rose, "Commercial Break," *Wired*, February 1999.

CHAPTER 2: BREAKING THE CONTRACT

²⁹ As a private person: Ogilvy, David. *Confessions of an Advertising Man* (New York: Ballantine, 1971), 112.

³⁰ In the introduction to this book, I mentioned: Gunther, John. *Taken at the Flood: The Albert Lasker Story* (New York: Harper & Brothers, 1960), 192–196.

³⁶ The Newspaper Association of America notes: Shin, Annys, "Newspaper Circulation Continues to Decline," *Washington Post*, 3 May 2005.

³⁷ For instance, studies show that ritual: "The Power of Cinema: An independent qualitative study by SPA Research," *Digital Cinema Media*, http://www.dcm.co.uk/why-cinema/fragmentation.aspx.

⁴³ His war service, his passion: Smith, Donald B. (contributor), "Belaney, Archibald Stansfeld," *The Canadian Encyclopedia, Vol. VI* (Edmonton: Hurtig Publishers Ltd., 1985), 158–9.

CHAPTER 3: THE RISE AND FALL AND RISE OF BRANDED ENTERTAINMENT

[49] When executing advertising: O'Toole, John. *The Trouble with Advertising* (New York: Chelsea House, 1981), 96.

[50] In July 2008, the *International Herald Tribune*: Robert Levin, "Corporations Lend a Hand to Hip-Hop and R&B Artists," *International Herald Tribune*, 7 July 2008.

[51] Sara Lee Frozen Dinner Entres: Ries, Al, and Jack Trout. *Positioning: The Battle for Your Mind* (New York: Warner, 1981), 143.

[51] Bic Underwear: Haig, Matt. *Brand Failures* (London: Kogan Page, 2005), 85.

[51] Hooters Air: Jana, Reena, "Bad for the Brand? Here's a look at seven brand extensions that are a real stretch," *Business Week*, http://images.businessweek.com/ss/06/07/brand_extensions/source/1.htm.

[53] One million sesterces: "Monete_en," *The Colosseum* website, http://www.the-colosseum.net/history/monete_en.htm.

[53] After Commodus moved on: "Ancient Rome: Roman Entertainment," *SPQR Online*, http://library.thinkquest.org/26602/entertainment.htm.

[55] These early rainmakers earned: Meyers, Cynthia Barbara, "Admen and the Shaping of American Commercial Broadcasting." (Thesis, 2005), 100. Accessed through the University of Texas digital repository: https://repositories.lib.utexas.edu/handle/2152/1632.

[55] On December 4, 1933: Dunning, John. *On the Air: The Encyclopedia of Old-Time Radio* (New York: Oxford University Press, 1998), 420–422.

[55] Rival brands, most of them soaps: "Transcription Records," *archive.org* transcription records of a complete broadcast day, WJSV Washington, D.C., 21 September 1939, http://www.archive.org/details/CompleteBroadcastDay.

[56] As the early trade bible: Marchand, Roland. *Advertising the American Dream: Making Way for Modernity, 1920–1940* (Berkeley: University of California Press, 1985), 66.

[56] By the mid-thirties, Frank Hummert: "Hummert's Mill," *Time*, 23 January 1939, http://www.time.com/time/magazine/article/0,9171,760635–2,00.html.

[58] It might easily have been forgotten: Gunther, John. *Taken at the Flood: The Albert Lasker Story* (New York: Harper & Brothers, 1960), 195.

[59] In 1946, fewer than 1 percent: "Number of TV Households in America," *Television History—The First 75 Years*, http://www.tvhistory.tv/Annual_TV_Households_50–78.JPG.

[61] When the entrance fee of twenty francs: James, Tom, "The Origins of the Tour de France," *Veloarchive.com*, 28 July 2003, http://www.veloarchive.com/races/tour/origins.php.

[61] And sure enough, by 1904: Ibid.

[62] No one was more surprised: "The History of the Book," *Guinness Book of Records Online*, http://guinness.book-of-records.info/history.html.

[64] The previous record was held by: "Quantum of Solace Sets Product Placement Record," *Filmonic.com*, 27 October 2008, *filmonic.com/ quantum-solace-sets-product-placement-record*.

[65] Subsequently, when HarperCollins published: Rose, M.J., "Your Ad Here," *Salon.com*, 5 September 2001.

[65] Naysayers, meanwhile, blasted Weldon's: Ibid.

[68] Nearly a quarter of all the actors: "Hallmark Hall of Fame," *Hallmark Cards Online* http://corporate.hallmark.com/company/Hallmark-Hall-of-Fame-Facts.

[68] Hallmark became the first TV sponsor: Kittleson, Timothy, "The First Fifty Years," *UCLA Television and Film Archive Online*, http://www.cinema.ucla.edu/hallmark.

[69] Advertising trade magazines: Macarthur, Kate, "BK Sets High Score with its Adver-Games," *Advertising Age*, 8 January 2007.

[73] [young people are] threatened: Clark, Eric. *The Want Makers: Inside the World of Advertising* (New York: Penguin, 1998), 371.

[74] A majority of American teenagers own cellphones: Macgill, Alexandra Rankin Research Manager, "Parents, Teens and Technology," *Pew Internet & American Life Project*, 24 October 2007, http://pewresearch.org/pubs/621/parents-teens-and-technology.

[74] In 1985, 23 percent of teens: Bahrampour, Tara, "More Newly Licensed Teens Score Pricey Wheels," *Washington Post*, 8 November 2004.

[75] "Tweens" (people eight to twelve years old): Groppe, Laura, CEO, Girls Intelligence Agency (marketing firm), "Marketing to 'Tweens' Going Too Far?" *CBS News Online*, 15 December 2004, http://www.cbsnews.com/stories/2007/05/14/earlyshow/living/parenting/main2798400.shtml.

[75] Kids aged four to twelve years old: Waters, Jennifer, "Young with Tons of Purchasing Power," *MarketWatch Online*, 11 Oct. 2006, http://www.marketwatch.com/ story/young-americans-a-giant-influence-on-buying-decisions-study?dist=newsfinder&siteid=google&keyword=.

[75] Though estimates vary: Ibid, interview within audio link.

[77] Cream of Wheat is so good to eat: Reynolds, Doris, "Let's Talk Food: This traditional cereal exemplifies the 'cream of the crop,'" *Naples News Online*, 21 April 2009, http://www.naplesnews.com/news/2009/apr/21/lets-talk-food-traditional-cereal-exemplifies-crea/.

[77] What do I care for snow or sleet: "Cream of Wheat," *BookRags Online*, http://www.bookrags.com/wiki/Cream_of_Wheat.

[79] Granted, today this isn't the stuff: Goodwin, Danny, "Music Jingle Saves Wheaties from Extinction," *Old-Time.com*, http://www.old-time.com/commercials/.

[80] Jim Ameche, lesser-known: Dunning, John. *On the Air: The Encyclopedia of Old-Time Radio* (New York: Oxford University Press, 1998), 352.

[81] And research would later affirm: "Children and Advertising," *National Institute of Media and the Family Online*, 7 Aug. 2002, http://www.mediafamily.org/facts/facts_childadv.shtml.

[82] The Orphan Annie decoder pin: Olsen, John, "Radio Orphan Annie's Secret Decoder Society," *Radio Archives Online*, http://www.radioarchives.org/annie.

[85] That crazy Head and Shoulders: "Shampoo and Toiletries Commercials: Head and Shoulders," *Roadode* (website), http://www.roadode.com/groom_2.shtml.

[87] No VietCong ever called me: "Oprah Talks to Muhammad Ali," *Oprah.com*, June 2001, http://www.oprah.com/article/omagazine/oprahscut/omag_200106_ocut/3.

[89] Don Cherry appeared in ads: "Controversy on tap for Don Cherry beer ads," *CTV.ca*, 8 May 2003, http://www.ctv.ca/servlet/ArticleNews/story/CTVNews/1052402958501_268?s_name=&no_ads.

[90] Despite the objection of scores: Walsh, Mark, "USA: Commercials in the Classroom," *The UNESCO Courier Online*, April 2000, http://www.unesco.org/courier/2000_04/uk/apprend.htm.

[90] In Canada a similar venture: "Controversial Canadian Youth News Network Goes Off the Air until January," *The Canadian Press Online*, http://www.asu.edu/educ/epsl/CERU/Articles/CERU-0010–86-OWI.doc.

[91] Early in 2008 Dave Droga: "'F-C-U-K' apparel made quite the splash—for awhile, at least," www.droga5.com and *BBC News Online* http://news.bbc.co.uk/2/hi/uk_news/1258961.s .

[94] Major corporations are actually turning: Safer, Morley. "Here Come the Millennials," (TV Broadcast) *60 Minutes*, CBS Television, 11 November 2007.

CHAPTER 5: THE YOUTUBE REVOLUTION

[97] The consumer isn't a moron: Ogilvy, David. *Confessions of an Advertising Man* (New York: Ballantine, 1971), 84.

[98] Years earlier, England's King George III: "King George III: Mad or Misunderstood?" *BBC News Online*, 13 July 2004, http://news.bbc.co.uk/2/hi/health/3889903.stm

[99] So what happened when Jawed Karim: Karim, Jawed, *(YouTube)* "*From Concept to Hyper-growth*," lecture, University of Illinois, 23 October 2006, http://www.youtube.com/watch?v=nssfmT07SZg

[100] In February, 2006, YouTube obliged: Biggs, John, "A Video Clip Goes Viral, and a TV Network Wants to Control It," *The New York Times*, 20 Feb 2006.

[107] In full damage control mode: Wells, Jane, "How hard can it be to cancel an AOL account?" *MSNBC Online*, http://www.msnbc.msn.com/id/13447232.

[108] On a relatively low budget: Notes emailed to the authors by Tim Piper.

[108] It was among *Time* magazine's: Ibid.

[114] Breast exam: $100: "Mastercard Priceless Parody to Promote Breast Cancer Awareness," *Breastcancervictory.com*, 19 June 2008, http://www.breastcancervictory.com/mastercard-priceless-parody-to-promote-breast-cancer-awareness.

[115] A brand can, in fact, be a medium: McMains, Andrew, "TBWA's Media Arts Lab Rebundles for Apple," *AdWeek*, 19 June 2006, http://www.adweek.com/aw/esearch/article_display.jsp?vnu_content_id=1002690245.

CHAPTER 6: GUERILLAS IN OUR MIDST

[119] To explain responsibility to advertising men: Gossage, Howard Luck. *The Book of Gossage* (Chicago: Copy Workshop, 1995), 29.

[120] In the spring of 2002: Oliver, Mark, "Game publicity plan raises grave concerns," *The Guardian*, 15 March 2001.

[121] Here I lie: Wallechinsky, David, and Irving Wallace. *The People's Almanac #2* (New York: Bantam, 1978), 1207.

[121] There was enough fuss: Oliver, Mark, "Game publicity plan raises grave concerns," *The Guardian*, 15 March 2001.

[122] The Spanish word guerrilla: Chantrell, Glynnis, ed. *The Oxford Dictionary of Word Histories* (Toronto: Oxford University Press, 2002).

[123] Clusters of the temporary abodes: Connolly, Chris, "Six Great Guerrilla Marketing Campaigns," *Mental Floss*, July-August 2007.

[123] Oddly enough, similar signs: Blankstein, Andrew, "Devices Placed in Boston Also Intended for L.A.," *LA Times*, 1 February 2007.

[124] An outfit worth more: "Fortune 500 2007: Full List 1–100," *CNN Money Online*, http://money.cnn.com/magazines/fortune/fortune500/2007/full_list/index.html.

[126] Dr Pepper called off the contest: Ellement, John R., and Mishra, Raja, "Marketing treasure hunt trips in historic graveyard," *Boston Globe Online*, 23 February 2007, http://www.boston.com/news/local/articles/2007/02/23/marketing_treasure_hunt_trips_in_historic_graveyard.

[127] A gum-swallowing thirty-five knots: "Charles Parsons," *University of Cambridge Engineering* (website), http://www-g.eng.cam.ac.uk/125/1875–1900/ parsons2.html.

[128] It's widely believed that Edison: Berton, Pierre. *Niagara, a History of the Falls* (Toronto: McClelland & Stewart, 1994).

[128] Condemned prisoners could then: Rasenberger, Jim, "Fade to Black," *The New York Times*, 2 January 2005.

[131] I believe that your decision: Brandt, Peter, "PETA's Ingrid Newkirk," *Salon.com*, http://archive.salon.com/people/conv/2001/04/30/newkirk/index.html.

[131] A head-turning roster: Rotella, Mark, "boldThe PETA Celebrity Cookbook: Delicious Recipes from Your Favorite Stars," *Publishers Weekly*, 16 December 2002.

[131] Since its creation in 1990: "About PETA," PETA website, http://www.peta.org/about.

[133] A home pregnancy test allegedly used: Wilps, Lindsay, "GoldenPalace.com corners 'weird' market with auction purchases," *North Texas Daily Online*, 21 September 2005, http://media.www.ntdaily.com/media/storage/paper877/news/2005/09/21/Arts/Goldenpalace.com.Corners.weird.Market.With.Auction.Purchases-1894136.shtml.

[136] There were identical billboards: Bosman, Julie, "Public Hath no Fury, Even When Deceived," *The New York Times*, 24 July 2006.

[137] They were fined $50 for littering: Crawford, Krysten, "Gotcha! Ads Push the Envelope," CNN *Money* (website) 17 August, 2004, http://money.cnn.com/2004/08/13/news/economy/weirdads/index.htm.

CHAPTER 7: THE LESSON OF CLARK GABLE'S UNDERSHIRT

[139] Don't confuse selling with art: Rothenberg, Randall, *Where the Suckers Moon: An Advertising Story* (New York: Alfred A. Knopf, 1994), 113. Accessed online: http://advertising.utexas.edu/resources/quotes/PROD75_016451.html.

[141] She accepted gracefully: Spicer, Chrystopher J. *Clark Gable* (Jefferson: MacFarland & Company, 2002), 111.

[144] The Star Wars Merchandising Explosion: "Special Features," *Star Wars* DVD, Beverly Hills, California: 20th Century Fox Home Entertainment, 2004.

[144] The Star Wars Merchandising Explosion: Serwer, Andrew E., "Who Gets What in the Star Wars Toy Deal," *Fortune Magazine Online*, 18 August 1997, http://money.cnn.com/magazines/fortune/fortune_archive/1997/08/18/230223/index.htm.

[145] Two years earlier Steven: "The Monster that Ate Hollywood," *PBS Documentary*, 22 November, 2001; "Special Features," *Jaws (DVD) Anniversary Edition*, Universal Studios, 2005.

[147] Projected revenue from a Universal Studios: Bulik, Beth Snyder, "Harry Potter: the $15 Billion Man," *Advertising Age*, 16 July 2007.

[149] Pull in more than a half-billion dollars: Box *Office Mojo* (website) www.boxofficemojo.com.

[150] Sting and Jaguar: Donation, Scott, "Sting-Jaguar deal serves as a model for the music world," *Advertising Age*, 22 Sept, 2003.

[152] One headline read: Stevenson, Seth, "Paul McCartney? Is That You?" *Slate Magazine Online*, 19 September 2005, http://www.slate.com/id/2126568.

[155] There was Frank Sinatra: "Colgate Shampoo Says 'Halo' with Musical Jingle," *Old-Time Radio* (website) http://www.old-time.com/commercials/1940%27s/Halo%20Everybody%20Halo.htm.

[157] There was also an ironic twist: "Waits v. Frito Lay, 978 F. 2d 1093 (9th Cir. 1992)," *markrowesler.com*, http://markroesler.com/pdf/caselaw/Waits%20v.%-20Frito-Lay%20Inc.%20_1992_.pdf.

[159] Would climb to Number 7: Quenqua, Douglas, "boldWhat's That Catchy Tune?" The New York Times, 31 December 2007.

[160] *Wired* magazine reported: Smith, Ethan, "Organization Moby," *Wired*, May 2002.

CHAPTER 8: THE LANGUAGE OF PERSUASION

[163] Advertising practitioners are interpreters: "Texas Advertising and Public Relations: Practice & Practitioners," *University of Texas* (website), http://advertising.utexas.edu/resources/quotes/PROD75_016470.html.

[165] Thousands of stores spread: "A Brief History of Starbucks," *Starbucks* (website), http://www.starbucks.ca/en-ca/_About+Starbucks/History.htm.

[170] Health conscious customers: Horsley, Scott, "Wendy's 'Biggie' Portion Gone in Name Only," *NPR* (website), 20 June 2006, http://www.npr.org/templates/story/story.php?storyId=5498454.

[170] Plenty of room in women's clothing: Jackson, Kate M., "As waistlines grow, women's clothing sizes shrink incredibly," *Boston Globe*, 5 May 2006.

CHAPTER 9: A SENSE OF PERSUASION

[186] One famous study concluded: Lindstrom, Martin, "Smelling a branding opportunity," *Marketing Digest Online*, 28 July 2005, http://www.ameinfo.com/65026.html.

[187] Shoppers make up their minds: Hollis, Nigel, "Smelly Business," *Millward Brown* (website), www.millwardbrown.com.

[188] Yielded only curt: Diefendorf, David, *Amazing . . . but False!: Hundreds Of "Facts" You Thought Were True, But Aren't* (New York: Sterling, 2007), 221.

[188] Media philosopher Neil Postman: Postman, Neil. *Amusing Ourselves to Death* (New York: Viking Penguin, 1985), 44.

[190] In 1915 a New York audience: "Symphony No. 5 in F sharp major for piano, organ, chorus & orchestra ('Prometheus, Poem of Fire'), Op. 60," *Allmusic* (website), http://www.allmusic.com/cg/amg.dll?p=amg&sql=42:97431~T1.

[190] A mood of "melancholy womanliness": *Yale Library* (website), www.library.yale.edu.

[190] Stellar musicians who likely: http://en.wikipedia.org/wiki/List_of_people_with_synesthesia

[191] If Johnny Hodges is playing: George, Don. *Sweet man: The real Duke Ellington* (New York: G.P. Putnam's Sons, 1981), 226.

[195] Created by children's illustrator: "Vernon Grant's History," *Cultural & Heritage Museums* (website), http://chmuseums.org/myco/vernon-grant.php.

[195] Consumers consider Rice Krispies: Lindstrom, Martin. *BRAND sense: Build Powerful Brands through Touch, Taste, Smell, Sight, and Sound* (Toronto: Free Press, 2005), 12.

[197] Introduced a scent into a Philadelphia: Herz, Rachel and Napoli, Lisa, "How to Make it Smell Like a Sale," transcript from *American Public Media* (website) http://marketplace.publicradio.org/display/web/2007/11/22/how_to_make_it_smell_like_a_sale.

[198] Reported a sales spike: ibid

[199] The audience, overcome with sleep: Pile, Stephen. *The Incomplete Book of Failures* (Toronto: Musson, 1979), 113.

NOTES TO CHAPTER NINE

[200] The removal of the posters: Gordon, Rachel, "Aromatic ads pulled from city bus shelters," *San Francisco Chronicle*, 6 December 2006.

[201] Hence, just before a new: Lindstrom, Martin. *BRAND sense: Build Powerful Brands through Touch, Taste, Smell, Sight, and Sound* (Toronto: Free Press, 2005), 94.

[201] To make amends: "New Car Smell may become a thing of the past," *Taipei Times*, 3 October 2005.

CHAPTER 10: THE HUMAN FACE OF PERSUASION

[205] In general, my children: Bombeck, Erma, *Four of a Kind: A Suburban Field Guide*, (BBS Publishing, 1985).

[206] Aunt Jemima: "Nancy Green," *Notable Black American Women, Book 3*, (Kitchener Public Library: Gale Group, 2002).

[208] Advertising, wrote the legendary: Simpson, James B., *Contemporary Quotations*. (Binghamton, NY: Vail-Ballou Press, 1964), 84.

[209] Over the years, real life: Lacitis, Erik, "Burien man is American icon: oldest active Fuller Brush Man," *Seattle Times*, 20 April 2008.

[211] By 1945 she was voted: "The Advertising Century," *Advertising Age*, http://adage.com/century/icon04.html.

[212] Madge the Manicurist: "Jan Miner," *Internet Movie Database* (website) www.imdb.com.

[212] Duncan Hines: "The History of Duncan Hines," *Duncan Hines* (website), http://www.duncanhines.com/newDuncan/pub/about-us.

[212] Chef Boyardee: Boiardi, Hector, "Obituary," *The New York Times*, 23 June 1985.

[212] Wendy's: Williams, Mark, "Wendy's founder Dave Thomas dies," *Seattle Times*, 8 January 2002.

[212] Sara Lee: "Our History," *Sara Lee Corporate website*, http://www.saraleebakery.com.au/special.php?page=history.html.

[214] In 1992 Kiam semi-retired: BBC News obituary, *BBC News Online*, 29 May 2001, http://news.bbc.co.uk/2/hi/americas/1356903.stm.

[214] Deadenbacher: Elliott, Stuart, "A Year for Quick Hits and Fast Flops as Campaigns Broke New Ground," *The New York Times*, 17 December 2007.

[215] His widow and son: "Marlboro Manslaughter," *Snopes.com*, 6 Aug. 2007, www.snopes.com/radiotv/tv/marlboro.asp.

[215] And that pleased-looking chap: "Is the guy on the Quaker Oats box John Penn?" *The Straight Dope*, http://www.straightdope.com/columns/read/1553/is-the-guy-on-the-quaker-oats-box-john-penn.

[216] The logo altered to look: Mcgill, Douglas C., "Colgate to Rename a Toothpaste," *The New York Times*, 27 January 1989.

[217] Frito Bandito: Rath, Arun and Segal, David, "On the Media," *National Public Radio*, 27 April 27 2007.

[217] American Library Association's list: "100 Most Challenged Books," *Library Spot* (website), http://www.libraryspot.com/lists/100mostchallengedbooks.htm.

[217] Pillsbury once marketed: "Vintage Ad," *YouTube.com*, http://www.youtube.com/watch?v=PuUlWnYkYtw.

[219] That famous handshake: Price, S.L., "The Visionary," *Sports Illustrated*, 26 May 2003.

[220] It's just amazing: Colombo, John Robert. *The Dictionary of Canadian Quotations* (Toronto: Stoddart, 1991), 7.

[221] Rival golfers dream: "The World's Top Earning Athletes," *Forbes Magazine*, 26 October 2007.

[221] Michael Jordan still ranked: ibid.

[223] Arnold Schwarzenegger hawked: Faiola, Anthony, "U.S. Stars Shine Again in Japan Ads," *Washington Post*, 14 Jan 2007.

[223] Harrison Ford made ads: "Harrison Ford," *Japander* (website), http://www.japander.com/japander/ford.htm.

[223] Madonna endorsed Shochu: "U.S. Stars Shine" *Japander* (website), http://www.japander.com/japander/madonna.htm.

[224] Ben Kingsley and Sam Waterston's: *VOICEBANK.NET*, www.voicebank.net.

[226] Janet Jackson lingerie: Rhone, Nedra, "boldCelebrities don't just set the style, they market it," *The Atlanta Journal and Constitution*, 23 November, 2008.

CHAPTER 11: THE LONG AND SHORT OF IT

[229] We find that advertising works: Mayer, Martin. *Whatever Happened to Madison Avenue? Advertising in the '90s* (Boston: Little, Brown, 1991), 179–80

[229] Myself and time: Colombo, John Robert. *The Dictionary of Canadian Quotations* (Toronto: Stoddart, 1991), 381.

[230] A few years later, Honda: Petracca, Laura, "Five-second ads try to counter TiVo," *USA Today*, 7 June 2006.

[231] I put instant coffee: Wright, Stephen. *I Have a Pony*, Warner Brothers, 1985.

[234] When Abraham Lincoln: Postman, Neil. *Amusing Ourselves to Death* (New York: Viking Penguin, 1985), 44–49.

[236] Caples, who served: "John Caples," *Gale Biography Resource Centre*, Kitchener Public Library, 28 October 2003.

[236] I have seen one advertisement: Ogilvy, David. *Ogilvy on Advertising* (New York: Vintage, 1985), 9.

[236] When you have written your headline: Ogilvy, David. *Confessions of an Advertising Man* (New York: Ballantine, 1971), 92.

[237] At 60 miles an hour: Ogilvy, David. *Ogilvy on Advertising* (New York: Vintage, 1985), 10.

[239] The amazing story of a Zippo: Ogilvy, David. *Ogilvy on Advertising* (New York: Vintage, 1985), 81.

[239] Influence a congressman's vote: Bendinger, Bruce. *The Copy Workshop Workbook* (Chicago: Copy Workshop, 1993), 24.

[239] Answer these ten questions: ibid.

[241] Not a cake of Lifebuoy: "Life Buoy serial," *Old-Time.com*, http://www.old-time.com/commercials/1930%27s/LifebuoyMiniStories.htm.

[241] It gets better: Hall, Sarah, "Veteran singer-actor who found fame in TV ad dies, 95," *The Guardian*, 30 November 2001.

[243] There's a lovely story: Fadiman, Clifton, and André Bernard, eds. *Bartlett's Book of Anecdotes* (New York: Little, Brown, 2000), 24.

[244] Beyoncé for Emporio Armani: "Beyoncé Making of the Emporio Armani Diamonds Commercial," *YouTube.com*, http://www.youtube.com/watch?v=7nLm0c6n940.

[245] George Clooney for the Nespresso: "Making of Nespresso Commercial with George Clooney," *YouTube.com*, http://www.youtube.com/watch?v=cUy65zvwukA.

[245] Here's one of my favourite Lincoln: Gross, Anthony, *Lincoln's Own Stories* (New York: Sun Dial Press, 1940), 24.

[247] Some scientists argue: Clayton, Victoria, "What's to blame for the rise in ADHD?" *MSNBC Online*, 8 Sept 2004, http://www.msnbc.msn.com/id/5933775.

[247] A new media malady: Fields, Suzanne, "How TV can 'rewire' brands of tiny tots," *Washington Times*, 19 April 2004.

[247] Part of that movie's soundtrack: "Kenny Loggins: Danger Zone," MVD-BASE.com, http://www.mvdbase.com/video.php?id=16837.

[247] He'd been a camera operator: "Tony Scott Interview," *YouTube.com*, http://www.youtube.com/watch?v=LYcZIt71_rM&feature=related.

[248] In 1941 Roosevelt: Fadiman, Clifton, and André Bernard, eds. *Bartlett's Book of Anecdotes* (New York: Little, Brown, 2000), 465.

[249] Winston spent the best years: Fadiman, Clifton, and André Bernard, eds. *Bartlett's Book of Anecdotes* (New York: Little, Brown, 2000), 112–113.

[249] Slipped the surly bonds of earth: Rees, Nigel. *Brewer's Quotations* (London: Cassell Wellington House, 1994), 231.

[250] The Strange Death: Saatchi, Maurice, "The Strange Death of Modern Advertising," *Financial Times*, 22 June 2006.

CHAPTER 12: THE WALL OF CYNICISM

[255] History will see advertising: Clark, Eric. *The Want Makers: Inside the World of Advertising* (New York: Penguin Books, 1988), 371.

[255] Advertising is only evil: Ogilvy, David. *Ogilvy on Advertising* (New York: Vintage, 1985), 207.

[255] All of us who professionally: Bernbach, Bill. Bill Bernbach Said (DDB Needham Worldwide, 1989). http://advertising.utexas.edu/resources/quotes/PROD75_016453.html

[256] His product was snake oil: Schwarcz, Joe, "Why are snake-oil remedies so-called?," *Montreal Gazette*, 23 Feb 2008, and Nickelle, Joe, "Snake Oil: A Guide for Connoisseurs," *Committee for Skeptical Inquiry* http://www.csicop.org/sb/2006–09/i-files.html and "Peddling Snake Oil," http://www.csicop.org/sb/9812/snakeoil.html.

[257] Some popular British brands: "Balm of America," *Smithsonian National Museum of American History Online*, http://americanhistory.si.edu/collections/object.cfm?key=35&objkey=4718&gkey=51.

[257] Lydia Pinkham's formula: Pace, Eric, "Books of the Times," *The New York Times*, 21 June 1984.

[258] Dishonesty in advertising: Starch, Daniel, *Principles of Advertising* (Chicago: A.W. Shaw Company, 1923), 437.

[258] This skepticism had been fuelled: "Crucible of Empire: Yellow Journalism," *PBS Online*, http://www.pbs.org/crucible/journalism.html.

[258] A strikingly similar radio hoax: "The Riot that Never Was," *BBC 4* (website), 16 June 2005, http://www.bbc.co.uk/radi04/factual/ the_riot_that_never_was.shtml, and "Show that Sparked a Riot," *BBC Newswatch*, 13 June 2005, http://news.bbc.co.uk/newswatch/ifs/hi/ newsid_4080000/newsid_4081000/4081060.stm.

[261] Welles won a major Hollywood contract: *The Battle of Citizen Kane*, Warner Home Video, 1996.

[261] One New Jersey hospital: Tribble, Scott, "War of the Worlds" *St. James Encyclopedia of Pop Culture*, accessed online: http://findarticles.com/p/articles/mi_g1epc/is_/ai_2419101298.

[262] I have discovered the most exciting: Andrews, Robert. *The Columbia Dictionary of Quotations* (New York: Columbia University Press, 1993), 18.

[262] Never before could advertising: Lears, Jackson, *Fables of Abundance: A Cultural History of Advertising in America* (New York: BasicBooks, 1994), 238–9.

[262] By the 1940s: Skeat, Walter W. *A Concise Etymological Dictionary of the English Language* (New York: G.P. Putnam's, 1980), 248.

[262] Fort Lee, New Jersey: Rogers, Stuart, "How a Publicity Blitz Crated The Myth of Subliminal Advertising," *P/R Quarterly*, Winter 92/93.

[265] Either by the Government: Ogilvy, David. *Confessions of an Advertising Man* (New York: Ballantine, 1971), 87.

[265] As ad giant Leo Burnett: "100 LEO's," *Leo Burnett Company*, http://advertising.utexas.edu/resources/quotes/PROD75_016433.html.

[265] There's no evidence that P.T. Barnum: Rees, Nigel. *Brewer's Quotations* (London: Cassell Wellington House, 1994), 41.

NOTES TO CHAPTER TWELVE

[266] According to psychologist Richard Wiseman: Alleman, John, "We Can't Handle the Truth," *Globe and Mail*, 28 September 2002.

[267] It no longer is strictly: "Texas Advertising and Public Relations: Belief," *Chairman of The University of Texas Advertising Department*, http://advertising.utexas.edu/resources/quotes/PROD75_016422.html.

FURTHERMORE

[269] More than a century ago: Rousseaux, Charles, "Brilliant mind, faulty instincts," *Washington Times*, 21 Feb 2004.

[272] In 1787 Thomas Jefferson: Bartlett, John. *Bartlett's Familiar Quotations* 14th ed. (Toronto: Little, Brown, 1968), 471.

BIBLIOGRAPHY

Andrews, Robert. *The Routledge Dictionary of Quotations.* London: Routledge and Kegan Paul, 1987.

Bartlett, John. *Bartlett's Familiar Quotations,* 14th ed. Toronto: Little, Brown, 1968.

Berton, Pierre. *Niagara, a History of the Falls.* Toronto: McClelland & Stewart, 1994.

Bendinger, Bruce, *The Copy Workshop Workbook.* Chicago, Copy Workshop, 1993.

Chantrell, Glynnis, ed. *The Oxford Dictionary of Word Histories.* Toronto: Oxford University Press, 2002.

Clark, Eric. *The Want Makers: Inside the World of Advertising.* New York: Penguin, 1998.

Cohen, Herb. *You Can Negotiate Anything.* Secaucus, NJ: Lyle Stuart, 1980.

Colombo, John Robert. *The Dictionary of Canadian Quotations.* Toronto: Stoddart, 1991.

Diefendorf, David. *Amazing . . . but False!: Hundreds of "Facts" You Thought Were True, but Aren't.* New York: Sterling, 2007.

Dunning, John. *On the Air: The Encyclopedia of Old-Time Radio.* New York: Oxford University Press, 1998.

301

Fadiman, Clifton, and André Bernard, eds. *Bartlett's Book of Anecdotes*. New York: Little, Brown, 2000.

Gossage, Howard Luck. *The Book of Gossage*. Chicago: Copy Workshop, 1995.

Gunther, John. *Taken at the Flood: The Albert Lasker Story*. New York: Harper & Brothers, 1960.

Haig, Matt. *Brand Failures*. London: Kogan Page, 2005.

Hicks, Brian. *Ghost Ship: The Mysterious True Story of the* Mary Celeste *and Her Missing Crew*. New York: Ballantine, 2004

Lindstrom, Martin. *BRAND sense: Build Powerful Brands through Touch, Taste, Smell, Sight, and Sound*. Toronto: Free Press, 2005.

Marchand, Roland. *Advertising the American Dream: Making Way for Modernity, 1920–1940*. Berkeley: University of California Press, 1985.

McDonald, David, "The Man Who Invented Modern Advertising," *The Beaver*, Aug-Sept 2004.

Meyers, Cynthia Barbara, "Admen and the Shaping of American Commercial Broadcasting." (Thesis, 2005), 100. Accessed through the University of Texas digital repository: https://repositories.lib.utexas.edu/handle/2152/1632.

Ogilvy, David., *Confessions of an Advertising Man*, New York: Ballantine, 1971.

———. *Ogilvy on Advertising*. New York: Vintage, 1985.

Pile, Stephen. *The Incomplete Book of Failures*. Toronto: Musson, 1979.

Postman, Neil. *Amusing Ourselves to Death*. New York: Viking Penguin, 1985.

Rees, Nigel. *Brewer's Quotations*. London: Cassell Wellington House, 1994.

Ries, Al, and Jack Trout. *Positioning: The Battle for Your Mind*. New York: Warner, 1981.

Rose, Frank. "Commercial Break," *Wired*, Feb 1999.

Skeat, Walter W. *A Concise Etymological Dictionary of the English Language.* New York: G.P. Putnam's, 1980.

Shenk, David. *Data Smog.* San Francisco: Harper Edge, 1997.

Strasburger, Victor C. "Children and TV Advertising: Nowhere to Run, Nowhere to Hide," *Journal of Developmental & Behavioral Pediatrics*, 22 June 2001, 185.

Walker, Rob. *Buying In: The Secret Dialogue Between What We Buy and Who We Are.* New York: Random House, 2008.

Wallechinsky, David, and Irving Wallace. *The People's Almanac #2.* New York: Bantam, 1978.

PERMISSIONS

Grateful acknowledgment is made to the following sources for permission to reprint from previously published material.

Quotation (p. xi) by Marshall McLuhan used with permission from the estate of Marshall McLuhan.

Quotation (p. xi) from *Keep the Aspidistra Flying* by George Orwell (Copyright © George Orwell, 1936), used by permission of Bill Hamilton as the Literary Executor of the Estate of the late Sonia Brownell Orwell and Secker & Warburg Ltd.

Quotation (p. 1) from the *Times* (London), 1886, used by permission.

Quotations (p. 11, 16, 29, 48, 93, 97, 236, and 265) from *Confessions of an Advertising Man* by David Ogilvy, (Simon & Schuster, 1964).

Quotation (p. 16) from *David Ogilvy: An Autobiography* by David Ogilvy, used with permission from Global Rights Dept., John Wiley & Sons, Inc.

Quotations (p. 16, 17, 239, and 255) from *Ogilvy on Advertising* by David Ogilvy (Crown Publishing, a division of Random House Inc., and Andre Deutsch, 1983).

Four lines (p. 27) from the poem "Song of the Open Road" by Ogden Nash, Copyright © 1933 by Ogden Nash, renewed. Reprinted by permission of Curtis Brown, Ltd.

Quotation (p. 49) used with permission courtesy of JasonLove.com.

Quotation (p. 49) from *The Trouble With Advertising* (Chelsea House Publishers, New York, 1981) by John O'Toole, used with permission from Chelsea House Publishers.

Quotations (p. 56, 275) from *Printers Ink* magazine.

Quotations (p. 73, 255) from Bill Bernbach used with permission.

Quotations (p. 119, 178) from *The Book of Gossage* by Howard Luck Gossage, used with permission from The Copy Workshop.

Quotation (p. 139) from Jack Taylor in *Where The Suckers Moon* by Randall Rothenberg.

Quotations (p. 163, 267) used with permission courtesy of Jef I. Richards.

Quotation (p. 185) courtesy of the American Foundation for the Blind, Helen Keller Archives.

Quotation (p. 205) by Erma Bombeck from her book *Four of a Kind: A Suburban Field Guide,* reprinted with permission from The Aaron Priest Literary Agency, 2009.

Quotation (p. 229) from Andy Tarshis in *Whatever Happened to Madison Avenue?* by Martin Mayer, used courtesy of Little, Brown & Company Publisher.

Quotation (p. 242–243) used with permission courtesy of Tom Murray.

Quotation (p. 255) from Malcolm Muggeridge, used with permission from The Malcolm Muggeridge Society.

Advertisement (p. 273–274) used with permission courtesy of Bob Levenson.

Every effort has been made to contact the rightful copyright holders; in the event of an inadvertent omission or error, please notify the publisher.

PERMISSIONS

INDEX

309

INDEX

convergence concept, 148
Coolidge, Calvin, 20
Coombs, Ernie, 83
Cooper, Anderson, 89
Coors, 17
Copeland, Miles, 150, 151
Coppertone girl, 215
Coppola, Francis Ford, 37, 145, 223, 225
Coppola, Sophia, 223
copyright, 100–1, 156–58
Copywriters Hall of Fame, 16
Copywriting, xxiii–xxiv, 164–82, 231,
    236–43
Cora the Coffee Lady, 213
Cord, E.L., 171, 172
Coty Inc., 196
Court TV, 136
CP24, 17–18
Craigslist, 99
Crawford, Joan, 142
Cream of Wheat, 77
Crispin, Porter + Bogusky, 69, 109
Crispy Critters cereal, 88
Cronkite, Walter, 250
Crosby, Bing, 31, 58
Cross-Canada Hit Parade, 84
Crow, Sheryl, 158
"Crush" stunt, 127
Crush, William G., 127
Cruz, Penelope, 225
"culture jammers," 91
Curtis, Jamie Lee, 131
customer service, 117, 209, 271
Cyber Grand Prix, 113

Da Brat, 50
da Cesena, Biagio, 143–44
"Danger Zone," 247
"Darkie" brand toothpaste, 216
data mining, 40–41
Data Smog (Shenk), 4
Davis, Bette, 140, 143
Davis, R.T., 206, 207

Dawson, Rosario, 179
death, 120–22, 239
Deaver, Michael, 266
DeMille, Cecil B., 22
demography, 4–5
"Desert Rose," 150–51
Desgrange, Henri, 61
Desperate Housewives, 19–20
Devine, Andy "Jingles," 82
Dharma and Greg, 160
DialAmerica Marketing, 36
Dick Tracy, 80, 81
Dickson, Tom, 100–11
Die Another Day , 64
Diefenbaker, John, 233
Diet Coke, 50, 90–100
Diet Pepsi, 50
Dietrich, Marlene, 142
DigiScents, 200
digital cameras, 99
digital music players, 75
DIM lingerie, 247
DiMaggio, Joe, 209
Dion, Céline, 196
direct mail, 39
disclaimers, 22–23
dishonesty in advertising, 258–66
Disney, Elias, 207
Disney, Walt, 189–90, 207
displacement, law of, 202
"Do This or Die" ad, 273–75
"Do You Want to Dance?," 157
Doritos, 105
double broadcast, 31
Douglas, Michael, 224
Douglas, Norman, xiii
Douglas, Stephen, 234, 248
Dove, 65–66, 107–8
Doyle Dane Bernbach (DDB), xxiii–xxiv,
    237–38, 273–74
Dr Pepper, 126
Dr. Care toothpaste, 42
Dreyfus Affair, 61

311

INDEX

314

315

Lee, Ang, 66
Lee, Peggy, 155
Lefèvre, Géo, 61
"Lemon" ad, xxiii, 237–38
Lennen & Mitchell, 55
Lennon, John, 152, 153
Lenny, 213
Leonard, Sheldon, 88
Let's Go to the Museum, 83
Let's Pretend, 77
Letterman, David, 100, 111
Levenson, Bob, 273–74
Levenson, Larry, 273
Levi's, 157
Levinson, Barry, 67
Lexus, 269
Lifebuoy, 240–41
Lincoln, Abraham, 181, 234, 245, 248
Lindbergh baby, 80
Linder, Cec, 84
Lindstrom, Martin, 195, 202
Link, Henry, 263
Linton, Doug, 182
Linus the Lionhearted, 88, 211
Liotta, Ray, 193
Liszt, Franz, 190
Little Black Sambo, 217
Little Orphan Annie, 80, 82
Liu, Lucy, 179
Livingston, Jay Conrad, 122, 123
Loesser, Frank, 155
Loggins, Kenny, 247
Lois, George, 187
long-form print ads, 231, 234–39
Lopez, Jennifer, 196
Lord & Thomas (L & T), xvii–xx, xxi, 30, 31, 58
L'Oréal, 225
Lost in Translation, 223
Louis Vuitton brand, 225
Louis XVI, king of France, 98
Louis, Joe, 220
Lubars, David, 108

Lubin, Charles, 213
Lubin, Sara Lee, 213
Lucas, George, 37, 144–48
Lucky Charms, 211
Lucky Strike, 30, 59, 63
Lucky Strike Auctioneer, 58
Lucky the Leprechaun, 211
Lumsden, Norman, 241
"Lust for Life,"158
Lux, 50
Lux Radio Theatre, 22, 57

Ma Perkins, 55
Macdonald, John A., 53, 234
MacNeil, Robert, 83
MacNeil-Lehrer Report, 83
Mad magazine, 251
Mad Men, 64
Madame Tussaud (London), 191
Madge the Manicurist, 212–13, 215, 251
Madison, James, 272
Madonna, 156, 223
Magee, John Gillespie, 249
"making of" stories, 244–45
Mahovlich, Frank, 226
Mail Pouch Tobacco, 35
make-good ad, 11
Manchurian Candidate, The, 264
Mandel, Howie, 224
Manson, Marilyn, 66
Marathon of Hope, 125
"marblegate," 264–65
Marciano, Rocky, 227
marketing language, 168, 170–76
Marketing magazine, 69
Marks, John, 264
Marlboro Man, 215
Mars candy company, 63, 216
Martha Reeves and the Vandellas, 156
Mary Kay and Johnny, 87
Mary Tyler Moore Show, 120
mass audience, 31–32
mass marketing, xvii, 117, 218, 257, 268

317

320

323

INDEX